Noticing Oral Corrective Feedback in the Second Language Classroom

Noticing Oral Corrective Feedback in the Second Language Classroom

Background and Evidence

Eva Kartchava

LEXINGTON BOOKS
Lanham • Boulder • New York • London

Published by Lexington Books
An imprint of The Rowman & Littlefield Publishing Group, Inc.
4501 Forbes Boulevard, Suite 200, Lanham, Maryland 20706
www.rowman.com

6 Tinworth Street, London SE11 5AL, United Kingdom

Copyright © 2019 The Rowman & Littlefield Publishing Group, Inc.

All rights reserved. No part of this book may be reproduced in any form or by any electronic or mechanical means, including information storage and retrieval systems, without written permission from the publisher, except by a reviewer who may quote passages in a review.

British Library Cataloguing in Publication Information Available

Library of Congress Cataloging-in-Publication Data

ISBN 978-1-4985-3677-6 (cloth)
ISBN 978-1-4985-3679-0 (pbk)
ISBN 978-1-4985-3678-3 (electronic)

For Mom
От всей души, Спасибо!

Contents

Acknowledgments ix

Introduction 1

1 What Is Corrective Feedback? 9
2 Noticeability and Effectiveness of Oral Corrective Feedback 39
3 Training Learners to Notice Corrective Feedback 81
4 Learner Beliefs and Corrective Feedback 117
5 Nonverbal Behavior and Corrective Feedback 141
6 Conclusion 163

Endnotes 173
References 177
Index 199
About the Author 205

Acknowledgments

No worthy undertaking is possible without the help and support of a myriad of people, who each play a role in seeing the work come to fruition. The volume before you is no exception and in large part owes its existence to numerous people who provided inspiration and assistance during the various stages of the project. I would like to express my sincere gratitude to the editorial team at Lexington Books, in particular Jana Hodges-Kluck, for recognizing the need for this book and for making the process of writing the volume a supportive one. I would also like to thank David Wood, a colleague and long-time supporter of my work, for persuading me to present the results of my research program in the form of a book. My journey to this point would not have been possible without the support of my academic mentors—Ahlem Ammar, Elizabeth Gatbonton, Hossein Nassaji, Leila Ranta, Randall Halter—who have tirelessly given their time, guidance, encouragement, and unwavering support from my very first steps in the field.

The research reported in this book owes its existence in no small part to the English language learners and their teachers in two Canadian educational institutions in the provinces of Quebec and Ontario. I am forever indebted to Marlene Lundy, Nicolas Walker, Mel Shantz, and Mike Levine for their interest, patience, and dedication to this research. I would also like to thank David Schwinghammer and Evan Lavoie for having afforded me the opportunity to carry out these investigations at their institutions. Special thanks are owed to Jeanne Pugin for her help in examining the link between corrective feedback and gesture (Chapter 5) and Judy Seal for her outstanding editing work. Any and all remaining errors are, of course, my own.

Finally, I would like to profoundly thank my family for their understanding and patience during what may have seemed a never-ending endeavor. I dedicate this book to my precious Mother, a woman-extraordinaire, who has always encouraged and believed in the value of my dreams.

Introduction

Corrective feedback (CF), defined as "utterances that indicate to the learner that his or her output is erroneous in some way" (Nassaji & Kartchava, 2017a, p. ix), has preoccupied both second language (L2) teachers and researchers alike. This is because CF, in the words of Ellis (2017), is an "interface issue" that "brings together the concerns" (p. 3) of the two groups. For teachers, the main concern rests on understanding whether correcting learner errors is at all necessary and if so, then how may this practice be made effective in notably improving their students' linguistic accuracy. Researchers, in turn, are interested in determining the role of CF in L2 development and its effects on the processes that underlie L2 acquisition. The need to comprehend the underlying processes stems from the main preoccupation of the Second Language Acquisition (SLA) field to determine how languages are learned. This quest to understand involves, among others, the study of cognitive processes that include "how the L2 is represented in the mind of the learner, the role played by attention in reception and production, and the processes that can account for interlanguage change" (Ellis, 2015, p. 202).

Various L2 cognitive theories[1] articulated to date have allocated *attention* a central role in language learning for it is believed to heighten the level to which input (i.e., "second or foreign language learners are exposed to, be it aural or written, [authentic or pedagogical]," Leow, 2015, p. 17) is activated in working (i.e., short-term) memory. That is, since working memory is limited in storage capacity, attention is thought to increase the amount of time information remains available for processing or for adoption into long-term memory, whose capacity is believed to be unlimited. Increased attention is especially important for L2 learners, who often struggle to focus on both meaning and form of an utterance at the same time, often prioritizing meaning at the expense of form (VanPatten, 2002, 2004). Specifically, attention is said to: (1) have limited storage capacity, (2) be selective in terms of focus, (3) drive individual goals and intentions, and (4) control access to consciousness (Ortega, 2009). It is this last definitional aspect of attention (i.e., access to consciousness) that is of interest to this book.

It is, however, important to note that the view of attention to be discussed here can be seen as arguably narrow, especially in light of Leow's (2015) "finer-grained" theoretical framework for the L2 learning process in SLA. The traditional view of the L2 learning process (i.e., the "coarse-grained framework," Leow, 2015) can be thought of as a continuum of stages with "input" and "output" at each end, and "intake" and "internal system" placed between them. Here, "input" represents the target language that learners are exposed to or seek with the goal of attending to it and/or its parts (e.g., grammar, lexis, pronunciation). "Intake," in turn, is what a learner registers in the input and may or may not subject to further processing in the "internal system," the place where the learner's interlanguage or existing knowledge of the L2 is amassed. Finally, "output" is the L2 that the learner produces and is seen as a representation of his or her internal system.

In his 2015 model, Leow expanded the four stages to include processes and products that each subsumes. He argues that "viewing the learning process in terms of processes and products is important to differentiate between learning as a process, that is, an event taking place, and learning as a product, that is, something learned or internalized or produced" (Leow, 2015, pp. 20–21). Here, "input" and "output" are seen exclusively as external products, whereas "intake" and "internal system" are further divided into three processes (input processing, intake processing, and knowledge processing) and two products (intake and L2 knowledge). The seven-phase L2 learning process, then, is a movement from exposure to input (Input—product) to processing of that input (Input—process), selection of the input to attend to (Intake—product), further processing (e.g., hypothesis testing and modification) of the intake (Intake—process), incorporation of that intake into the learner's internal system (L2 knowledge—product), additional processing of the learner's L2 knowledge for use within specific situations/parameters (L2 knowledge—process), culminating in an overt demonstration of the learned L2 knowledge (Output—product).

Leow (2015) argues that with the exception of Gass (1997), most SLA theoretical explanations of attention do not account for the product and process stages, with the majority focusing on either the input to intake stage alone (Ellis, N., 2002; Schmidt, 1990, 1994, 2001; Tomlin & Villa, 1994), the input to intake stage in combination with the intake processing stage (McLaughlin, 1987; Robinson, 1995, 2003; VanPatten, 2004, 2007), or solely on the L2 knowledge processing stage (Swain, 2005). This book will consider research on the role of attention in the early stages of L2 learning (i.e., the input to intake stage) to determine how it may effectively be applied to the L2 classroom. Researchers working within this focus area have been primarily concerned with whether attention is necessary for L2 success. Specifically, they wanted to know whether learners needed to pay explicit/conscious attention to L2 elements in the input to learn the L2 or if such overt focus on linguistic forms was not required for learning to occur. In other words, the debate centered around the role of consciousness in attention, with two of the most influential theories on attention in SLA (Ellis, 2015) taking opposite sides. That is, while Tomlinson and Villa (1994) claimed that *detection*—subliminal registration of information outside focal attention (i.e., attention without consciousness)—alone is sufficient for L2 learning, Schmidt (1990, 1995, 2001) posited that learning without conscious attention is not possible since "people learn about the things they attend to and do not learn much from the things they do not attend to" (Schmidt, 2001, p. 30). Hence, to Schmidt, *noticing*—conscious detection of information plus its rehearsal in short-term memory prior to encoding it in the long-term memory (Robinson, 1995, p. 296)—involves awareness that is necessary for any learning to take place (i.e., for input to become intake).

The importance of noticing in language learning was first highlighted by Schmidt, who having studied a Japanese artist living in Hawaii who learned English exclusively through exposure (Schmidt, 1983) and Schmidt's own learning of Portuguese (Schmidt & Frota, 1986) proposed the Noticing Hypothesis (Schmidt, 1990), according to which learning any aspect of an L2 requires conscious noticing (not just detection) of the relevant linguistic data in the input. That is to say that "in order to acquire phonology, one must attend to phonology; in order to acquire pragmatics, one must attend to both linguistic forms and the relevant contextual features; and so forth" (Schmidt, 1995, p. 17). Hence, it is focused attention on specific aspects in the input, Schmidt claimed, that brings about L2 knowledge—"what learners notice in input is what becomes intake for learning" (Schmidt, 1995, p. 20). Learners can notice: (1) linguistic forms of an L2, (2) gaps between their (i.e., learner) and native-speaker input (i.e., noticing-the-gap), and (3) "holes" (i.e., missing elements) in their interlanguage (Schmidt, 1995; Swain & Lapkin, 1995). Arguments against Schmidt's assertion that only those elements that have been consciously attended to by the learner in the input can be learned[2] led him to adjust his original claim from seeing noticing as "the necessary and sufficient condition for conversion of input into intake' (Schmidt, 1993, p. 209) to assigning it a facilitative role in L2 learning. Thus, in its present form, the Noticing Hypothesis states that noticing is helpful for L2 learning (Schmidt, 2001). Yet, it is important to acknowledge that, to Schmidt (2001), noticing may be necessary for learning *new* things and that only established features can be registered non-consciously: "non-conscious registration applies to well learned rather than new information. Syntactic categories may also be non-consciously activated once they are well established. . . . However, comprehending what is new requires conscious processing" (p. 31).

If noticing is helpful, then how can/should it be affected in the L2 classroom? In other words, what can teachers do to help their learners to take advantage of the L2 input they are exposed to, and what could learners themselves do to self-regulate their learning? Interaction (Long, 1991, 1996), comprehensible output (Swain, 1985, 1993), and corrective feedback (Doughty & Williams, 1998; Lightbown, 1998; Long & Robinson, 1998; Lyster, Lightbown, & Spada, 1999), to name a few, have been suggested as effective ways to promote noticing when learning an L2. Corrective feedback, in particular, is seen as effective in facilitating noticing of errors that L2 learners make in the classroom setting.[3] This is because CF not only provides learners with information about what is incorrect or impossible (i.e., negative evidence) in the L2, and does it at the time when this information is necessary (generally, during meaning-focused interactions) or in reaction to a linguistic difficulty the learner is experiencing, but also helps them to notice the gaps, and possibly holes, in their interlanguage (Long, 1996). For feedback to be effective, however, learners need to recognize its didactic focus (Carroll, 1995). That is, they need to acknowledge that CF aims to alert them to the problem of form (not meaning) in their utterance, prompting learners to recognize the L2 norm and/or remedy the inaccuracy. In this way, CF, when noticed, can help learners make target-like form-meaning connections necessary for L2 development (e.g., Doughty & Varela, 1998; Long & Robinson, 1998).

Investigations of CF noticeability have often operationalized the concept of noticing differently from Schmidt's definition (e.g., Ammar, 2008; Mackey, Gass & McDonough, 2000). Ammar (2008), for example, generated three data-based categories of noticing: detection, uptake of teacher's correction, and recognition of teacher's help. When the following example for "detection" is considered—"I was thinking that Miss X correct person when they did past tense mistake," it becomes clear that the learner is engaged in analyzing language metalinguistically in that he/she is attending to the rule underlying the given structure. Yet, Schmidt (2001) distinguished "noticing" from "metalinguistic awareness" in his conceptualization of noticing "by assuming that the objects of attention and noticing are elements of the surface structure of utterances in the input—instances of language, rather than any abstract rules or principles of which such instances may be exemplars" (p. 5). In this view, Schmidt's conceptualization of noticing is much narrower than that employed in Ammar. Mackey et al. (2000), in turn, stayed away from using the term "noticing" altogether, choosing to instead explore "learners' reports about their perceptions [operationalizing the term 'perceptions'] in a nontechnical sense because we see our study as a first step in the process of investigating theoretical claims about interaction, learner attention, and L2 development" (p. 477). In this volume, noticing is operationalized differently from Schmidt's definition and refers to learners' reports of (i.e., perceptions) and/or reaction to CF (i.e., uptake).

Interest in corrective feedback has produced an immense body of research that has considered the issue from many facets. These include: the place of corrective feedback in L2 classrooms (Chaudron, 1977; DeKeyser, 1993; Long, 1991, 1996; Lightbown, 1998; Doughty & Williams, 1998), types of feedback (Lyster & Ranta, 1997; Lyster, 1999) and their in-classroom distribution (e.g., Brown, 2016; Lyster & Ranta, 1997; Panova & Lyster, 2002; Sheen, 2004), the effectiveness of these techniques (e.g., Ammar & Spada, 2006; DeKeyser, 1993; Doughty & Varela, 1998; Ellis, Loewen, & Erlam, 2006; Lightbown & Spada, 1990; Lyster, 2004; Yang & Lyster, 2010), and the noticeability of CF (e.g., Ammar, 2008; Ammar & Sato, 2010b; Egi, 2007b; Kim & Han, 2007; Mackey, Gass & McDonough, 2000; Mackey, Philp, Egi, Fujii & Tasumi, 2002; Philp, 2003; Trofimovich, Ammar, & Gatbonton, 2007). Furthermore, numerous meta-analyses and reviews on the topic (e.g., Li, 2010; Lyster & Saito, 2010; Lyster, Saito, & Sato, 2013; Mackey & Goo, 2007; Nassaji, 2015, 2016; Russell & Spada, 2006) have shown various benefits for CF provision and reiterated the positive role CF plays in language learning. A recently edited volume on CF (Nassaji & Kartchava, 2017) has expanded the focus of previously reported investigations to include examination of the role of timing, context (face-to-face versus technology-mediated environments), mode (oral, written, computer-mediated), peer and non-verbal feedback, various individual learner differences, learner and teacher attitudes, as well as feedback explicitness on CF effectiveness. While the volume confirms the facilitative role of CF, it also highlights the complexity of the topic and the need for additional research on both known and new facets of CF. Among these are: (1) the role and importance of feedback explicitness and noticing, (2) the need for feedback training, and (3) the role of nonverbal feedback in the delivery of verbal CF (Nassaji & Kartchava, 2017b, pp. 174–175). These issues are among those explored in this publication.

The goal of the book before you is to contribute to the accumulated knowledge regarding the noticeability of CF in the field of L2 teaching and learning. It does so by synthesizing available research on the noticeability of CF in the language classroom and linking it to four original research studies that examined: (1) learners' ability to notice and learn from teacher-generated CF, (2) the impact of training learners to notice CF, (3) a relationship between learners' beliefs about CF and noticing, and (4) the role of non-verbal feedback in the noticeability of oral CF. While this book is based on research conducted for a large research project, the original focus has been expanded to include two new studies conducted since. That is, Studies 1 and 3 will report on the work completed for the project, whereas Studies 2 and 4 will detail aspects considered and researched afterwards. Each study, in turn, connects theory with research evidence to support practical recommendations offered to language teachers at the end. This volume embodies a journey of exploration into the role of noticing in CF and the many factors that may affect it. This journey was motivated by my own experience as a language learner and language teacher, who has been lucky enough to live this issue from both sides of the desk. Consequently, I hope that this book may appeal to researchers and graduate students in applied linguistics and Teaching English as a Second Language (TESL), as well as language teachers and teacher educators who are interested in the role of corrective feedback in L2 teaching and learning.

The book consists of six chapters. Chapter 1 reviews the literature necessary to set a background to the area of corrective feedback. Specifically, this analysis first defines the term "corrective feedback," identifies the various contexts in which feedback can be provided, and explains facets of CF that have been researched. It then focuses on the types of oral feedback and gestures used in the language classroom. Major L2 theories as they relate to CF are discussed next; the discussion includes an examination of the theoretical importance of noticing (as championed by Schmidt) in general and in regards to CF. Pedagogical perspectives on oral CF are detailed at the end.

Chapter 2 examines the various measures of noticing that have been used to study the noticeability of CF. Investigations that empirically examined the noticeability and effectiveness of CF in instructional settings are discussed next. An analysis of the research that considered the relationship between the noticing of CF and L2 learning is also provided. Then, a study that examined the noticeability and effectiveness of CF in the language classroom (Study 1) is presented. The implications of this study and its contribution to the area of study are outlined at the end. Several tools and materials from the study are available on the book's website at www.rowman.com/ISBN/9781498536776.

Study 2, in the third chapter, investigated whether training in recasts prior to their provision would make them more noticeable, yielding increased uptake and larger gains on the post-intervention scores. The implications of these findings and the instructions for the training are discussed.

A case for the need to study learner beliefs about CF as they relate to the noticeability and effectiveness of feedback is made in Chapter 4. First, the review of literature on beliefs and their impact on language learning in general and CF in particular is presented. This is followed by a study that investigated whether learners' beliefs about CF mediate what is noticed and learned in the language classroom (Study 3). The chapter ends with a discussion of the study's contributions. A copy of the questionnaire is also provided on the book's website.

Chapter 5 examines the role of nonverbal behavior in the provision of oral CF in the L2 classroom. This topic is not new but has received very little attention in SLA overall and CF studies in particular. Yet, since there is evidence that nonverbal feedback in general and, specifically, gestures that accompany feedback can increase its noticeability and effectiveness, the study reported here describes the nonverbal behavior of an instructor teaching in a university-based intensive ESL program in Canada (Study 4). The findings add to this under-researched area of inquiry and respond to a call for studies that not only explore different types of nonverbal techniques, but also examine learners' reactions to them. The chapter concludes with a discussion of implications that these results may yield for the classroom.

In conclusion, Chapter 6, summarizes the findings of the four research studies and highlights the resulting implications for the language classroom. The chapter discusses the overall significance and contribution of the volume as well as identifies its limitations. Future research directions in the study of CF are suggested at the end.

Chapter One

What Is Corrective Feedback?

1.1 DEFINITIONS, MODES, LINGUISTIC TARGETS, TIMING

Feedback has long been considered an important and, arguably, indispensable part of the learning process. Its power lies in the information (positive or corrective) it carries about the effectiveness of one's performance on a given task—feedback is, hence, "a 'consequence' of performance" (Hattie & Timperley, 2007, p. 81). To be effective, the learner needs to understand the intent of the provided feedback; without such understanding, the learner may feel threatened by the feedback or, worse, take no further action in response to it (Hattie & Timperley, 2007). Yet, because the learner has the power to adopt, refuse, or adapt feedback he/she recognizes (Kulhavy, 1977), Good and Brophy (2000), in their guide for classroom teaching, argued that feedback needs to be provided on both correct and incorrect learner output. This sentiment is echoed in other teacher guides that strive to provide teachers with tools to support learners in their L2 learning. In fact, many of the guides pay more attention to positive feedback that is seen as offering "an affirmation of the content or correctness of a learner utterance" (Nassaji, 2015, p. 11) than negative feedback (i.e., corrective feedback), which is often relegated to instances of accuracy work (Ellis, 2017). Because corrective feedback may invoke negative reactions in learners, the guides argue, it should not be provided during fluency activities, but if attention to form is needed during those instances, then CF should be as brief and unobtrusive as possible. Although attention to error is deemed important in general, the guides stress possible negative repercussions for learners that teachers should be aware of when providing CF, urging teachers to supply CF "in an atmosphere of support and warm solidarity, so that learners feel that the teacher's motive is honestly to promote and encourage their learning, not to push them down" (Ur, 1996, p. 255). Ur worries about "the accompanying implications of aggression on the side of the assessor and humiliation on the side of the assessed" (ibid). L2 researchers, in contrast, while aware of the possible affective variables in the provision of correction, are interested in the role of CF in the study of an L2 and its effects on cognition.

Corrective feedback is the focus of this book. Different terminology has been used to define and operationalize "corrective feedback." Despite the differences in their original definitions, the literature on the subject has often used the terms "negative evidence," "negative feedback," "error correction," and "corrective feedback" interchangeably. To avoid possible confusion this practice may cause, it is necessary to describe and define each term. The concept of "negative evidence" arises from two types of input language learners are generally exposed to when learning L2: positive evidence and negative evidence. While positive evidence provides learners with models of what is possible and grammatically acceptable in the target language, negative evidence supplies learners with information about what is unacceptable in the L2 (Long 1996, 2006). Negative evidence can either be direct or indirect. While *direct* negative evidence refers to a teacher's reaction to an error[4] with the purpose of attracting the learner's attention to it, *indirect* negative evidence provides learners with signals that a certain construction is not possible in the L2 due to its absence from input (Chomsky, 1981). In light of this, negative feedback—"any reaction of the teacher which clearly transforms, disapprovingly refers to, or demands improvement of the learner's utterance" (Chaudron, 1977, p. 31)—is a subset of *direct* negative evidence, not its counterpart. However, when corrective feedback is defined as "any indication to the learner [by the teacher] that his/her use of the target language is incorrect" (Lightbown & Spada, 2006, p. 197), it can be equated to negative feedback, and the two terms may be used interchangeably. Hence, negative/corrective feedback may be explicit and include metalinguistic explanation or implicit and range from mere silence or expression of confusion to confirmation checks and recasts. Finally, it is important to note that "corrective feedback" is not the same as "error correction" and as such, the two terms should not be used interchangeably. According to Chaudron (1977), the term "error correction" is used to refer to corrective moves that *lead to repair*/correction of the non-target-like forms. Corrective feedback, on the other hand, signals the presence of an error *in hopes of repair*. Hence, in this book, corrective feedback is defined as any teacher's reactive move (explicit or implicit), whose aim is not only to warn the learner about the presence of an error, but to also move him/her to attend to the accuracy of their production (i.e., repair the error) (Carroll & Swain, 1993; Sheen, 2011).

Corrective feedback can be provided for oral, written, and technology-mediated output. It can also be supplied in instructed (i.e., the classroom, study abroad programs, self-study, Loewen, 2015) and naturalistic contexts by teachers, peers, other interlocutors, and the self. Furthermore, any feedback (including corrective) "can also be sought by students, peers, and so on, and detected by a learner without it being intentionally sought" (Hattie & Timperley, 2007, p. 82). CF can target errors of grammar, lexis, phonology, and pragmatics.[5] Among these, grammatical errors have been shown to be addressed the most by all interlocutors, including language teachers (Brown, 2016; Kim & Han, 2007; Lyster 1998b; Mackey et al., 2000). Yet, because learners tend to recognize and repair CF aimed at lexical and phonological errors more than that aimed at grammatical errors (Lyster, 1998a; Lyster, Saito, & Sato, 2013; Mackey & Goo, 2007), their vocabulary knowledge has been shown to develop more readily than the grammatical knowledge (Mackey & Goo, 2007). Positive effects of CF on pronunciation development have also been observed (e.g., Saito & Lyster, 2012). These benefits, some have argued, are due to the negative effects that an inappropriately chosen vocabulary item or mispronounced word can have on the comprehensibility of the intended message (Egi, 2007a; Isaacs & Trofimovich, 2012; Mackey et al., 2000).

Despite these findings, "teachers' CF is more likely to target grammar than other error types" (Brown, 2016, p. 453). This is perhaps due to research showing that instruction, coupled with CF, facilitates acquisition of the majority of L2 features that learners need to master (Doughty & Williams, 1998; Lightbown, 1998). These usually include features that lack salience in the input, are misleadingly similar to certain first language (L1) structures, and affect the intended meaning in ways that can lead to communication breakdowns (Doughty & Williams, 1998). Still, cautions Sheen (2011), "we cannot assume that because CF has been shown to assist the acquisition of one grammatical feature it will necessarily do so for all features" (p. 165).

English grammatical features that have been investigated by CF research include possessive determiners, passive forms, articles, comparative /–er/, past tense, and questions (Lyster et al., 2013). The studies reported in this book examine the noticeability and effectiveness of CF on the latter two morphosyntactic features—namely, the simple past and questions in the past. This is because they represent features that are generally problematic for all English learners regardless of their L1, exemplify different levels of complexity (DeKeyser, 1998, 2005), and are subject to L1 interference (e.g., Ammar, Sato, & Kartchava, 2010; Collins, 2002). Despite their inherent challenges, the English simple past and question formation occur frequently in the input (Doughty & Varela, 1998), which facilitates their elicitation during communicative tasks (McDonough, 2007), and have received much attention in developmental research that showed them as good candidates for learner improvement when CF targeting them is provided (e.g., Mackey & Philp, 1998; McDonough, 2005; McDonough & Mackey, 2006; Mackey, 2006 for questions; Doughty & Varela, 1998; Ellis et al., 2006; Han, 2002; McDonough, 2007; Nobuyoshi & Ellis, 1993; Yang & Lyster, 2010 for past tense). Finally, research has shown that noticing of feedback leads to language development, but that it, in large part, depends on the technique employed and on the nature of the error (e.g., Ammar, 2008; Ammar & Sato, 2010a).

CF can also be supplied immediately after an error has occurred (immediate CF) or following a delay (i.e., delayed CF). That is, CF can be provided during a task or after completing the task. While much research on oral CF has championed immediate CF, to date, there is no conclusive evidence that it is more effective than delayed CF. In fact, new evidence suggests that delayed feedback may be as effective as its counterpart and that each type can contribute differently to language learning as a whole (Ellis, 2017; Quinn & Nakata, 2017) as well as in terms of particular context, CF type, and learner (Nassaji, 2016). With these considerations in mind, this volume investigates the impact of teacher corrections delivered during in-class communicative tasks on the noticeability and effectiveness of oral immediate CF that targeted errors of the past tense and questions.

1.2 CF TECHNIQUES AND GESTURES, THEIR DISTRIBUTION, AND LEARNER UPTAKE

1.2.1 Oral CF Techniques and Their Distribution

Building on a number of early descriptive classroom studies of corrective feedback (e.g., Chaudron, 1977; Fanselow, 1977), twenty years ago, Lyster and Ranta (1997) conducted what is now considered by many a landmark study that described the types of techniques language teachers used (in French immersion classrooms) to provide L2 learners with oral CF. The resulting framework of six feedback types—recasts, explicit feedback, elicitation, metalinguistic feedback, repetition, and clarification requests—has received much attention from both researchers and language teachers. It has also been modified and built on by the authors themselves (Lyster, 2004; Ranta & Lyster, 2007) as well as other scholars (Sheen & Ellis, 2011). The six feedback techniques were first re-classified by Lyster (2004) into three categories of (1) recasts, (2) explicit correction, and (3) prompts, and most recently regrouped again by Ranta and Lyster (2007) into "reformulations" and "prompts" (see Table 1.1). Recasts and explicit

Table 1.1. CF Techniques (Based on Lyster & Ranta, 1997)

	Technique	Definition	Example
Teacher corrects = Reformulations (input-providing)	Recast	"Teacher's reformulation of all or part of a S's utterance minus the error" (p. 46). Recasts can be whole (complete utterance is reformulated) or partial (only the error is reformulated).	Student: "I go to the movies yesterday." Teacher: "Oh, you went to the movies yesterday."
	Explicit correction	"Explicit provision of the correct form" by the teacher (p. 46).	Student: "I go to the movies yesterday." Teacher: "No. Go, past tense."
Student self-corrects = Prompts (output-prompting)	Metalinguistic cue	"Contains comments, information or questions related to the well-formedness of the S's utterance, without explicitly providing the correct form" (p. 47).	Student: "I go to the movies yesterday." Teacher: "No, not *go* [stressed]. It happened *yesterday* [stressed]. So, what should you say?"
	Elicitation	Teachers either: (1) elicit "completion of their own utterance by strategically pausing to allow Ss to fill in the blank, (2) use "questions to elicit correct forms," or (3) ask Ss to "reformulate their utterance" (p. 48).	Student: "I go to the movies yesterday." Teacher: "He *what* [stressed] yesterday?"
	Repetition	"Teacher's repetition, in isolation, of the S's erroneous utterance" (p. 48).	Student: "I go to the movies yesterday." Teacher: "I *go* [stressed] to the movies yesterday [stressed]? Go yesterday [stressed]? *Go* [stressed]?"
	Clarification request	"Indicates to Ss either that their utterance has been misunderstood by the teacher or that the utterance is ill-formed in some way and that a repetition or reformulation is required" (p. 47).	Student: "I go to the movies yesterday." Teacher: "Pardon me? Sorry?"

correction were categorized together under "reformulations" because they both supply the learner with either an implicit or explicit reformulation of the target form and are thus input-providing (Ellis, 2006). The "prompt" category (formerly referred to as the "negotiation of form" (Lyster & Ranta, 1997) and "form-focused negotiation" (Lyster, 2002)), in turn, is made of four output-prompting (Ellis, 2006) corrective techniques, namely, metalinguistic feedback, elicitation, repetition, and clarification request, all of which are designed to push learners to recognize the corrective intent of CF and to help them correct the error on their own.

It is, however, important to remember that each category can differ greatly in terms of implementation and the degree of explicitness and/or implicitness of the technique as dictated by a given context.[6] This was precisely why Sheen and Ellis (2011) proposed an amended framework of CF types that accounted for the differences between explicit and implicit reformulations and prompts as well as distinguished didactic recasts from conversational recasts and explicit correction from explicit correction with metalinguistic explanation. In addition to possible differences in the length of recasts (i.e., whole vs. partial), their focus can be pedagogical (i.e., didactic) or communicative (i.e., conversational). It is pedagogical when a teacher reformulates the error to draw a learner's attention to it (Example 1); conversational recasts are used to check whether the message intended by the learner is what was actually understood by the interlocutor (Example 2)—in this way, conversational recasts act as comprehension checks.

Example 1 (Sheen, 2011, p. 3)

Student: Women are kind than men.

Teacher: Kinder. (partial recast)

Example 2 (Sheen, 2011, p. 3)

Student: How much weigh?

Teacher: What?

Student: How weight are you?

Teacher: How much do I weigh? (Conversational recasts)

Sheen and Ellis (2011) also distinguished between explicit correction that clearly identifies the error and provides the correct form (Example 3) and explicit correction with metalinguistic explanation that identifies the error, provides the correct form, and supplies a metalinguistic comment about the erroneous form (Example 4).

Example 3 (Sheen, 2011, p. 3)

Student: I'm late yesterday.

Teacher: You should say 'I was late,' not 'I'm late.'

Example 4 (Sheen, 2011, p. 3)

Student: Fox was clever.

Teacher: The fox was clever. You should use the definite article 'the' because fox has been mentioned.

As for the implicitness and explicitness of the techniques, Sheen and Ellis (2011) saw conversational recasts, repetition, and clarification requests as implicit whereas didactic recasts, explicit correction, explicit correction with metalinguistic explanation, metalinguistic cues, elicitation, and paralinguistic cues (non-verbal signals) were seen as explicit CF types. Among these CF techniques, recasts tend to occur more frequently than the other strategies, a finding that has recently been confirmed by Brown (2016) in his meta-analysis of descriptive studies that showed recasts as being the most common type of CF (57%), followed by prompts (30%), in the language classroom. Lyster et al. (2013), however, warn that "this [situation] is not necessarily the case across all instructional settings that have been observed" (p. 7).

1.2.2 Gestures and Their Distribution

To date, CF research has focused almost entirely on feedback that is provided verbally, without looking at nonverbal cues that teachers may utilize to alert learners to a linguistic issue in their L2 production. Limited research done on nonverbal/paralinguistic signals in the L2 classroom has shown that gestures used during CF provision make the corrective intent of oral CF not only noticeable to learners, but also that gestures help learners to develop their L2 knowledge "because learners are better able to understand the linguistic target of feedback and because learning is better retained" (Nakatsukasa & Loewen, 2017, p. 167). These findings are perhaps why Sheen and Ellis (2011) tagged paralinguistic cues as explicit CF types. In terms of distribution, ESL teachers have been observed to couple their verbal CF with non-verbal cues 60% of the time, with head movements and pointing being among the most commonly occuring paralinguistic cues (Wang & Loewen, 2016). The taxonomy used to classify gestures in studies of CF and gestures (e.g., Nakatsukasa, 2016; Wang, 2009; Wang & Loewen, 2016) has been that of McNeill (1992). This classification includes emblems, iconic, metaphoric, deictic, and beats gestures, which are described and illustrated in Table 1.2. Study 5 described

Table 1.2. Gestures (McNeill, 1992 with Description and Examples from Nakatsukasa & Loewen, 2017, p. 160)

Gesture	Definition	Example
Emblems	Meaning of gestures is culturally specified and understood without speech	"Thumb and index finger making a circle with the other fingers extended upward is an example of [signifying] 'okay' in the United States, but signifies 'money' in Japan."
Iconic	Illustrate images of concrete items or actions	"Thumbs and index fingers of both hands create a circle while saying, 'Please shape the dough into *a round shape.*'" (original italics)
Metaphoric	Illustrate images of abstract concepts	"Right and left arms are extended outwards slightly and moved vertically and repeatedly. Palms are held upwards as if they are holding something inside while saying, 'We discussed two options. Which one is better—*Option A or B?.*'" (original italics)
Deictic	Pointing with hands or other body parts to indicate concrete and abstract objects	"An index finger points to two types of cat food one by one while saying, 'Which one is better for our cat? *This one or that one?.*'" (original italics)
Beats	Vertical or horizontal hand movements made in rhythm with speech	"Extended right arm moves in accordance with the emphasis of a sentence, 'First, I will describe the procedure. *Then,* you will make your own sauce.'" (original italics)

in this volume uses this classification in its analysis of gestures used in the provision of CF.

1.2.3 Learner Uptake

An important consideration in the study of CF is learner uptake. Although the term "uptake" has been used in a variety of research fields (e.g., kinetics, pharmacology, language learning) to refer to different concepts, Lyster & Ranta (1997) were perhaps the first to operationalize the term in the context of CF. They defined uptake[7] as "a student's utterance that immediately follows the teacher's feedback and that constitutes a reaction in some way to the teacher's intention to draw attention to some aspect of the student's initial utterance" (p. 49). Uptake can occur in the form of "repair" or "needs repair." While the "repair" episodes are usually evidenced by repetition/incorporation/provision of the correct form depending on the CF technique utilized, the

Table 1.3. Types of "Repair" Uptake (Adapted from Lyster & Ranta, 1997, p. 50)

Type of Repair	Definition	Example
Repetition	Repetition of the correct form provided by the teacher	St: *Là, je veux, là je vas le fairs à pied.* [Error-lexical] T4: *. . . avec mon pied.* [Feedback—recast] St: *. . . avec mon pied.* [Repair repetition]
Incorporation	Repetition of the correct form supplied by the teacher in the feedback, which is then incorporated into the student's longer utterance	St: *Mais, mais, elle nous a appelles le matin pis uhm Dimanche Diana et son frère ils ont venu chez moi* [Error-grammatical]; T3: *Sont venus* [Feedback—recast] St: *Sont venus chez moi pour jouer* [Repair—incorporation]
Self-repair	Self-correction made by the student who made the original error in response to the teacher's feedback that did not include the correct form of the error	St: *La marmotte c'est pas celui en haut?* [Error—gender] T3: *Pardon?* [Feedback—clarification] St: *La marmotte c'est pas celle en haut?* [Repair—self]
Peer-repair	Correction made by a student, other than the one who made the initial error, in response to the teacher's feedback	St: *J'ai apporté du pita bread. Le pita, c'est le meme chose* [Error-multiple] T: *Oké, mais pita bread, comment tu pourrais dire ça tu penses?* [Feedback—elicitation] Stdif: *Le pain pita* [Repair—peer]

"needs repair" instances require additional feedback. The "repair" instances include four sub-categories and are detailed in Table 1.3.

The "needs-repair" category, in turn, is comprised of the following six types of responses (Lyster & Ranta, 1997, pp. 50–51):

1. *Acknowledgement*—a simple "yes" or "no" in response to the teacher's feedback.
2. *Same error*—uptake that includes a repetition of the student's initial error.
3. *Different error*—uptake that is in response to the teacher's feedback but that neither corrects nor repeats the initial error; instead, a different error is made.
4. *Off target*—uptake that is clearly in response to the teacher's feedback turn but that circumvents the teacher's linguistic focus altogether, without including any further errors.

5. *Hesitation*—a student's hesitation in response to the teacher's feedback.
6. *Partial repair*—uptake that includes a correction of only part of the initial error.

Since the "needs repair" category generally requires additional feedback from the teacher, it allows for multiple-turn feedback, as is illustrated in this example (Lyster & Ranta, 1997, p. 51):

> St: *J'ai la difficulté à . . . comment expliquer que em . . . pour lui qui . . . qui nous envoie une lettre dans se future.* [Error—lexical]
>
> T3: *Je ne comprends pas.* [Feedback—clarification]
>
> Sts: *Moi non plus.*
>
> Stsame: *J'ai de la difficulté à . . . à formuler une phrase pour dire em . . . pouvez-vous renvoyer une lettre de re . . . une lettre de retour.* [Needs—different]
>
> T3: *Une lettre de retour?* [Feedback—repetition]
>
> Stsame: *Oui.* [Needs—acknowledgement]
>
> T3: *Bien regarde. Dans la conclusion, qu'est-ce qu'on dit? . . . Qu'est-ce qu'on disait dans la conclusion?* [Feedback—elicitation]
>
> Stdif: *J'attends avec impatience votre lettre.* [Repair-peer]

Arguably, the need to study uptake first emerged on the SLA landscape with the appearance of Chaudron's (1977) descriptive study of the different types of CF provided by teachers in French immersion. The study revealed that some CF techniques (e.g., repetition with emphasis) led to more immediate reformulation (i.e., uptake) on the part of the learners than did other techniques (e.g., repetition without emphasis), suggesting that uptake can help determine the effectiveness of provided CF. Later, in another descriptive study, Doughty (1994) observed a variety of CF types used by a teacher in a beginner level French-as-a-foreign-language classroom. The most frequent types of feedback were clarification requests, repetitions, and recasts; of these, recasts were supplied the most (60%). Although the teacher responded to over 40% of *both* correct and incorrect learner utterances, there seemed to be a pattern to the teacher's responses—while feedback given in response to a correct utterance was in the form of repetition, feedback targeting a single-error utterance was either in the form of a recast (68%) or a clarification request (23%). In terms of uptake, the results revealed that the learners did not react very often to any of the three types of feedback, but when they did, their responses usually followed recasts (61 of 284 recasts were repeated). This led researchers to consider various characteristics of recasts and their relationship to L2 learning. Other descriptive classroom studies confirmed that the most frequent type of feedback provided to learners was the recast, but they were less likely to lead to learner uptake in that they often failed to produce *immediate* reaction to the feedback from the learner (Havranek, 1999; Lochtman, 2002; Lyster & Ranta, 1997; Panova & Lyster, 2002; Sheen, 2004, 2006).

In their observational study of four French immersion classrooms (grades four and five), Lyster and Ranta (1997) analyzed 18.3 hours of interaction between 104 students and four French-English bilingual teachers in Canada. The data were coded in terms of the six types of feedback the teachers provided (i.e., recasts, explicit feedback, elicitation, metalinguistic feedback, repetition, and clarification requests) and the kinds of uptake these produced. The analysis revealed that while recasts were used the most by the teachers (55% of the total number of teacher CF moves), they yielded the least uptake (31%). However, even though the other corrective techniques were less frequent, with elicitation accounting for 14% of the total teacher corrective moves, clarification requests for 11%, metalinguistic feedback for 8%, explicit correction for 7%, and repetition for 5%, they produced higher rates of uptake. Specifically, elicitation led to uptake 100% of the time, clarification requests 88%, metalinguistic feedback 86%, repetition 78%, and explicit correction 50%. Furthermore, the researchers noted that recasts were least likely to lead to student-generated repairs (0%), which contrasted sharply with the results generated for elicitation (43%). Interestingly, these findings were confirmed by other classroom observation studies, which found a high frequency of recasts with little learner uptake in adult ESL (Panova & Lyster, 2002) and English as a Foreign Language (EFL) (Slimani, 1991) classes as well as in German foreign language classes in Belgium (Lochtman, 2002). In her investigation of the occurrence of the different CF techniques and the uptake they produce, Sheen (2004) investigated four instructional contexts— French immersion, ESL in Canada, ESL in New Zealand, and EFL in Korea. While for the most part, the results were comparable across the contexts in terms of frequency of occurrence and the amount of generated uptake, recasts seemed to occur more often and yield more uptake in the New Zealand (frequency: 68.3%; uptake: 72.9%) and Korean (frequency: 82.8%; uptake: 82.5%) contexts. This was explained by the fact that the corrective intent of recasts becomes more apparent to learners in highly structured foreign language contexts than it often is in the highly communicative language learning environment of Canada (Sheen, 2004).

Other studies have shown that certain characteristics of a recast can affect the rate of uptake it generates. Sheen (2006), for example, found that recasts that are pronunciation-focused, declarative, short, reduced (focus on just one word/small part of the learner's erroneous utterance), repeated, with a single error-focus, or involve substitutions instead of deletions or additions are more likely to lead to uptake and repair than their long, interrogative, incorporated, and metalinguistic counterparts. This is because recasts of the first type are more explicit than implicit and make the target of correction more salient, rendering the teacher's feedback more noticeable to learners. The findings of Sheen's (2006) study empirically support Lyster's (1998a) observation that reduced recasts make it easier for learners to compare the erroneous form of their utterance and the correct form of the target because such recasts help to identify the locus of the error, thus reducing some of the attentional burden on the working memory (WM). In fact, research shows that recasts that are short and focus on a single error in a learner's incorrect utterance are more likely to lead to uptake and repair than their longer counterparts with multiple errors (e.g., Chaudron, 1977; Loewen & Philp, 2006; Philp, 2003; Roberts, 1995; Sheen, 2006). Furthermore, reduced recasts lead to more noticing (e.g., Ammar & Sato, 2010a; Nicholas, Lightbown & Spada, 2001). Uptake has also been used as a measure of noticing. The findings of that research along with a discussion of other instruments used to operationalize noticing in L2 research are detailed in Chapter 2. It is useful to note that uptake was used to measure noticing in Study 2 and Study 4 of this volume; the remaining two studies employed online recall protocol to examine learners' noticeability and perceptions of CF.

1.3 CF AND SLA THEORIES

Researchers generally agree on ten key theories that explain the linguistic and cognitive aspects of SLA (VanPatten & Williams, 2015a): Behaviorism, Nativism/Innatism, Autonomous Induction Theory, Associative-Cognitive CREED Framework, Skill Acquisition Theory, Input Processing Theory, Processability Theory, Concept-Oriented Approach, Interaction Framework, and Vygotskian Sociocultural Theory. This publication, however, will consider the Behaviorism, Nativism/Innatism, Interactionism, and Cognitive/Psycholinguistic theories to explain the role of error and feedback in L2 learning—for a review of other theories on the topic, please see Nassaji and Kartchava (in press).

1.3.1 Behaviorism

Within the behaviorist theory, habit formation was seen as key to learning any skill (Skinner, 1957) and the environment was considered the most important factor in learning. All behavior was explained as a response to external factors in the environment and not as a function of internal processes. It was believed that learning resulted in the acquisition of new behavior when it consisted of imitation, practice, and appropriate feedback. While imitation of sounds and structures heard in the environment was the essential first step in learning a language, feedback on production (output) was instrumental in the formation of good habits. In fact, feedback was a whole system called *behavioral conditioning*, which trained learners to engage in new behaviors through reinforcement and punishment. That is, positive feedback (*reinforcement*) would result in the repetition of error-free L2 output by a learner, but negative or non-existent reaction (*punishment*) would make replication of such behavior less probable. As such, active and repeated engagement in the target behavior was considered crucial to the learning process. The behaviorist approach to language learning and teaching was closely linked to structural linguistics, which viewed language as based on a finite set of predictable patterns. Thus, the learner's job was to imitate and internalize predetermined linguistic patterns without having to think about what he/she was doing, since learners were seen as receivers of language, programmed to listen and repeat what they heard in as error-free a fashion as possible.

The behaviorist theory suggested direct and tangible pedagogical practices and stressed the importance of correct models, practice, and feedback. The importance of CF lay in the belief that successful L2 learning could only be achieved through the eradication of old habits (i.e., errors) and the formation of new (correct) ones. That is, errors were believed to impede the learning process. As such, teachers would not allow learners to engage in spontaneous speech, fearing that they would make errors, which could then develop into bad habits if left untreated. Instead, teachers provided correct models, ensured abundant repetition without learner reflection, did everything to avoid errors in the student output, and provided appropriate feedback. In fact, language teachers trained in the Audiolingual Method were instructed to avoid errors at all costs. If an error did occur, the teachers were told to "correct student errors immediately, use reinforcement, use repetition and imitation till the student masters the problem" (Courchêne, 1980, p. 9). Hence, the treatment of errors was consistent, overt, and immediate. The two CF techniques that seem most compatible with behaviorism are those that provide the learner with the correct form (i.e., recasts and explicit correction). Recasts supply learners with grammatically correct (full or partial) models of the target language, and explicit feedback signals the presence of an error by providing an overt reformulation of the problem, thus prompting repetition of the correction.

The behaviorist stimulus-response model of language learning and the structuralist approach to language description were challenged in the 1960s, when the first language acquisition researchers (Chomsky, 1957, 1966) began to show that the linguistic system was too complex to be learned through imitation alone and that children learning their L1 were able to produce language (and language rules) far richer and more diverse than any sample of language they could have picked up in the input. Furthermore, regardless of any context or other external factors, all children learning their L1 appeared to acquire grammatical features in fixed orders and made only certain kinds of errors instead of making all errors that were theoretically possible. Empirical investigations into the role of negative evidence in L1 acquisition demonstrated that, as a rule, parents rarely paid attention to the form of their children's output, but instead paid more attention to the truth value of what was said (Brown, 1973; Brown & Hanlon, 1970). These observations led researchers to suggest that language learning was unique and relied on an innate ability available to all humans at birth. According to Chomsky (1957), this innate ability is stimulated by the linguistic input one is exposed to. This input, in turn, shapes one's knowledge of the rules of a given language, which allows for the production of an infinite number of sentences, a large portion of which is unique and, as such, cannot be imitated or rehearsed.

As L1 researchers were transforming the theory of language acquisition, SLA researchers found that behaviorism, together with Contrastive Analysis,[8] could not predict or explain the errors that L2 learners make. Moreover, grammatical morpheme studies revealed that L2 learners acquired grammatical features in a consistent order and made errors that resembled those made by children learning their L1. This led them to conclude that L2 learning is not dependent on L1, but that it is internally driven and involves unconscious testing of hypotheses derived from the L2 input. Furthermore, largely due to Corder's (1967) influential paper that questioned the place of error in L2 learning, errors were no longer viewed as problems, but as a necessary part of language development. This is because they not only provide evidence of where learners are in respect to the target norms, but they also reveal the process by which L2s are acquired.

1.3.2 Nativism/Innatism

Stephen Krashen's Monitor Theory (1982) was the first innatist theory developed specifically for SLA. Although Krashen has never openly stated this, many in the field believe that his theory is based on Chomsky's theory of language (e.g., Gass & Selinker, 2001; Larsen-Freeman & Long, 1991; VanPatten & Williams, 2015b). The connection between the two theories lies in their shared belief that humans possess a unique innate ability to learn languages—Chomsky's "the language acquisition device." Krashen argued that this ability is not exclusive to L1 but that, under appropriate conditions, it can also extend to L2 acquisition. According to his model, which comprises five interrelated hypotheses,[9] the only thing needed for L2 acquisition to occur is for a learner to be exposed to comprehensible input that he/she can 1) readily process for meaning and 2) learn from. Krashen suggested that comprehensible input is readily available to learners by means of listening and reading texts, and that if the content is relevant and learners are able to comprehend its meaning, grammar learning will happen naturally and CF will not be necessary. Krashen based this role for input on L1 acquisition research that claimed that "in order to build an L1 grammar, children only need to be exposed to the language that parents or caretakers direct them to for the purpose of meaning making" (Ortega, 2009, p. 60).

According to Krashen's acquisition-learning hypothesis, L2 learners have two independent ways to develop L2 knowledge: subconsciously (acquisition) and consciously (learning). Acquisition is subconscious in both process and product. The process of acquisition is similar to the way children learn their L1 in that learners acquire language without being aware of it. The only thing they are aware of is that they are using the language to communicate meaning and as such, all their attention is focused on the task at hand. The result of acquisition (product) is also subconscious because "we are generally not consciously aware of the rules of the languages we have acquired. Instead, we have a 'feel' for correctness. Grammatical sentences 'sound' right, or 'feel' right, and errors feel wrong, even if we do not consciously know what rule was violated" (Krashen, 1982, p. 10). Unlike acquisition, learning is conscious in both process and product. The process of learning is through intentional study of the L2 rules and patterns, resulting in explicit knowledge of the "grammar" or "rules" of the language. Interestingly, according to Krashen, these two systems can never interact; knowledge gained by means of one system can never be transferred or incorporated into another for the purpose of spontaneous use. Instead, each system functions independently and has a different task to perform: the acquired system is used to produce language, and the learned knowledge monitors the resulting output.

Since Krashen saw acquisition as central in language learning, the learned system only had a peripheral role to play. Its primary function was to monitor the acquired knowledge during language production. This "Monitor," however, could not be used at all times; it could only be activated when three conditions were met: (1) learners needed to have enough time to access the learned system, (2) they had to also focus on form (not just the meaning) of what they were saying, and (3) their learned system needed to be rich enough to allow for the retrieval of case-appropriate rules. Thus, the Monitor can only be used in situations when it does not interfere with communication (e.g., writing or test-like tasks).

The natural order hypothesis states that L2 learners acquire grammatical morphemes (e.g., *-ing*, *-s*, *-ed*) in a predictable order, regardless of their L1 and whether or not they received instruction. The "natural order" originates in the acquired system and receives no interference from the learned system. It has been argued that the "order" is regular across L2 learners because all language acquisition is guided by the innate human language learning ability.

Given that there is a natural order of acquisition, how do learners move from one point to another? According to Krashen, L2s are acquired by "understanding messages or by receiving 'comprehensible input'" (Krashen, 1985, p. 2), which he defined as language that is slightly above the learner's current grammatical knowledge. This type of input was represented as "*i+1*," where "*i*" referred to the learner's current interlanguage level and "*i+1*" identified a point just above the learner's current level. Krashen considered comprehensible input as the most valuable for L2 acquisition since exposure to input that is both comprehensible and comprehended allows for the spontaneous acquisition of the L2 to take place. As such, instruction that focused on meaning instead of form was promoted, and learners were encouraged to produce language only when they felt ready to do so since premature (and forced) production was believed to inhibit the acquisition process by taking learners' attention away from the primary task of communication. In short, for SLA to occur, one simply needs access to his/her innate language ability and exposure to rich comprehensible input. Furthermore, if comprehensible input is available, SLA is inevitable (VanPatten & Williams, 2015b).

Finally, in his affective filter hypothesis, Krashen states that in order for L2 learners to acquire language, they need to feel comfortable and be receptive to the input they are exposed to. Factors such as motivation, attitude, self-confidence, and anxiety can all affect the success of language learning. Krashen thus proposed the *affective filter* construct: learners whose filters are "down" are more likely to feel comfortable and motivated to learn an L2, allowing for comprehensible input to flow in freely and for acquisition to occur. If the filter is "up," however, learners are likely to block the input, thus preventing acquisition from taking place. Stressful environments where learners are asked to pay attention to form and/or are forced to produce language before they are ready to do so characterize *high* affective filter situations and need to be avoided. According to Krashen, for successful language acquisition to occur, two conditions are necessary: (1) rich comprehensible input (at the right level) and (2) a low/weak affective filter.

While the behaviorist theory profusely advocated CF, Krashen's Monitor Theory shied away from it altogether. Krashen argued against treatment of errors that did not impede understanding of the intended message, saying that although CF may be helpful, comprehensible input alone is sufficient for SLA. According to his model, knowledge that entails deliberate attention to form as well as formal instruction can be used only to monitor (i.e., make minor form-related changes) the output generated by the acquired system. Furthermore, since the Monitor is not always available during communicative tasks, feedback to form may be of little use, since even if it is provided, nothing can guarantee that learners will notice, understand, and adopt it. As such, Krashen maintained that learners should be engaged in tasks that are rich in comprehensible input and that provide opportunities for meaningful interaction instead of those that focus on instruction of grammatical categories and include feedback on errors. Truscott (1996) went even further to claim that grammar teaching and CF are to be avoided as they are likely to result in the breakdown of the communicative flow.

Krashen's theory that comprehensive input alone is enough for successful language learning was challenged (e.g., Long, 1991, 1996; Swain, 1985, 1993, 1995; White, 1987). It has been suggested that attention to form is necessary "if native-like proficiency is the goal" (Long, 1996, p. 423). Several studies, conducted in both natural and classroom contexts (e.g., Harley & Swain, 1984; Lightbown & Spada, 1994; Sato, 1990; Schmidt, 1983; Schmidt & Frota, 1986; Swain, 1985), have demonstrated that despite abundant exposure to comprehensible input and ample opportunities to use L2 in meaningful ways, the learners' grammatical development was minimal. For example, in his well-known case study of Wes, a young Japanese artist, Schmidt (1983) reported a remarkable transformation in the communicative ability of someone who arrived in the United States with limited L2 skills and who was able, in the course of a three-year intensive exposure to the L2 input, to carry on conversations as well as to conduct all of his dealings entirely in English. Despite his success, Wes' speech fell short in terms of accuracy, which Schmidt attributed to the lack of formal instruction and Wes' preference for "message content over message form" (p. 169). A lack of instruction in the L2 norms has also been blamed for the low grammatical accuracy among learners in immersion (Harley & Swain, 1984; Swain, 1985) and highly communicative intensive ESL contexts (Lightbown & Spada, 1990, 1994), where the primary focus is placed on the communication of meaning and interaction. This research has shown that students enrolled in purely communicative classes attained advanced abilities in reading and listening skills (and even fluency) but failed to achieve native-like accuracy in writing and speaking. Hence, researchers agree that while input is necessary in SLA, it is not enough on its own, and that other factors are needed to explain the processes involved. Several theories have been put forth to explain additional sources of L2 learning. Of these, the interactional and psycho-cognitive theories are detailed next.

1.3.3 Interactionism

In today's communicative classrooms, much of the L2 input is provided through oral interaction with one or more interlocutors. Thus, modifications to one's speech are important for successful communication. These modifications are initiated by either of the speakers, who, having perceived a comprehension problem, adjusts his/her speech to make the intended meaning more comprehensible. This process of meaning adjustment, termed "negotiation for meaning," has become the primary tenet of the Interaction Hypothesis, proposed by Michael Long (1983, 1991, 1996). The original formulation of the Hypothesis (1983) argued that it is modified interaction (e.g., linguistic simplification, slower speech rate, gestures, and contextual clues) that renders input comprehensible, and in turn promotes L2 acquisition. While there is agreement regarding the positive effects interaction has on comprehension in general (e.g., Doughty & Pica, 1986) and on language development in particular (e.g., Mackey & Philp, 1998), Pica (1994) identified an additional way in which interaction may encourage language learning. She observed that whenever an interlocutor could not understand the intended meaning, he/she would signal the problem by using the following negotiation strategies: clarification requests, confirmation checks, comprehension checks, and recasts. While clarification requests (e.g., *what? uh? pardon me?*) elicit an explanation of the interlocutor's preceding utterances, comprehension checks (e.g., *do you want me to repeat? did you understand?*) verify that the intended message has been understood. Confirmation requests (e.g., *a base? you mean X?*), in turn, are used to elicit confirmation that the interlocutor has correctly understood the message. Finally, recasts provide a correct reformulation of an erroneous utterance while maintaining the original meaning intact. These interactional moves, Pica argued, were instrumental in alerting the learner that a breakdown in communication has occurred and that a reformulation or clarification is needed. Furthermore, the learner's recognition of the problem could invoke noticing, which would then lead to L2 learning (Schmidt, 1990, 2001; Schmidt & Frota, 1986). This view was also advocated by Gass (1997), who claimed that interaction can draw the learner's attention to linguistic problems and that noticing of mismatches between input and learner output is the first step in interlanguage development.

These observations, along with Swain's Comprehensible Output hypothesis (detailed below), led Long to revise his Interaction Hypothesis (1996) by giving CF more importance. In his revised Hypothesis, Long asserted that information about the correctness and, more importantly, the incorrectness of learners' utterances received through interaction leads to greater L2 acquisition. Thus, in its new form, this Hypothesis claims that modified input coupled with CF obtained through interaction bring about L2 learning.

Swain (1985) took the idea of interaction modification further by positing that output is inevitable in the L2 development process. Prior to her Comprehensible Output hypothesis, output was seen as a way to practice already-existing knowledge or to elicit additional input (Krashen, 1985) and not as a way to create knowledge. Swain argued that learners need to be pushed to produce L2 in a precise, coherent, and appropriate fashion. This is important because "output may stimulate learners to move from the semantic, open-ended, nondeterministic, strategic processing prevalent in comprehension to the complete grammatical processing needed for accurate production. Output, thus, would seem to have a potentially significant role in the development of syntax and morphology" (Swain, 1995, p. 128). Furthermore, Swain (1995) claims that output serves four functions in the learning process. First, producing output allows learners to test their interlanguage hypotheses about the structures and meanings of the L2, leading either to the reinforcement or rejection of a hypothesis, which ultimately results in language learning. Second, output promotes noticing of gaps (and holes) between what a learner wants to say and what he/she actually says. This noticing, in turn, pushes the learner to direct attention toward the problematic utterances and to revise them. Another function of output is to promote automaticity—(that is, control over one's linguistic knowledge), which involves "consistent mapping of the same input to the same pattern of activation over many trials" (McLaughlin, 1987, p. 134). Swain extended this notion to output, claiming that consistent and successful mapping of grammar to output brings about automatic processing, an argument reiterated by DeBot (1996). In other words, continued practice of language ensures more fluent and automatic L2 production. Finally, output carries a metalinguistic function "of using language to reflect on language, allowing learners to control and internalize it" (Swain, 1995, p. 132).

While most interactionist researchers agree that CF is beneficial for learning, they argue as to the techniques that will bring about acquisition. For example, Long (1996, 2006) has advocated the use of recasts and the "three C's," namely Clarification requests, Confirmation checks, and Comprehension checks (Gass & Mackey, 2015). Because of their implicit and reactive nature, these techniques lend themselves well to communicative classrooms, where the focus is primarily on meaning and communication. Long claims that CF needs to be reactive and should only occur when teachers or other learners perceive difficulty in understanding the message or its form (Long & Robinson, 1998). Recently, interaction research has "augmented and in some cases replaced the three C's with other constructs, including recasts" (Gass & Mackey, 2015, p. 188). Recasts provide learners with target-like reformulations of the learner's original utterance. They do not need to involve repetition of the entire utterance and may include additional elaborations not present in the original statement, but they are contingent on the learner's utterance, which they temporarily juxtapose. This juxtaposition frees the working memory from processing for meaning, therefore increasing the chances of processing for form. While this juxtaposition is instrumental in simultaneously providing the learner with both positive (correct form) and negative evidence (non target-like form), it may also confuse the learner as to its intent. That is, if a recast occurs after an ungrammatical utterance, it may be perceived as responding to the content of the statement (instead of its form) or even as another way of saying the same thing (Lyster, 1998a, 1998b; Lyster & Ranta, 1997). Although Swain (1985) did not openly advocate one corrective technique over the other, the notion that learners need to be pushed to produce more target-like output suggests that prompts are possibly the best way to facilitate L2 learning in that context. Since prompts push learners to correct the error on their own, they are instrumental in focusing the learners' attention on certain aspects of their speech, leading them to notice the gaps and/or holes in their output.

1.3.4 Psycho-cognitive Theories

Cognitive SLA theories aim to explain how the L2 is processed and learned by the human brain. Unlike the behaviorist stimulus-response model for human learning, cognitive psychologists view the brain as a processor that operates on mental representations, which mediate input and output. Output is measured in terms of performance, which is inferred from observations of information processing. SLA research on cognition has adopted three key assumptions made by information processing psychologists: 1) learning is made of representation and access or process (Skehan, 1998), 2) mental processing is divided into automatic/fluent (unconscious) and voluntary/ controlled (conscious) modes, and 3) attention and memory—a central preoccupation in SLA cognition—are limited (Ortega, 2009). To begin, representation refers to knowledge of the L2 in terms of its grammar, lexicon, and schemata. Access involves the processing (i.e., access and retrieval) of that knowledge when it is needed for comprehension (input) or production (output). This processing is supported by both automatic and controlled mechanisms, which create all human perception and action through interaction. When a task is automatic, its processing requires little effort and, as such, uses few cognitive resources, allowing for simultaneous execution of several tasks (i.e., parallel processing). Controlled processing, on the other hand, involves more effort and cognitive resources, which limits the number of elements one can attend to at the same time (i.e., serial processing). The latter is activated when mental and conscious effort is required to perform any task. This *limited capacity model* of information processing

(Ortega, 2009) predicts that tasks performed under controlled processing will yield a performance that is variable and vulnerable.

To become an effective L2 user, one would need to achieve a certain level of automaticity, i.e., "automatic performance that draws on implicit-procedural knowledge and is reflected in fluent comprehension and production and in lower neural activation patterns" (Ortega, 2009, p. 85; Segalowitz, 2003), where he/she will be able to use the language with relative ease and speed. According to the Skill Acquisition Theory, adapted from John Anderson's Adaptive Control of Thought (ACT) theory (Anderson, 1983), learning is the gradual transformation of knowledge from controlled to automatic through repeated practice. That is, over time, practice replaces controlled processes with automatic ones through the conversion of declarative/explicit knowledge into procedural knowledge. While the initial change happens rather quickly, the subsequent automatization of procedural knowledge occurs at a much slower rate. Automatization can be defined in several ways: 1) the whole process of knowledge change (from declarative to procedural), 2) "the slow process of reducing error rate, reaction time, and interference with/from other tasks that takes place after proceduralization," or 3) "quantitative change in the subcomponents of procedural knowledge to the exclusion of any qualitative change or restructuring" (DeKeyser, 2007a, p. 3). Regardless of the definition one adopts, researchers agree that knowledge developed at the later stage is more specific than at the beginning, often becoming so specialized that it does not transfer well, even to similar tasks (DeKeyser, 2007b). Thus, the development of the two kinds of knowledge is needed for effective language learning: procedural knowledge for use in predictable contexts and declarative knowledge for application of rules in new situations. More important, however, is that the right conditions be present for the automatization of knowledge to succeed. That is, abstract rules need to be repeatedly illustrated with concrete examples (to create mental associations between the two) to move learners from the "that" to the "how" stage of skill acquisition (Anderson, Fincham, & Douglass, 1997), and this is precisely what is missing in L2 teaching (DeKeyser, 2005).

A central concept in the study of skill acquisition is the "power law of practice/learning" (DeKeyser, 2007a; 2007b), which states that regardless of what is being learned, reaction time and error rate decline over time according to a specific power function (e.g., Anderson, 2000); in other words, practice with a given task brings about a gradual decline in both reaction time and error rate. Furthermore, automatization is highly skill-specific and, as such, it should involve practice that focuses on the production/comprehension of relevant abilities (e.g., practice of L2 production will help automatize production, not comprehension). Lastly, it is important to note that proceduralized knowledge is not the same as implicit knowledge. While absence of awareness is a necessary requirement for implicit knowledge, this is not so for automaticity (DeKeyser, 2007a). That is to say that knowledge can be implicit but not automatic (e.g., error rate is high but speed is low due to incomplete implicit learning, which causes the learner to feel unsure about what he/she knows), and vice versa—it can be automatic yet not implicit (speed is high and error rate is low, but the learner is still conscious of the rule).

The third key assumption in the study of cognition in SLA is that although memory and attention play an important role in language learning, their capacity is limited. Since long-term memory is about representation, its capacity is virtually unlimited. It comprises two types of memory: explicit-declarative, which aids in the recollection of facts and events, and implicit-procedural, which supports skills and habit learning.[10] Working (short-term) memory, in turn, is about access and involves on-the-spot "working out" (N. Ellis, 2005) of problems. Thus, it not only stores information, but also integrates new information with knowledge that has already been encoded in long-term memory. N. Ellis (2005) defines working memory as "the home of explicit induction, hypothesis formation, analogical reasoning, prioritization, control, and decision-making. It is where we develop, apply, and hone our linguistic insights into an L2. Working memory is the system that concentrates across time, controlling attention in the face of distraction" (p. 337). Its storage capacity, however, is limited, and stores information for only a few seconds before forgetting it altogether (unless it is practiced enough to enter long-term memory—*phonological loop,* Baddeley, 2007).

This limitation is offset by *attention,* which increases the amount of time information remains activated in working memory before it is sent for further processing or for storage in long-term memory. Attention, however, is also limited in capacity, allowing it to handle only one attention-demanding processing task at a time (Ortega, 2009, but see Robinson & Gilabert, 2007; Wickens, 2007). But what determines the order in which information is processed? In his Input Processing hypothesis, Bill VanPatten (2002, 2004) suggests two principles that guide learners in the processing of input during real time comprehension. First, learners process input for meaning before they process it for form. In grammatical terms, this means that: 1) they process content words before anything else (e.g., in "The cat is sleeping," learners will process "cat" and "sleep" before "the" and "is," VanPatten, 2007, p. 117), 2) they tend to rely on lexical items as opposed to grammatical form to get meaning when both encode the same semantic information (e.g. "yesterday" will be processed before the verb-final "-ed"; "he" before the third person singular marker "-s"), and 3) they interpret the first noun in a sentence to be the subject (e.g., "Mary hates John," Mary = doer = subject, VanPatten,

2007, p. 121). Second, for learners to process form that is not meaningful, they must be able to process informational or communicative content at no or little cost to attention. This means that the learners' attention needs to be drawn to form in ways that ensure awareness.

The importance of awareness in learning an L2 was first highlighted by Schmidt, who proposed the Noticing Hypothesis (Schmidt, 1990). According to this hypothesis, learning any aspect of an L2 requires conscious noticing of the relevant linguistic data in the input. It is focused attention on specific aspects in the input that brings about L2 knowledge: "what learners notice in input is what becomes intake for learning" (Schmidt, 1995, p. 20). In other words, learning all aspects of an L2 cannot occur without awareness. What is more, subliminal learning is impossible (Schmidt, 1990). Schmidt (1990, 1994, 1995, 2001) attributed two levels to awareness: higher and lower. While the higher level of awareness is associated with understanding and is seen as facilitative but not necessary for language learning, the lower level is equated to noticing and is judged as crucial to L2 acquisition.

Various positions have been taken on the Noticing Hypothesis (Ellis N., 2002; Gass, 1997; Robinson, 1995; Schmidt, 2001; Tomlin & Villa, 1994). Nick Ellis (2002), for example, has sided with Schmidt's position, saying that the Noticing Hypothesis can be deemed "correct," provided that it is complemented by the following two conditions (stipulated in his Implicit Tallying Hypothesis, 2002): (1) noticing is necessary only for new elements, whose learning cannot be achieved without conscious attention; and (2) noticing may be necessary only for first, and not for consecutive, encounters with "difficult" elements because "once a stimulus representation is firmly in existence, that stimulus [. . .] need never be noticed again; yet as long as it is attended to for use in the processing of future input for meaning, its strength will be incremented and its associations tallied and implicitly catalogued" (Ellis, 2002, p. 174). Robinson (1995) also agreed that noticing is a necessary condition for language learning, but specified that this is only so as long as noticing is seen as involving awareness (focal attention) plus rehearsal of input in the short-term memory. The focus here is on the rehearsal function, which is claimed to control the sending of information stored in the short-term memory to the long-term memory.

Others, however, have disagreed with Schmidt, suggesting that only *detection* is necessary in learning an L2 (Tomlin & Villa, 1994) and that while *noticing* facilitates L2 development, it is not required (Gass, 1997; Tomlin & Villa, 1994). In their functional model of input processing, Tomlin and Villa (1994) divided attention into three components: (1) alertness (a general readiness to deal with the incoming stimuli), (2) orientation (the direction of attention resources to a certain type of stimuli), and (3) detection (the cognitive registration of the stimuli) (p. 190). Of the three, they accord *orientation* and *detection* central roles in the process of second language acquisition. For them, "the key idea of orientation is that the specific aligning of attention ('orienting') on a stimulus has facilitative or inhibitory consequences for further processing depending on whether or not information occurs as expected or not as expected" (p. 191). Despite the importance of orientation as a function of attention, Tomlin and Villa argue that it is detection *alone* that is necessary for acquisition to occur because once a particular exemplar is registered in memory, the learner can then use it to make and test hypotheses about the L2 standard. As such, the model maintains that while alertness and orientation may increase the chances of detection, they (separately or together) are not necessary for detection to take place (p. 197). In other words, there is no link between learning and awareness; instead, it is the detection of linguistic input (without awareness) that is necessary to ensure L2 learning. Similarly, Gass (1997) claimed that although noticing is helpful in L2 learning, it is not essential.

In light of this, Schmidt adjusted his original claim of noticing being the "necessary and sufficient condition for converting input to intake" (Schmidt, 1990, p. 129) to assigning it a facilitative role in L2 learning. Thus, in its present form, the Noticing Hypothesis states that noticing is helpful in L2 learning and that "more noticing leads to more learning" (Schmidt, 1994, p. 18). Noticing can come from within the learner or can be encouraged by external factors, such as a lesson or a reaction from the teacher/interlocutor. These factors make learners become aware of (1) the forms in the target language (Schmidt, 1995), (2) the gaps between their utterances and the L2, and (3) the holes (what is missing) in their interlanguage (Swain & Lapkin, 1995). In this weaker form, the Hypothesis has attracted much support among researchers, who, for the most part, have been able to demonstrate that noticing (detection plus awareness) is facilitative of L2 learning.

In terms of the corrective techniques, the theories herein do not explicitly subscribe to one type over the other, but simply reiterate the importance of feedback as an awareness-raising tool. However, it may be possible to conclude that VanPatten's Hypothesis advocates recasts. Since learners (especially low level learners) cannot attend to meaning and form simultaneously, one of the potential benefits of recasts is that they keep the meaning constant. Once the meaning is understood (even if partially), the resources needed to process meaning will be reduced, allocating more attention to form, and consequently, facilitating form-function mapping (VanPatten, 1990). Furthermore, in relation to cognitive psychology, prompts may also be seen as a "good" CF technique as they can help with proceduralizing declarative knowledge and automatizing retrieval of correct forms (DeBot, 1996). In other words, recasts may be advantageous for first-time encounters because they can serve as models of what is possible in the target language. Once these models are provided, prompts may be employed to push learners to retrieve these correct forms from declarative knowledge to proceduralize them and to make their retrieval automatic.

To sum up, the four theories described here represent different views on the process of L2 learning and the role of CF in this process. The behaviorist viewpoint suggests that language is learned through imitation of the supplied models and that errors are to be avoided for successful acquisition. If errors occur, the best way to treat them is through immediate and overt correction that includes the identification and remediation of the problem as well as the provision of additional target-like models. Hence, recasts and explicit correction are the preferred techniques to remedy ill-formed utterances—recasts provide the models of the target form, and explicit correction signals the locus of the error, explains the problem in grammatical terms, and ensures ample repetition of the correction. Innatists, on the other hand, believe in the sufficiency of comprehensible input and see no need for grammar teaching or CF, which instead of promoting acquisition, impede it by raising the affective filter, decreasing motivation, and interrupting the flow of communication. Arguing against the sufficiency of comprehensible input in SLA, interactionists agree on the importance of having the learners' attention drawn to the formal properties of the target language by means of feedback. Their theoretical stances, however, imply different corrective techniques. While some (Long, 1996, 2006) see recasts as effective in that they are implicit and are provided in reaction to a comprehension or production "roadblock," others (Swain, 1985, 1995) seem to prefer pushing learners to produce output, which may favor prompts over recasts. Finally, although the psycho-cognitive theories have not made explicit claims about which CF techniques bring about more language learning, they see both recasts and prompts as important, though at different stages in the language learning process. CF is attributed an important role in these types of theories as it draws the learners' attention to form during communication and thus allows them to notice the gap between what they said and what they meant to say. While the major language theories advocated today generally agree on the facilitative effect of CF on language learning, there is no consensus on whether certain feedback techniques are more effective than others in leading to learning gains—a question (among others) that is of interest to language teachers.

1.4 PEDAGOGICAL PERSPECTIVES ON CF

Corrective feedback is an important consideration for language teachers. This is primarily because "error correction is an expected role for the teacher"

(Hedge, 2000, p. 288) and learners generally expect to receive some information about the accuracy of their L2 output. Learners also hold beliefs about the types of CF they find most useful and are not as concerned about the affective consequences that teachers tend to attribute to CF. As such, Li (2017), in his research synthesis of teacher and learner beliefs about CF, urges teachers to inform, and, if needed, reconsider, their views on correction by taking into account students' views on the subject and the findings that CF research has produced. While language teachers generally resist reading and at times, lack access to reports of empirical investigations (Bartels, 2003; Borg, 2007; Shkedi, 1998), consuming CF research in particular may help teachers to reflect on and understand their own CF practices as well as to respond to numerous questions they may have about CF implementation in the classroom (Kamiya & Loewen, 2014). Even though research often cannot answer all the questions teachers may have or the answers may not directly apply to a particular teaching situation, it can "stimulate reflection on the complex phenomenon of instructed language learning and a willingness to experiment with new approaches in accordance with [teachers'] local conditions" (Ellis, 2005, p. 44, cited in Kamiya & Loewen, 2014).

CF is one such phenomenon that affects L2 learning. It is also a complex phenomenon in that its application is not clear-cut and is often affected by numerous factors inside and outside the classroom (Nassaji & Kartchava, 2017). The advice that teachers receive about correction from teacher guides (Ellis, 2017) and selected scholars (e.g., Krashen, 1981; Schwartz, 1993; Truscott, 1999) can also complicate the matter. Truscott (1999), for example, has called on teachers to eradicate oral error correction altogether due to the difficulties they may experience in recognizing and correcting a student's error, providing personalized correction, and doing so consistently while maintaining a communicative focus. Students, Truscott argued, may also be challenged to notice, understand, and incorporate the provided correction. These concerns notwithstanding, growing research on CF has demonstrated that it is better to provide correction than to withhold it (e.g., Li, 2010; Lyster & Saito, 2010; Mackey & Goo, 2007; Russell & Spada, 2006).

Yet, it is still not clear whether or not to correct learners' errors, when to correct, which errors to address, how, and by whom. These concerns were first articulated by Hendrickson (1978), and today, they continue to be the focus of teacher guides when it comes to discussions of CF. Ellis (2017) has compared the advice teachers find in the guides with that proposed by L2 researchers. He concluded that guides: (1) see oral CF as important, (2) worry about the negative affect that CF can invoke, (3) distinguish between CF in accuracy versus fluency work, preferring it in the former rather than the latter, (4) promote immediate correction in accuracy work, but delayed correction during fluency practice, (5) encourage correction of selected errors, (6) advise the use of various strategies to address errors, and (7) endorse learner involvement in self or peer correction, leaving the teacher to help students find the locus of the error (Ellis, 2017, p. 13). Because these recommendations are largely based on the authors' teaching experiences and intuitions about what may be most effective, Ellis claims, it is not surprising that CF research has produced different advice.

While the importance of CF is not disputed, research has shown that correction plays an essential role in both controlled (accuracy-focused) and free (fluency-driven) types of production. In fact, attention to form during meaningful communication makes the problem of form more noticeable (Long, 1996), providing the learner with an opportunity for in-time learning (Lightbown, 1998). Furthermore, form-focused instruction (FFI), defined as "pedagogical events which occur within meaning-based approaches to L2 instruction, in which a focus on language is provided in either spontaneous or predetermined ways" (Spada, 1997, p. 73), is believed to promote noticing of form for it allows teachers not only to react to learners' errors as they occur in communication (i.e., CF), but also to plan activities that focus on remedying any form-related issue(s) their students may face in the learning process (i.e., pro-active or pre-emptive grammar teaching). Similar to the teacher guides, much CF research advises teachers to use a variety of corrective techniques (e.g., Lyster et al., 2013), but the research presents the techniques as taxonomies, whose application is largely dictated by a given context, learner needs, teacher's goals, and other factors that may affect the effectiveness and usability of a particular CF strategy. In this way, researchers advise "a principled way" (Nassaji, 2016, p. 553) to use the different CF types whereas the guides offer a "simple list of strategies" (Ellis, 2017, p. 14) that are expected to work with any teacher, in any classroom, and under any condition. As for who should provide CF, unlike the guides, researchers see an important role for both students and teachers, not students alone. Yet, while teacher guides see value in delaying feedback (especially in fluency work), CF research has not yet been able to determine whether immediate correction is more, less, or equally as effective as delayed CF (Quinn & Nakata, 2017). Finally, while there is a consensus that not all errors should be addressed, the process of error selection is viewed differently by teacher educators and researchers. Teacher guides suggest that errors that affect sentence structure as a whole (i.e., "global" errors) should be addressed whereas errors that concern a part of a sentence (i.e., "local" errors) should be omitted. This is because local errors are unlikely to result in a message breakdown, but global errors may. CF research, in turn, does not distinguish errors in this way but studies how CF impacts acquisition of particular linguistic (mostly, grammatical) features.

These features are usually chosen based on their non-saliency in the input, redundancy of structure, or interference from the learners' L1. While the list of features studied is not exhaustive (e.g., French articles (Lyster, 2004); French grammatical gender (Lyster & Izquierdo, 2009); English past tense (Yang & Lyster, 2010); English possessive determiners (Ammar & Spada, 2006)), research findings have shown that provision of CF improves learners' accurate use of these structures.

Ellis' (2017) analysis concludes with an understanding that both teacher educators and CF researchers can learn from each other. While advice given to teachers should go beyond worrying about the students' well-being alone to considering cognitive factors, studies of CF should investigate issues that have either not been addressed before (e.g., nonverbal feedback, role of positive feedback) or have been the target of research that has produced non-generalizable/partial findings (e.g., effect of immediate versus delayed CF). This recommendation finds support in the fact that the five questions posed by Hendrickson so many years ago continue to motivate CF research and puzzle language teachers even today.

1.5 CONCLUSION

This chapter reviewed the concept of corrective feedback, identified contexts in which it can occur, detailed the various oral CF types that have been observed in language classrooms, and pointed out several factors that may influence its effectiveness. The role of CF and CF techniques as they figure within major L2 acquisition theories has also been explored, pointing out both the differences and similarities in the viewpoints. The chapter also explored pedagogical relevance of CF and detailed the differences between the type of advice teachers are generally given about oral error correction and the advice that is research-based. What this chapter makes clear is that CF is a multi-faceted phenomenon and that there are no clear-cut answers on how best to implement it in the classroom. Indeed, while CF research has provided some answers about the role of CF and its effectiveness, much remains in need of further investigation. The role of noticing is one of these underexplored areas. This is because while noticing is deemed important, and for some researchers, a necessary condition for L2 development, it is not clear what teachers can do to help learners notice the corrective intent of the feedback they provide. Making CF explicit by training learners to recognize the function of feedback has been one suggestion; another is to consider learner individual factors and tailor feedback expressly to them. Better still, combining feedback with paralinguistic features has been shown to increase the explicitness of feedback.

Studies detailed in this book address all these issues to determine whether these suggestions may indeed be effective in facilitating learners' ability to notice CF in the classroom setting. To begin this exploration, however, it is important to determine whether all techniques teachers have been shown to use when providing oral CF are equally effective in highlighting the corrective focus of feedback. The next chapter describes a study that investigated this question.

Chapter Two

Noticeability and Effectiveness of Oral Corrective Feedback

This chapter will describe a study that investigated the noticeability and effectiveness of three CF techniques (recasts, prompts, and a combination of the two) delivered in the L2 classroom. To explain the relevance of the study, a review of literature that informed it is provided. The review includes an examination of the various measures of noticing that have been used to study the noticeability of CF as well as a discussion of investigations that empirically examined the noticeability and effectiveness of CF in instructional settings. Then, my quasi-experimental study originally published in *Language Teaching Research* (Kartchava & Ammar, 2014a[11]) is reproduced. The chapter concludes with a consideration of the pedagogical implications the study's results may have for the language classroom.

2.1 BACKGROUND

2.1.1 Measures of Noticing

As explained in Chapter 1, corrective feedback is considered an effective tool to facilitate noticing of errors a student makes when speaking an L2. The importance of this role is grounded in the belief among several researchers (Schmidt, 1990, 2001; Long, 1996; Long & Robinson, 1998; VanPatten, 2007) that attention to form plays an important role in learning an L2. Schmidt (1990, 1994), in particular, has claimed that it is the conscious noticing of the formal aspects of an L2 in the input that allows learners to turn input into intake, and to eventually learn these features, provided that the intake is processed in working memory. Processing of the noticed forms—"mapping meaning and function onto formal properties of language" (VanPatten, 2007,

p. 125)—as opposed to merely noticing them is necessary to ensure learning (i.e., integration of noticed forms into long-term memory). After all, according to Schmidt (2001), "people learn about the things that they attend to and do not learn much about the things they do not attend to" (p. 30). The noticeability of CF has generally[12] been examined via questionnaires and journals (Alanen, 1995; Izumi, 2002; Mackey, 2006; Schmidt & Frota, 1986; Slimani, 1989), verbal protocols (e.g., Egi, 2007a; Egi, 2010; Izumi, 2002; Mackey 2006; Mackey & Philp, 1998; Mackey et al., 2000; McDonough & Mackey, 2006; Philp, 2003; Rassaei, 2012; Trofimovich et al., 2007), as well as uptake (Lyster & Ranta, 1997; Mackey & Philp, 1998; Sheen, 2004). What follows is a discussion of each of these instruments, their strengths and limitations, as well as the findings of the investigations in which they were used are detailed.

2.1.1.1 Questionnaires and Journals

To provide introspective data on learners' noticing and L2 learning, several researchers have used questionnaires and diaries/journals (e.g., Slimani, 1989; Schmidt & Frota, 1986; Izumi, 2002). Questionnaires are one of the most common ways to collect data on a wide variety of topics, from attitudes and opinions to perceptions of noticing.[13] They allow researchers to gather information that learners are able to report about themselves and/ or their learning experiences. These reports are typically not available from tests alone and, as such, provide a complementary view on learners' beliefs and motivations about learning or their reactions to learning and classroom events (Mackey & Gass, 2016). Slimani (1989), for example, developed specialized types of questionnaires to study the role of topicalization (i.e., "who initiates the topics of interaction," Slimani, 1989, p. 223) in an Algerian EFL classroom. It was argued that a detailed study of classroom interaction could explain "uptake," defined as what learners report learning at the end of the lesson, and that topicalization would be influential in substantiating learners' claims about uptake. These questionnaires were highly customized and ranged in terms of type in that some were closed-ended and others open-ended. The closed-ended questionnaires (e.g., *The learners' operating principle questionnaire*, Slimani, 1989, pp. 233–234) included questions, to which answers were predetermined by the researcher for the purpose of (1) ensuring uniformity of measurement and consecutively, greater reliability, as well as (2) facilitating quantification and analysis of the results. The open-ended questionnaires, in turn, (e.g., *Uptake recall chart* and *Uptake identification probe*, Slimani, 1989, p. 233) allowed the participants to express their thoughts and ideas in relation to the specific questions of interest to the researcher (i.e., about the topics they noticed and learned in a given lesson).

Such questions as *"What points have come up in today's lesson?"* and *"Of all the things you wrote on your 'Uptake recall chart,' which do you think you learned today?"* were designed to probe learners' reactions to the instruction they were experiencing.

Questionnaires, as described above (and in general), can provide both qualitative and quantitative data about a number of subjects in a short period of time. Furthermore, administration of questionnaires is not only economical and practical, but it also lends itself to implementation through mail, e-mail and telephone. A major drawback of questionnaires, however, is that they do not provide a complete picture of the complexities of particular contexts (Mackey & Gass, 2016). That is, the responses yielded may be inaccurate or incomplete because of a learner's inability to describe his/her perceptions and beliefs. This can be exacerbated by: (1) open-ended questions and (2) the mode of execution (written vs. oral), as well as (3) learner's limited ability in the L2. To counteract this limitation, more than one type of question should be used and the participants should be given the option to respond to the questions verbally and/or in their L1. Another limitation has to do with the validity of questionnaires as an elicitation tool in that the data elicited may be an artifact of the device. As such, prior to mass implementation, questionnaires need to be piloted and reviewed by others. Finally, although Slimani's study yielded interesting results, using questionnaires as a sole instrument of noticing is problematic due to the fact that the respondents themselves generate the data. As with all self-reported data, it is necessary to collect information from more than one source to ensure a more holistic picture of noticing (Mackey & Gass, 2006) and to counterbalance the participants' varying abilities in making explicit what they notice. What's more, absence of awareness/noticing in reports cannot be taken as evidence of no awareness. As such, recent studies on noticing have incorporated a variety of measures to get at learners' noticing (e.g., Mackey, 2006; Mackey et al., 2000; Philp, 2003).

Diaries, or L2 learning journals, have been used to allow learners to write about their language learning experiences outside the constraints that other measures and perspectives may entail. They provide opportunities for learners to record their thoughts, reflections on classroom experiences, language items noticed and learned (Schmidt & Frota, 1986), as well as emotional issues (Schumann & Schumann, 1977). Journals can be either structured or not. In her study of the relationship between CF, noticing, and L2 learning, Mackey (2006) used journals to elicit the learners' impressions about the employed activities and general interaction in the classroom, as well as the instances of learning. To tap into noticing, Mackey provided a structure for the journals to have learners record: (1) the language forms and concepts they were noticing (i.e., pronunciation, grammar, vocabulary, content),

(2) the interlocutor who produced the reported items (i.e., learner, teacher, peer), and (3) the novelty of the reported items. The insights these provided pointed to a positive relationship between the learners' noticing of feedback in response to questions and its subsequent incorporation in the output. Journals are, however, limited in that (1) they need to be consistent and maintained over a certain period of time, (2) the insights generated cannot be generalized, and (3) analysis of unstructured journals can be complex and convoluted. Despite these drawbacks, journals can provide a more complete picture of the underlying processes at play.

2.1.1.2 Verbal Protocols

Introspective measures have been used extensively in SLA research to elicit data from an individual who has or is undergoing a language-related experience. The premise is that an individual is able to verbalize information that he/she has attended to while carrying out a task.[14] Unlike the early users of verbal protocols who assumed that individuals could directly report the mental processes that bring about different sensations and experiences, modern-day researchers do not make such an assumption (Green, 1998). Instead, verbal protocols are viewed as a source of information for the researcher to infer the cognitive processes involved. As inferences are usually made directly from the data, this technique is considered qualitative (in that standard statistical procedures cannot be applied to non-numerical data), but it can also be used quantitatively. If, for instance, the frequency with which a certain behavior (e.g., noticing of form) occurs is of interest, the data will first need to be coded (using, for example, Leow's (1997, 2001) categories of noticing: *unaware, aware, aware with understanding*) and only then, subjected to various statistical analyses. This was the case in Egi's (2007a) study, where she investigated the functions (i.e., responses to content, negative evidence, positive evidence, or a combination of positive and negative evidence) that L2 learners of Japanese assigned to recasts which they noticed in their interactions with native speakers of the language. The instances of noticing were collected by way of verbal reports and were then categorized in terms of: (1) learner noticing (or not noticing) the recast and (2) the aspect of the recast that was noticed. The raw frequencies of reported noticing were then tallied and later used in statistical analyses.

Verbal protocols represent a rich source of data for they allow access to cognitive processes that are difficult (if not impossible) to study via other means. Two types of verbal protocols have been used to measure noticing. The first type includes think-aloud or talk-aloud procedures that are carried out *during* a task. The second type involves retrospective protocols, which engage thinking about a *previously-performed* task. This (latter) type of protocol usually entails a prompted interview (i.e., stimulated recall), which may utilize video, audio or written prompts to engage the learner in retrospection. These two types of protocols may be grouped further into online (i.e., think-aloud and talk-aloud) and retrospective (i.e., stimulated recall) reports in terms of timing (Mackey & Gass, 2016). That is, whereas online reports require that the learner tells the researcher what he/she is thinking *while or immediately after* performing a task, retrospective measures call on the learner to report those thoughts *after* completing a given activity.

Think-aloud, a type of online report, requires learners to simultaneously observe and report their thoughts while completing a task (see Bowles, 2010, for a comprehensive treatment of think-alouds). This is usually achieved by engaging learners in problem-solving tasks, during which they are asked to describe what is happening in their minds as they solve the problem. The purpose is to shed light on the way people execute tasks and arrive at solutions. In SLA, this type of introspection has been used by Ronald Leow, who wanted to demonstrate that noticing *plus* awareness (see discussion on Schmidt) leads to L2 development (e.g., Leow, 1997; 1998; 2001; Rosa & Leow, 2004). In Leow's (1998) study of noticing among Spanish L2 university students, for example, he used crossword puzzles and instructed the participants in the following way (p. 54, original emphasis):

> Here is a crossword puzzle similar to the ones you have done in class. Use the clues provided and see if you can successfully complete this crossword [. . .]. As you do the crossword, *try to speak aloud into the microphone your thoughts WHILE you perform the task for each word, NOT AFTER*. Include the numbers of the clues also while you are thinking aloud. Please try to speak in a clear voice.

By using the think-aloud protocol, Leow was able to gather comments the participants made as they were solving the puzzle. He later classified these into (1) *unaware* (when introspective data revealed no noticing); (2) *aware* (when a learner acknowledged paying attention to the target in question); and (3) *aware with understanding* (when a learner signaled some understanding of a rule by making partial references to it). The results of his research program reliably show that those participants who are "aware" or "aware with understanding" score consistently higher on post-tests than their "unaware" counterparts.

The talk-aloud protocol (also known as "immediate recall") is another kind of online verbal report. It must be carried out *immediately after* the event of interest has been concluded to allow participants to "verbalize thoughts they had during a conversational turn immediately after a recall prompt" (Mackey

& Gass, 2016, p. 94). This measure of noticing is of particular interest to SLA researchers for two reasons: (1) the verbalized thoughts do not rely on memory and (2) the immediacy of recall facilitates retrieval of the mental processes at play. Effective administration of the tool, however, relies on the need to pilot-test the measure and to train the participants. Several researchers (e.g., Egi, 2007a; Philp 2003; Trofimovich et al., 2007) have investigated the noticeability of feedback using the talk-aloud protocol. While the findings of this research are detailed later in this section, for the purpose of illustration, Philp's (2003) study used the talk-aloud protocol to determine the extent to which L2 learners were able to verbalize their noticing of CF following a recall prompt operationalized by the sound of two knocks. Trofimovich et al. (2007), in turn, used the measure to examine how cognitive variables (i.e., working memory, phonological memory, attention control, and analytical ability) affect learners' ability to notice recasts, a CF technique.

Stimulated recall, a retrospective measure, prompts learners to verbally reflect on the thoughts they had while performing a task or taking part in an activity *after* that task/activity has been completed. To facilitate reflection, a prompt of some kind—usually in the form of a video/audio recording of a learner carrying out the activity or the learner's written product with changes made to it (Mackey & Gass, 2016)—is required. This is to enable the learner "to relive the original situation with great vividness and accuracy" (Bloom, 1954, p. 25) and to mitigate inaccuracies of recall (due to the time lapse between the actual task and the recall session) inherent to the tool. Learners may also be challenged to separate information attended to during the task from that dealt with after the task completion. This is why the instructions participants receive need to be uniform in both description and execution; after all, research has shown that "a single word or tense change can affect the nature of the participant's recall" (Gass & Mackey, 2000, p. 58). Moreover, a prolonged post-event wait may influence learners to say what they think the researcher wants to hear, and consequently, contaminate the data. In other words, in an effort to "please the experimenter" (Seliger & Shohamy, 1989, p. 170), learners may provide information that does not accurately reflect the actual thoughts they had, thus, altering the nature of their commentary.

This misrepresentation of information is a concern for validity, which is one of the major limitations associated with the use of verbal protocols in general. "Validity" refers to whether information captured in the verbal reports actually corresponds to the data yielded as the task is carried out. That is, if the reports are incomplete, if they produce contaminated information, or if they include additional data that were not expressed during the execution of the task, the validity of the reports may be compromised. Tool validity can, however, be improved by following a set of principles, which include: (1) using appropriate instructions, (2) asking participants to vocalize their thoughts only (without trying to explain them), (3) generating the reports either as a task is being performed or within as short a delay as possible after the event, and (4) limiting intervention from the researcher. Data triangulation (i.e., using more than one source and/or more than one technique to corroborate and analyze primary data) can further increase validity since it "aids in credibility, transferability, and dependability of qualitative research" (Mackey & Gass, 2016, p. 233). Exploring the relationships between feedback, instructed ESL learners' noticing of L2 form during classroom interactions and their subsequent L2 development, Mackey (2006), for example, used three tools to measure learners' noticing: (1) on-line learning journals, (2) stimulated recall, and (3) questionnaires.

2.1.1.3 Verbal Protocols in the Study of CF Noticing

Mackey et al. (2000) were perhaps the first to investigate the extent to which adult ESL learners ($n = 10$) and English L1 university learners of Italian ($n = 7$) were able to notice CF (noticing was operationalized as "learners' reports about their perceptions," p. 477) and to accurately identify its linguistic target. The non-native speakers (NNS) were paired up either with a native speaker (NS) (in the case of ESL) or a proficient L2 speaker (as was the case with Italian) to partake in two-way interaction activities (spot-the-differences and picture description tasks), during which native or proficient speakers of the L2 were asked to provide CF whenever and in whatever form seemed appropriate to them. Feedback was provided in response to errors on morphosyntax, phonology, lexis, and semantics. The interaction task was immediately followed by stimulated recall sessions, where the learners were asked to recall their thoughts at the time of the original interaction. To do this, they were asked to watch video replays of their interactions with the NSs. As they watched, the video was paused during instances of feedback and the learners were asked to report what they were thinking at the time. Noticing was operationalized as the learners' verbalization of what they perceived the focus of feedback to be. The results revealed that the accurate perception of CF was dependent on the type of error. That is, the ESL learners accurately recognized the corrective intent of feedback on their lexical (83.3%) and phonological (60%) errors, but not on the morphosyntactic problems (13%). The Italian learners, in turn, recognized the nature of feedback 66% of the time on their lexical errors, but not on the errors with phonology (21.4%) and morphosyntax (24%). A closer look at the feedback types in relation to error type showed that while recasts were used to treat most of the morphosyntactic errors (75%), negotiation was used to target the phonological errors (74%)—a move characterized as "suboptimal" by the authors "at least in terms of learners' perceptions about the feedback" (ibid, p. 493). Subsequent studies investigated the noticeability of CF in terms of learners' cognitive abilities, proficiency level, and types of recasts and compared the noticeability of recasts to that of prompts.

Following Robinson's (1995) suggestion that learners' ability to notice feedback may depend on the aptitude of their WM, Mackey, Philp, Egi, Fujii and Tasumi (2002) set out to investigate whether WM was in fact the mediating factor in Japanese L1 learners' ($n = 30$) ability to notice recasts in dyadic task-based interactions when learning English. In this pre-test/post-test design, all the participants received feedback from native speakers of English in response to their ill-formed questions and underwent psychometric tests of WM capacity. However, only a fraction[15] ($n = 11$) took part in the stimulated recall interviews to reflect on their thoughts during preselected feedback episodes. Noticing was identified as "the learner's articulation of response to the input, without distinguishing the degree of understanding involved, or the focus of noticing" (p. 188). The results suggested that learners with larger WM capacity were able to recognize recasts more readily than those with limited capacity.

This finding, however, was not corroborated by Trofimovich, Ammar and Gatbonton (2007), who explored whether individual differences such as proficiency level, attention span, phonological memory, WM and analytical ability along with error type (morphosyntax, phonology and the mixture of the two) affect ESL learners' ability to notice recasts. In addition to tests of the said individual differences,[16] 32 adult Francophone learners of ESL participated in an online description task, where they had to describe drawings depicting members of two families (with one male and one female child) engaged in everyday tasks (e.g., playing, eating, etc.). The pictures were designed to elicit one of the targeted features: (1) morphosyntactic (English possessive determiners = PDs), (2) lexical (intransitive verbs), or (3) both (transitive verbs followed by a possessive determiner-noun combination). The picture task proceeded as follows. First, on a computer screen, the learners were shown a picture of a person performing a task (e.g., a girl scratching her back). Then, after a short delay, a digitally-recorded voice of a native speaker of English prompted them to describe the event depicted in the picture (e.g., *What is she doing?*). At this point, the generated response could either be accurate (e.g., *The girl/she is scratching her back*) or inaccurate (e.g., *She is scratching his back*). Regardless whether the description was accurate or not, each response was followed by a digitally-recorded recast (e.g., *Yeah, she is scratching her back*). After that, the learners were asked to indicate, by saying "yes" or "no," if they noticed any difference between their original utterance and the recorded description (*Did you notice any difference? Please say yes or no*).

Finally, on the immediate post-test, the learners saw the same drawing again and were asked to describe it one more time. The delayed post-test was conducted 2–12 minutes later to examine the learners' ability to incorporate the earlier-supplied recast into their new description. Noticing of the recast was based on the immediate response to the "noticing" question and operationalized as proportion noticing (i.e., correctly detected recasts divided by the total number of incorrect productions). The learners' noticing scores for each of the linguistic targets (morphosyntactic, lexical, and mixed) were submitted to an analysis of variance. The results indicated that when the learners received feedback on their erroneous utterances, they noticed more recasts targeting lexical (intransitive verbs) than morphosyntactic errors (PDs), but none of the cognitive differences were found to predict noticing. The reason for this, the authors speculated, might have been due to the high frequency of recasts, which were supplied regardless of whether or not a learner's utterance contained an error. This might have increased the saliency of recasts in the input, making them highly predictable on the one hand, and limiting the learner's need to draw on his/her individual differences to notice them, on the other.

The noticeability of feedback was also investigated in relation to learner proficiency and the length of a recast. In her investigation of the extent to which L2 learners (NNS) noticed recasts in reaction to their ill-formed questions during oral interaction with native speakers of English (NS), Philp (2003) paired an NNS ($n = 33$) with an NS to perform a warm-up, a story-completion and a picture-drawing task. The warm-up task was used to train the participants in the methodology to be used. That is, the adult ESL learners were asked to listen as their NS partner read a string of 12 random numbers. The reading was interrupted at places by the sound of two knocks, at which time the NNS had to recall the last two numbers in the read sequence. No information as to the correctness (or incorrectness) of the recall was provided at that time. However, during the picture task, where the NNS had to ask the NS questions about the pictures, feedback (i.e., recast) was provided by the NS in response to any non-target-like structures. Each recast was followed by two knocking sounds (i.e., online/immediate recall), prompting the NNS to repeat the last thing he/she heard. An example of this follows (Philp, 2003, p. 108):

NNS: *Why he is very unhappy?*

NS: *Why is he very unhappy?* [2 knocks]

NNS: *Yeah, why is very unhappy?*

Noticing was measured through online protocol. Although Philp (2003) acknowledged that immediate recall is not a perfect measure of noticing since what is noticed is not always reported, she argued that "if recasts are recalled, it is evident that noticing at some level has taken place: input has been detected and further processed in working memory to the extent that it is available for recall" (p. 109). As such, the data were transcribed and analyzed as to the accuracy with which the recall was made: (1) correct, (2) modified, or (3) no recall. When the recast was repeated, the recall was judged as "correct." "Modified" recall applied to those instances when the recast was repeated but inaccurately (as in the example above). And finally, the "no recall" category described those utterances that either were not changed or failed to produce any response to the cue. The results showed that the advanced proficiency (high and intermediate, in this study) learners accurately recalled over 70% of the recasts compared to the 60% recalled by their low-level counterparts. Furthermore, the length of a recast affected the accuracy of the recall in that the shorter recasts were noticed more often (regardless of the proficiency) than the longer ones. Finally, recasts that resembled the original utterance the least (i.e., incorporated three or more changes) were not noticed as often as those with fewer changes. This result applied to all learners, irrespective of level.

To sum up, much of the research into the noticeability of feedback has primarily focused on noticing as a function of one type of CF, namely recasts. It has also showed that the noticeability of recasts as a function of recall protocols seems to depend on the error type, working memory, attention capacity and attention switching capacity, analytical ability, the learner's proficiency level, as well as the length and type (explicit/implicit) of a recast (Ammar & Sato, 2010a; Mackey et al., 2000; Mackey et al., 2002; Philp, 2003; Trofimovich et al., 2007).

2.1.1.4 Uptake

Uptake has also been used to measure noticing of CF. One such inquiry was conducted by Mackey et al. (2000), where uptake was defined as "the learners' modification of their original utterance following the NS's provision of feedback through recasts or negotiation" (p. 492). The results pointed to the learners accurately recognizing the corrective intent of feedback on their lexical and semantic errors, but not on the morphosyntactic and phonological problems. A further investigation revealed that in terms of uptake, only 52% of all feedback moves resulted in student modification of the original utterance. Of these, 45% of the feedback was accurately perceived in relation to phonological errors, followed by 16% to lexical and 5% to the morphosyntactic ones. Of the 48% of all the feedback that did not result in uptake, the target of feedback was not noticed by the learners 89% of the time. Hence, uptake is a sign of noticing in the sense that whenever it occurs, there is a 66% chance that the learners have noticed the CF. Mackey et al. (2000) posited that "uptake may be related to learners' perceptions about feedback at the time of the feedback" (p. 492).

Uptake was redefined once again in the study conducted by Ellis, Basturkmen and Loewen (2001), who investigated the amount of uptake in Form-Focused Instruction[17] (FFI) delivered during unplanned (reactive)[18] and planned (pre-emptive) discussions of form (i.e., Form-Focused Episodes, FFEs). Here, uptake referred to the learner's utterance, which was optional, and could occur not only after feedback, but also after any utterance (made by anyone) that provided information about a target feature. For Ellis et al. (2001), successful uptake in pre-emptive FFEs is equal to an overt indication on the part of the learner that the linguistic feature has been understood. Successful uptake in reactive FFEs, in turn, is demonstrated by the learner's use of the corrected form after receiving feedback. Two teachers and 24 adult ESL learners in New Zealand participated in twelve hours of communicative teaching interactions. The results revealed that overall 73.9% of all FFEs were followed by uptake, of which 74.1% were successful. Furthermore, uptake was observed after 75.3% of the reactive FFEs and 83.6% of the student-initiated pre-emptive FFEs. In terms of techniques, prompts, clarification requests and repetitions yielded 100% uptake when the focus was on form. Similarly, recasts also resulted in a high amount of uptake (71.6%), of which 76.3% was successful. This finding was further corroborated by Loewen (2004), who in an attempt to demonstrate the types of feedback that would be more successful in leading to more uptake, analyzed 1,373 FFEs to reveal that elicitation and explicit correction produced more uptake.

Yet another study suggested that learners do indeed notice recasts in a classroom setting. Ohta (2000) investigated the "private speech"—"oral language addressed by the student to himself or herself" (p. 52)—learners produced in reaction to the teacher's feedback. Set in a Japanese as a foreign language classroom, where the focus of instruction centered on grammar and metalinguistic knowledge, the study revealed that learners were more likely to notice recasts when they were directed either toward another student or to the whole class, and not when the recasts were directed to the learners' own errors. This finding, Ohta claimed, confirms that recasts are noticed by students in a class, even if they do not lead to uptake from the actual student who has originally made the error. This assertion, however, has been questioned since the accuracy-driven context in which the study was conducted coupled with the fact that the participants were wearing microphones (and were aware of the fact that their interactions were being recorded, which may have raised their awareness of the treatment at hand, thus rendering recasts more salient) could have influenced the learners' ability to notice recasts (Nicholas et al., 2001). In fact, as Nicholas et al. (2001) suggested, the grammar-oriented classroom in which the study was conducted may have afforded recasts more salience; a similar conclusion was reached by Sheen (2004).

Finally, Mackey and Philp (1998) examined the effects of "intensive" recasts—recasts that repeatedly focus on a particular linguistic item in a communicative discourse—on the production and learning of English questions. Working in 35 NS-NNS dyads, adult learners of English were asked to engage in three info-gap tasks (picture drawing, story completion and story sequencing) designed to elicit and produce questions. The NSs were instructed to recast any non-target-like utterances, paying special attention to the errors in questions and targeting these as much as possible. Responses to recasts were categorized in four different ways: (1) continue, (2) repeat, (3) modify, and (4) other. In the "continue" type of response, the learner could either acknowledge the recast with a sound (e.g., "hmm") or simply continue with the task. In the "repeat" response, the participant simply repeated the recast partially or in its entirety, while the "modify" condition called for some kind of modification (not repetition) of the recast. And finally, the "other" condition signaled that in some cases a response was not possible for one reason or another (e.g., change of topic). The results revealed that the participants rarely modified their utterances immediately after a recast, but if they were at a higher stage of question development (i.e., the "readies"), they were more likely to benefit from recasts than their less advanced counterparts ("unreadies"), for whom the presence or absence of recasts in an interaction seemed to make little difference. This led the researchers to conclude that the corrective nature of the recast is more likely to be perceived and learned from by more developmentally ready learners and that simple repetition of a recast does not constitute L2 learning or development.

To sum up, studies that have examined the noticeability of recasts as a function of uptake show conflicting results. While some descriptive studies suggest that recasts lead to the least amount of uptake (Lyster & Ranta, 1997; Panova & Lyster, 2002) because they are not always noticed by learners, others support the noticeability of recasts (Ellis et al., 2001; Ohta, 2000; Sheen, 2006). Still, some laboratory studies demonstrate that recasts may go unnoticed by learners (Mackey et al., 2000) and their noticeability is not contingent on uptake (Mackey & Philp, 1998; Nassaji, 2011a). In fact, the use of uptake as a measure of noticing has been questioned (e.g., Leeman, 2007; Ortega, 2009) because uptake is not seen as "a robust measure of learner noticing nor of the utility of feedback for L2 development, as it should not be assumed that learners will verbally acknowledge all feedback that they notice" (Leeman, 2007, p. 122). In other words, absence of uptake does not necessarily mean that feedback has not been noticed. It could simply imply that the learner: (1) does not see the importance of reacting to the teacher's correction or (2) is unable (due to context, for instance—as in interaction, where recasts do not require a reaction from the interlocutor) or developmentally "unready" to overtly react to the feedback. The use of uptake as a measure of noticing is particularly problematic for recasts because, as Long (2006) cautioned, learner reaction to a recast does not necessarily reflect the source of the learner's knowledge for it is impossible to tell whether the reaction to feedback is an example of newly-acquired knowledge or simple activation of the learner's prior knowledge.

In contrast, Mackey et al. (2000) reported that even though many NNSs claimed not to notice feedback, they produced output in response to such feedback. This was also the case in Yoshida's (2010) study. Hence, simple repetition of feedback cannot imply that the correction has been noticed, understood, or incorporated (Gass, 1997). Instead, the resulting repair may simply be "mimicking" (Gass, 2003, p. 236) of the feedback received, with no analysis or revision done to the learners' interlanguage. After all, repetition of recasts in NS-NNS interactions has been shown not to lead to L2 learning with Mackey and Philp (1998) calling them "red herrings." In the same vein, Philp (2003) found no relation between noticing of feedback and L2 production. Panova and Lyster (2002) attributed this lack of L2 development to the fact that recasts are both initiated and completed by the teacher and not worked out by the learners themselves.

However, the amount of repetition, in large part, depends on the context in which recasts are provided as feedback. This is because "the classroom context (particularly the communicative and/or content-based classrooms) may make it difficult for learners to identify recasts as feedback on form and hence make it difficult for them to benefit from the reformulation that recasts offer. The exception may be some foreign language classrooms in which students' and teachers' focus is more consistently on the language itself" (Nicholas et al., 2001, p. 744). Research has shown that recasts lead to uptake in Korean EFL classrooms (Sheen, 2004) as well as in ESL classrooms in New Zealand (Ellis et al., 2001; Sheen, 2004), but not in French immersion (Lyster & Ranta, 1997) or Canadian adult ESL (Panova & Lyster, 2002) contexts. The lack of uptake following recasts in content-based classrooms is rooted in their ambiguity. Lyster (1998a) reported that recasts have the same form as non-corrective repetitions and are used with the same frequency. As such, they may be perceived by learners as another way to say the same thing or as positive reinforcements of meaning and not as reactions to problems with form (Long, 1996). As mentioned earlier, Lyster and Ranta (1997) found that learners did not immediately respond to recasts as often as they did to the other corrective techniques, rendering the resulting limited uptake as a sign that learners did not notice the recasts' corrective intent. Sheen (2004), however, found that recasts lead to more uptake in the more structured foreign language classrooms and that reduced recasts are more noticeable by learners in communicative contexts (Ammar & Sato, 2010a; Sheen, 2006). Furthermore, the rate of uptake and successful repair depends on the type of recast used (Lyster, 1998a; Sheen, 2006) as was the case in Lyster's (1998a) study where isolated declarative recasts were repaired 23% more often than the incorporated recasts (0%).

2.1.2 Empirical Research on the Noticeability of CF

In light of the studies reviewed above, the noticing research has primarily focused on the noticeability of recasts, rarely comparing them to the other CF techniques. While some researchers interpreted the learners' ability to recall feedback online and retrospectively as a sign of noticing (e.g., Ammar & Sato, 2010a; Havranek, 1999; Mackey, 2006; Mackey et al., 2000; Mackey et al., 2002; Philp, 2003; Trofimovich et al., 2007), others designated uptake as evidence of noticing (e.g., Braidi, 2002; Doughty, 1994; Ellis et al., 2001; Loewen & Philp, 2006; Lyster & Ranta, 1997; Ohta, 2000; Panova & Lyster, 2002). Studies using recall protocols suggest that the learners' ability to recognize recasts as corrective moves is limited by error type (Mackey et al., 2000), length (Philp, 2003), explicitness of the recast (Ammar & Sato, 2010a), as well as by a cohort of individual variables that are mostly psycho-cognitive in nature, i.e., learner's proficiency level (Philp, 2003), working memory capacity (Mackey et al., 2002; Sagarra & Abbuhl, 2013), and attention switching ability (Ammar & Sato, 2010a). The studies that examined the noticeability of recasts as a function of uptake, on the other hand, show conflicting results. While some suggest that recasts lead to the least amount of uptake (Lyster & Ranta, 1997; Panova & Lyster, 2002) because they are not always noticed by learners, others support their noticeability (Ellis et al., 2001; Ohta, 2000; Sheen, 2006). Yet, some laboratory studies demonstrate that recasts may go unnoticed by learners (Mackey et al., 2000) and their noticeability is not contingent on uptake (Mackey & Philp, 1998).

What this research has not done consistently is compare the noticeability of recasts to that of other techniques. Though an early attempt at such a comparison was made by Mackey et al. (2000) where the noticeability of recasts was contrasted with negotiation for meaning techniques, the design of the study did not produce an even distribution of the two techniques across the four error types (lexicon, morphosyntax, phonology, and semantics), limiting any comparison between their noticeability. Although it was found that the learners were not able to accurately recognize recasts as feedback on morphosyntax, nothing was said about the negotiation techniques enabling or hindering the learners' ability to do the same. Similarly, while the learners were able to correctly identify negotiation feedback on phonological errors, no such comparison was made for recasts that addressed ill-formed phonological utterances.

Several researchers (e.g., Ellis, 2001, 2006; Loewen & Philp, 2006; Lyster & Saito, 2010) have called into question the rigidness of the distinction studies of interaction make between recasts and the negotiation for meaning techniques (e.g., Mackey, 2006; Mackey & Philp, 1998; Oliver, 2000) when comparing the effectiveness and noticeability of the two. The primary concern is that the negotiation techniques, as a group, include the CF types that provide input (e.g., confirmation checks) as well as those that require learners to produce output (e.g., clarification requests that prompt learners to self-repair), which blurs the boundaries between them, rendering any "analysis of the effects of different types of processing" (Lyster & Saito, 2010, p. 269) impossible. Clear comparisons between recasts and negotiation are further limited by the fact that confirmation checks, a negotiation technique, are similar in function to recasts, which "are often part of negotiation sequences and function as confirmation checks" (Loewen & Philp, 2006, p. 540). What's more, in their meta-analysis of 15 classroom-based studies that investigated the effectiveness of oral CF on L2 knowledge, Lyster and Saito (2010), questioning the feasibility of distinguishing recasts from negotiation, chose to exclude from their report those investigations that conflated the two techniques (e.g., Mackey, 2006; Muranoi, 2000).

Heeding this limitation, Ammar (2008) compared the noticeability of recasts to prompts among 48 young (11–12 year old) francophone learners of English. As part of the regular class work, the students engaged in information gap activities designed to target three morphosyntactic targets (question formation, third person possessive determiners, and past tense) and one phonological target (the "th" sound), during which the teachers provided feedback in the form of recasts or prompts. To measure noticing, the participants watched 20 video excerpts of CF instances and wrote down their thoughts about them. The responses were then analyzed along the three categories of noticing yielded by the data: (1) *detection* (e.g., "I was thinking that Miss X correct person when they did past tense mistake"); (2) *uptake* of the teacher's correction; and (3) recognition of *help*—when the learner recognized the teacher's attempt to help but did not necessarily identify the form of that help (e.g., "Mr. X was trying to help Mary"). The results showed that overall the learners noticed the corrective intent of prompts more readily than that of recasts. What's more, prompts, compared to recasts, yielded a higher rate of level one ("detection") noticing. To see if noticing of either CF type was a function of individual differences, Ammar assessed the learners' processing speed, phonological memory, attention control and analytical ability. No significant correlations between these four factors and the learners' noticing of prompts were found. However, while phonological memory, attention control, and analytical ability also came up as insignificant for the noticing of recasts, the results pointed to a statistically significant link between processing speed and the noticing of recasts, suggesting that the speed with which input is processed may affect learners' ability to notice and consecutively benefit from recasts.

To summarize, the noticing research has primarily focused on the noticeability of recasts only, rarely comparing it to other CF techniques. While studies that used uptake as a measure of noticing yielded conflicting and, for some, questionable results (Nassaji, 2009), investigations that implemented recall protocols suggested that learners' ability to recognize recasts as corrective moves is limited in a number of ways. What is needed is research that considers the differential noticing of recasts and other CF techniques as well as the use of a measure that allows for more reports of noticing. The study presented here recruited three groups that received CF by way of recasts, prompts or a combination of the two and used immediate protocol to measure noticing, which has been shown to predict learning more than does stimulated recall (Ammar & Sato, 2010a). Before considering the design and results of the study, it is necessary to examine the research that has looked at the effectiveness of CF, which is the focus of the next section.

2.1.3 Empirical Research on the Effectiveness of CF

While there is a general consensus that providing feedback brings about significant gains in learners' performance (Li, 2010; Lyster & Saito, 2010; Mackey & Goo, 2007; Russell & Spada, 2006), there is still disagreement regarding the effectiveness of the different CF types, with a large number of studies questioning the potential benefits of recasts compared to that of prompts (Ammar & Spada, 2006; Ellis et al., 2006; Havranek, 1999; Lyster, 2004; Yang & Lyster, 2010). This is because while classroom studies generally find prompts more effective, laboratory research attributes recasts a facilitative role in L2 development.

Lyster's (2004) study of young learners in the French immersion context, for example, found that when FFI is combined with prompts, it is more effective in facilitating acquisition of grammatical gender than when it is combined with recasts. Similarly, Ammar and Spada (2006) found prompts to be more effective than recasts in the acquisition of the English third person possessive determiners (PDs) *his* and *her* by young French L1 speakers, but the effect of feedback largely depended on the learner's proficiency level. That is, while high proficiency learners (with pre-test scores above 50%) benefited equally from the two CF techniques, their low proficiency counterparts (with pre-test scores below 50%) benefited much more from prompts than from recasts.

With adult ESL learners, Ellis et al. (2006) showed that metalinguistic feedback (i.e., a prompt that consists of error repetition followed by a clue as to the problem) was more effective than recasts in leading to the acquisition of the English regular past tense because the learners were able to recognize the corrective intent of this CF type more readily than that of recasts. In the EFL context, Yang and Lyster (2010) compared the effects of recasts, prompts, and no feedback on the learning of the English regular and irregular past tense by adult university-level learners in China. The results showed that the participants were able to benefit more from prompts than recasts on the acquisition of the regular past tense on both immediate and delayed post tests. Similarly, Loewen and Philp (2006), having analyzed 17 hours of meaning-based interaction in adult ESL classes, found that prompts led to more accuracy (75%) on the post-tests than did recasts (53%).

In the laboratory context, recasts have been shown to positively affect language learning when they were not compared to another CF condition (Han, 2002; Leeman, 2003; McDonough & Mackey, 2006) and when no control group was involved (Ishida, 2004). The studies that compared recasts to other CF types have either yielded positive results for recasts alone (Han, 2002; Leeman, 2003; Mackey & Philp, 1998) or for both recasts and prompts (McDonough, 2007; Lyster & Izquierdo, 2009). In the EFL context, for example, McDonough (2007) compared the effectiveness of recasts to clarification requests on the learning of simple past verbs among Thai L1 university students and found that both recasts and clarification requests were effective in bringing about development. Lyster and Izquierdo's (2009) investigation of adult L2 learners' acquisition of the French grammatical gender also found no differences in the effectiveness of prompts and recasts.

Moreover, the instructional context can also affect the explicitness and effectiveness of CF. That is, since CF in communicative yet accuracy-driven classrooms is usually delivered in a more explicit manner than in content-based classrooms, where L2 is the medium of instruction and not its subject (Sheen, 2004, 2006; Loewen & Philp, 2006), the learners in the former context are more likely to overtly acknowledge and thus, respond to the teacher's correction than are their counterparts in the immersion context. Yet, even in the immersion context, learner responses to feedback may differ depending on the type of focus (meaning or form) a classroom adopts. This was found to be true in Lyster and Mori's (2006) investigation of learner reactions to feedback in two immersion contexts—the French immersion in Quebec (the second language context) and the Japanese immersion in the United

States (the foreign language context). While the distribution of prompts and recasts was similar across the two settings, the French immersion learners showed a tendency to uptake and repair more of their ill-formed utterances after prompts (53%) than after recasts (38%). The reverse was found for the Japanese setting, where the learners repaired significantly less after receiving prompts (23%) than they did after recasts (68%). This difference in the learner reaction to the CF types between the contexts was explained by the authors via their Counterbalance Hypothesis. The Hypothesis posits that while the feedback techniques that add saliency to form are more likely to be noticed and learned from in meaning-based contexts (where the focus is placed on content and meaning making), grammar-oriented settings may benefit more from the implicit feedback types, which make the emphasis on meaning in the accuracy-driven culture stand out more in the minds of learners than an explicit prompt to attend to form.

Hence, the noticeability of recasts seem to depend on how salient they are in the input and on the opportunities they provide to infer their corrective intent. Prompts, on the other hand, provide learners with ample opportunities to recognize their corrective role through cues and output modifications. What still needs to be discovered is whether a combination of prompts and recasts yields differential learning from that of either recasts or prompts alone. This is necessary because, as Lyster and Ranta (1997) observed, language teachers regularly use combinations of feedback types ("multiple feedback") to address a learner's error, yet such mixing has not been investigated in previous research on the noticeability and/or effectiveness of CF (but see Algarawi, 2010).

It is important to note that because recasts and prompts are inherently different, each requires diverse processes to be noticed and effective (see Chapter 1). Recasts require a learner to retain his/her erroneous utterance and the teacher's target-like reformulation in the working memory long enough to: (1) shift attention from the meaning to form and (2) to identify the nature and locus of the error. The burden is significantly lightened with prompts, however, because they, with the exception of clarification requests, explicitly signal the presence and locus of the error, calling on the learner to self-repair. Metalinguistic feedback reduces the learner's task even further by identifying the nature of the error.

2.1.4 Empirical Research on the Link between Noticeability and Effectiveness of CF[19]

Because the ability to recognize the corrective information in the supplied feedback is considered a prerequisite to learning, it is important to identify whether such noticing affects L2 learning. In other words, it is necessary to study the relationship between noticing and L2 development. As the previous two sections show, empirical investigations of CF have either focused on the noticeability of CF or its effectiveness, with few studies addressing the link between the two (e.g., Ammar & Sato, 2010b; Mackey, 2006; Taddarth, 2010). Instead, conclusions about one element have been drawn from the findings of the other. That is, studies of CF effectiveness, for example, were used to draw conclusions about its noticeability without empirically investigating the type and how much CF was noticed. The same is true of the noticeability research where, based on the noticing scores, conclusions about the effectiveness of CF were made without observed proof.

Nabei and Swain (2002) were among the first to conduct a case study designed to test the potential link between noticing and L2 development. Shoko, a female Japanese university-level learner of English, was the subject of the study that examined the student's language learning in relation to the three aspects of input that she noticed: (1) meaning, (2) language, and (3) feedback. Noticing was measured by way of stimulated recall sessions that were repeated six times during the study. While "attention to meaning" was operationalized as the learner's comments that indicated her "understanding and reflection upon the content of discussion," "attention to language" referred to comments that the learner made in relation to "aspects of language" (p. 51). Attention to feedback, in turn, signaled that the learner interpreted recasts as CF. L2 development was assessed via grammaticality judgment tests that were administered after the weekly 70-minute lessons. Another grammaticality judgment test composed of all the previously given tests was completed at the end of the treatment and served as a delayed post-test. Feedback in the form of recasts was provided to errors on various linguistic structures (i.e., grammatical, lexical, phonological, and incomplete sentences) during the lessons. The stimulated recall revealed that the amount of noticing and learning depended on the engagement Shoko felt with the task. That is, there were three levels of listening for this learner: (1) listening for the meaning of the message, (2) listening for message meaning and language use, and (3) no listening. Shoko seemed to mostly concern herself with the meaning of what was said, and even when she was able to comment on the language form, this was rather superficial in that the learner was not able to identify the locus of the problem. In terms of language development, on the first test, Shoko was able to answer correctly 56% of the time and her accuracy increased to 78% on the delayed post-test. Even though the learner was exposed to very few corrective episodes ($n = 25$ in 420 minutes), she was able to learn from them when she understood that they targeted the form of the utterance, especially in the short-term. Specifically, the results of the immediate post-test demonstrated that when the corrective intent of recasts was accurately perceived, the learner's production improved significantly more (67%) than when she attributed recasts as having to do with the content of discussions (57%) or the linguistic structure (47%). While this study informs our understanding of what learners may attend to and how they learn an L2, the fact that only one learner was involved in the investigation suggests that the findings cannot be generalized.

Mackey (2006) employed a larger sample ($n = 28$) to investigate the noticing-learning relationship. High-intermediate participants enrolled in university-level intensive ESL classes took part in a game show, during which they received feedback in the form of negotiation and recasts when errors were made on questions, plurals, and the past tense. Noticing, which was assessed by way of a questionnaire, online learning journals, and stimulated recall protocols, referred to the learners' awareness of the gap between their interlanguage forms and the target norms (made salient by a recast). Learning, in turn, was measured by way of spot-the-differences and picture description tasks, administered immediately before and after the treatment. The results revealed that the learners were able to notice the CF and that there was a positive relationship between this noticing and L2 learning. Specifically, the learners' reports of noticing were mediated by error type, i.e., they reported more noticing for questions than for the other two targets, and their development on the questions target was superior (83% of those who noticed learned) compared to both the plural forms (50% of those who noticed learned) and the past tense forms (only one out of five learners who noticed learned, 20% of the total).

Similar results were found by Ammar and Sato (2010b), who investigated the relationship between the noticing of explicit and implicit recasts on errors with questions, the past tense, and the third person possessive determiners (PDs) among child francophone learners of English ($n = 53$). During the four-day treatment, participants engaged in seven activities that targeted morphosyntax. Noticing was measured by way of (1) online recall, executed during the activities, and (2) stimulated recall, done one day after the intervention. For the online recall, the researcher flashed a red-colored card during CF episodes; each time the card was displayed, the participants had to write down what they were thinking at that specific moment. There were a total of 14 stops after feedback was provided with implicit recasts and 16 after explicit recasts. The stimulated recall involved the learners watching student-teacher interactions from day 3 of the intervention and writing their thoughts on what was happening in the video each time the tape was stopped. There were 16 stops after the implicit recasts and 17 after the explicit recasts. Development on the past tense and PDs was assessed by way of a picture description task and a computerized oral picture description. Spot-the-differences tasks were used to measure the learning of questions. The results revealed that the explicit recasts were noticed more and led to more L2 knowledge gains than their implicit counterparts. Noticing was mediated by the target structure in that PDs and past tense recasts were noticed more than question recasts, which translated into positive changes for the learning of the past tense and PDs.

Finally, Taddarth (2010) studied the noticeability of CF (delivered by way of implicit and explicit recasts) and learner uptake. Two grade 6 classes ($n = 53$) participated in six oral activities designed to elicit the use of questions and PDs (three activities per target). Feedback was supplied in response to errors with the target features. Learning was measured by way of the pre-test/post-test design, where the learners participated in dyadic interactions with the researcher on three tasks, two of which targeted the development of questions (spot-the-differences task and a computerized picture description task) and one assessed the learning gains for PDs (picture description task). The results indicated that explicit recasts were more effective than implicit recasts in leading to uptake and language gains for both targets. The amount of uptake, however, appeared to depend on the target feature, such that errors with questions were repaired more than those with PDs. A positive relationship between uptake and the learning of questions was also reported, but the researcher cautioned against interpreting no uptake as evidence of not learning.

In summary, these studies suggest that when the corrective intent of recasts is accurately perceived, learner performance is likely to improve (Nabei & Swain, 2002; Taddarth, 2010). In terms of the relationship between noticing and learning, while there is evidence that noticing is dependent on the target feature, it is not clear what error types benefit most from such noticing. That is, while Mackey (2006) and Taddarth (2010) found that the noticeability of feedback to questions translated into the most learning gains, Ammar and Sato (2010b) found PDs to be affected more by the CF that was noticed, followed by gains with the past tense and questions. While intriguing, drawing final conclusions from this body of research is both imprudent and difficult. This is because the research is still embryonic and, as such, warrants additional studies to capture the extent of what appears to be a complex relationship between noticing and learning. It is also difficult to draw conclusions about the link from the studies that examined noticing as a function of learner recall (Ammar & Sato, 2010b; Mackey, 2006; Nabei & Swain, 2002) and/or uptake (Mackey, 2006; Taddarth, 2010) alone.

2.2 EVIDENCE: KARTCHAVA'S EXPERIMENTAL STUDY 1

Although the study presented next did not set out to investigate the direct link between CF noticing and L2 learning (see Kartchava & Ammar, 2013 for an example of a study that has), it did systematically compare the noticeability of several CF types across different targets, using various tools to measure noticing. Specifically, this study compared the noticeability of three CF techniques (recasts, prompts, and a mixture of the two) to determine whether such noticing translates into L2 learning outcomes. Noticing was assessed not only via recall protocols, but also by way of lesson reflection sheets and semi-structured interviews. The study was guided by the following research question: Does provision of CF promote noticing and learning of the English past tense and questions in the past?

2.2.1 Method

2.2.1.1 Setting[20]

The study was carried out in English language classes at a French-medium CEGEP, a post-secondary educational institution located in a predominantly French-speaking area of Montreal, Quebec, Canada. The acronym CEGEP (*Collège d'enseignement général et professional*) refers to the public post-secondary educational institution exclusive to the Quebec education system. Founded in 1967, today's CEGEP system includes 48 CEGEPs across the province, five of which are English language-medium. Roughly translated as "General and Vocational College," CEGEPs were designed to help young people to make a career choice by making post-secondary education more accessible and to provide proper academic preparation for those heading to university. As such, CEGEPs offer two types of programs: (1) the pre-university program, which is two years in length and leads to university studies, and (2) technical career programs, during which students have three years to acquire skills necessary for a profession or trade of their choice (e.g., nursing, policing, building engineering technology). Upon graduation, students receive a Diploma of Collegial Studies (known as "DEC" or *Diplôme d'études collégiales* in French), which allows them to either find immediate employment in the trade learned at college or to pursue an undergraduate degree in three instead of four years generally required at universities outside of Quebec. Regardless of the type of program chosen, all CEGEP students must pass four core subjects, which include French, English,[21] Humanities, and Physical Education. The guidelines for ESL instruction in Quebec (put forth by the Ministry of Education) require that upon completion of studies, college students be able to communicate in English well enough to comprehend and deliver messages of various levels of complexity (depending on the proficiency level) on both general and field-specific topics. As such, emphasis is placed on the development of speaking and listening skills (with some focus on reading and writing) and English teachers are encouraged to develop activities that reflect this goal.

The CEGEP in which this study was conducted numbers 6,100 students enrolled in both pre-university and technical programs as well as 4,000 learners registered in the continuing education courses. Among the 26 technical programs offered, many (e.g., Computer Technology, Business Management, Accounting, and Office Technology) are considered to be among the best in the city. To complete the English core requirement, the participating CEGEP requires that all students take two ESL courses. Although these can be taken at any time during the course of one's studies, the order in which they are pursued is predetermined. The first course is usually general in focus and targets improvement of learners' ability to speak, write, listen and read in English. The second course, in turn, is more specific to the student's program and works on improving his/her knowledge of English for the workforce or university studies.

The choice of setting was influenced by three factors: age of participants, opportunity to conduct research in the classroom context, and the particularity of English language instruction in predominantly French Quebec. SLA research has shown that the effectiveness of feedback is influenced by the age of learners (Lyster & Saito, 2010; Mackey, Oliver & Leeman, 2003) in that CF is more beneficial for younger (Mackey & Oliver, 2002; Oliver, 2000) than older (Mackey & Philp, 1998) learners because children appear to be more sensitive to feedback for "it engages implicit learning mechanisms that are more characteristic of younger than older learners" (Lyster & Saito, 2010, p. 293). A closer look at the studies on age and CF reveals that the age of children investigated ranged from 6–12 years, but the maturity of the adult participants was not always specified. It could, however, be assumed that these adults were of 18 years of age and older. Hence, there appears to be a gap in our knowledge of the impact of CF on learners between 13 and 18 years of age. In an attempt to initiate the bridging of this age gap, the present study recruited young adults aged 16 to 21 to investigate the effects of CF on their ability to notice and learn past tense forms and questions in the past.

The second reason for the setting choice stemmed from the opportunity to conduct research in intact classrooms. Because studies conducted in the laboratory setting (e.g., Carroll & Swain, 1993; Mackey & Philp, 1998; Leeman, 2003) found CF to facilitate L2 learning more than those conducted in the language classrooms (Ammar & Spada, 2006; Ellis et al., 2006; Havranek, 1999; Lyster, 2004; Yang & Lyster, 2010), it seemed important to investigate the noticeability and effectiveness of CF within the classroom environment. The importance of classroom research is furthered by the fact that much language learning happens in the classroom, "where the teacher is the only proficient speaker and interacts with a large number of learners" (Spada & Lightbown, 2009, p. 159) and that drawing conclusions about language learning from laboratory studies of dyadic interactions is rather limiting (Lyster

& Saito, 2010) since teacher-student exchanges are pedagogically different from those between a researcher and a research participant (Lyster & Mori, 2006). Furthermore, investigations on the efficacy of CF conducted in the classroom are of special significance because, while the provision of feedback to form is often considered to be "the primary role of language teachers" (Chaudron, 1988, p. 132), instructors often struggle to provide feedback with more than one technique (Lyster & Ranta, 1997; Sheen, 2004) as well as to be consistent in their provision of CF when treating certain linguistic targets (Nicholas et al., 2001).

Instructional context and the characteristics of learners within it is the final reason for the choice of research context (see Kartchava, 2016 for a full description). This is because since 1977 French has been the language of education, workplace, and public signage across the province of Quebec. Although this development did not abolish English-medium public schools, the number of children eligible[22] to enter them became restricted (Sarkar, 2004). Today, more than 90% of Quebec schoolchildren (regardless of their proficiency in or knowledge of English) attend French language schools. English, however, is still a required subject in French-medium institutions as is French in English-medium educational establishments. Yet, in the case of English, exposure outside the classroom is restricted for the language is not necessary to obtain employment or participate in the everyday life of the province. This situation brings a unique dimension to the investigation of CF noticeability since it allows for an examination of a predominantly French-speaking population that is required to study English as a school subject within the wider ESL context of Canada.

2.2.1.2 Participants

Three ESL teachers and 99 francophone college students participated in this study. The students were high beginners, with a mean age of 20.75. While many spoke more than one language (language mean: 2), the majority (78.8%) reported French as their mother tongue. The classes met once a week for three hours, two of which were spent in the classroom and one in the language laboratory. Prior to the study, the participants were exposed to ESL instruction for three years in primary school (~120 hours) and five years in high school (~670 hours). The teachers were English/French bilinguals, who had taught English extensively in various settings. They were observed in order to identify the way in which each provided CF. While Albert responded to errors primarily with recasts, Brian showed a clear preference for prompts. Charles, in turn, consistently alternated between recasts and prompts. Since it was not possible to find another teacher from the same college who provided no feedback, Kartchava taught the control group. Table 2.1 shows the group distribution.

Table 2.1. Group Distribution

Group	Teacher	n
Recast	Albert	31
Prompt	Brian	25
Mixed	Charles	23
Control	Kartchava	20

2.2.1.3 Feedback Conditions

Recasts were operationalized as a teacher's reformulation of the learner's incorrect utterance. The Recast teacher was instructed not to comment on the grammaticality of the students' incorrect utterances and to never push learners to correct their ungrammatical utterances. Instead, the teacher could react with a full, partial, interrogative, or integrated reformulation (see examples below). In response to a student's utterance *He go to the movies yesterday*, any of the following approaches could be adopted:

Full reformulation: Okay. He went to the movies yesterday.
Partial reformulation: (He) Went
Interrogative reformulation: Where did you say he went yesterday?
Integrated reformulation: He went to the movies yesterday. Did he go alone or with someone?

Prompts were defined as techniques that elicited self-correction from the learner. These included: (1) repetition, where the teacher repeated the student's incorrect utterance either as a whole with rising intonation or partly by zooming in on the error while withholding the correct form; (2) elicitation, where the teacher repeated part of the learner's utterance and paused at the error to provide a clue as to the problem, as well as to invite the student to self-repair; and (3) metalinguistic information, where the teacher provided metalinguistic clues but did not provide the correct form, pushing the learner to self-correct (see examples below). Hence, the Prompt teacher could adopt any of the following in response to *He go to the movies yesterday:*

Full repetition: He go to the movies yesterday?
Partial repetition: Go yesterday? Go?
Elicitation: He *what* [stressed] yesterday?
Metalinguistic information: It happened yesterday. So what should we say?
  (How do we form the past in English?)

The Mixed group's teacher was asked to alternate between recasts and prompts as equally as possible during the activities.

2.2.1.4 Linguistic Targets

The past tense and questions in the past were chosen as the linguistic targets because they: (1) are problematic for ESL learners, regardless of L1; (2) represent different levels of complexity (DeKeyser, 1998, 2005); (3) are subject to L1 interference (Ammar, Sato & Kartchava, 2010; Collins, 2002); (4) occur frequently in the input (Doughty & Varela, 1998), which facilitates their elicitation during communicative tasks (McDonough, 2007); and (5) have been shown to be good candidates for learner improvement when they are targeted with CF (Mackey & Philp, 1998; McDonough, 2005; McDonough & Mackey, 2006; Mackey, 2006 for questions; Doughty & Varela, 1998; Ellis et al., 2006; McDonough, 2007; Yang & Lyster, 2010 for past tense). Research has also shown that the noticing of CF leads to language development, though it largely depends on the technique employed and on the nature of the error (Ammar, 2008; Ammar & Sato 2010a; Mackey et al., 2000).

2.2.1.5 Instructional Intervention

The treatment consisted of two 120-minute sessions, during which the participants engaged in a communicative task designed to promote the use of both linguistic targets (adapted from Gatbonton, 1994). For each task, the students worked in groups to create accounts of their whereabouts (activity 1) or those of an accident victim (activity 2), which were then questioned by the whole class. CF was provided during the student-fronted portions of the activities, which lasted anywhere from 60 to 80 minutes each. No instruction on the two targets was provided prior to the intervention.

2.2.1.6 Noticing Measures

Noticing was measured with immediate recall protocols (Appendix 2.1, available on the Features tab at www.rowman.com/ISBN/9781498536776), administered during class activities, and with lesson reflection sheets (Appendix 2.2, available on the Features tab at www.rowman.com/ISBN/9781498536776) that were completed after each session. Following some CF instances, the researcher lifted a red-colored card, which by prior agreement, prompted each learner to write down (in English or French) his/her thoughts about what was happening in the class ("*Each time you see the RED CARD, write what you are thinking in relation to the lesson*"). The breakdown of the CF immediate recall instances across groups is shown in Table 2.2. While the total number of stops and distractors was similar for the Recast and Prompt groups, these were increased for the Mixed group to ensure a comparable distribution of errors corrected with recasts and prompts. The distractors were used to divert the participants' attention and were limited to disciplinary comments and task instructions.

Table 2.2. CF Immediate Recall Instances Across Groups

CF type	Past Tense	Questions	Distractors
Recast	13	12	3
Prompt	12	12	3
Mixed: Recast	10	8	7
Mixed: Prompt	8	7	
Total:	43	39	13

Table 2.3. Immediate Recall Corrective Episodes

CF Type	Past Tense	Questions
Recast	"WE WENT TO THE AIRPORT" S1: What did you do when you woke up? S2: Ahh, we don't do anything special. T: You did not do anything special? S2: No. S2: And after, we go to the airport. T: You went to the airport? S2: No, we go to the airport.... [looks at the teacher confused]. ... Yes. T: You went to the airport? S2: Yes.	"DID SHE TALK WITH YOU?" T: Where did you meet Britney Spears? T: Shopping? S1: Yeah ... [laughter] ... at the hotel, it was one star but ... at the beach ... T: Really? S1: Yeah. She was performing at the beach. S2: She talk with you? S1: No. T: Did she talk with you? S1: No.
Prompt	"WE TOOK THE AIRPLANE" T: In the airplane you ate McDo? [Class laughs.] S3: We bought the food and after that we take airplane. T: After that we ... (pauses, then gestures the need for the past tense) ... "take" in the past tense S3: Took. T: Good.	"WHAT DID YOU DO?" T: Questions! S1: What do you eat at McDonald's? T: What. ... S1: What did you eat?

Similar to previous research on uptake (Lochtman, 2002; Panova & Lyster, 2002; Sheen, 2004), the red card was flashed after full corrective episodes ("error treatment sequence," Lyster & Mori, 2006, p. 280), where the teacher reacted to the error and then waited for the learner to respond. This was done to allow learners extra opportunities to notice the teacher's cues. Table 2.3 provides examples of the immediate recall corrective episodes used.

The immediate protocols were analyzed in two ways. First, the reports were examined to identify the types of noticing the participants engaged in.

Then, percentage noticing scores were calculated for each learner (i.e., total reports of noticing divided by total recall instances, multiplied by 100) to determine the differential noticing of recasts, prompts and a mixture of the two. The first analysis yielded three types of noticing: (1) detection of CF and/or the correct form, (2) exact repetition, and (3) noticing of help (Table 2.4). Instances when the learners referred to context or did not respond to the recall prompt were categorized as "no noticing." The inter-rater reliability was 93% based on simple agreement; disagreements were solved through discussion. This analysis was done in order to understand the types of noticing achieved in general, not to attribute more importance to one category over the other.

Following Mackey (2006), lesson reflection sheets elicited the participants' impressions about the learning done in class and were analyzed qualitatively for additional evidence of noticing. Despite many participants submitting incomplete or blank sheets, an ad hoc analysis of the completed reflections supported the noticing reported in the immediate recall.

Table 2.4. Evidence of Noticing

Noticing	Description	Example
Detection of CF and/or correct form	Awareness of error or what the correct form is/should be and thought processes are made explicit	"fall, mistake;" "mistake" Fanny has difficulty with the verb tense. The past of "throw" is "threw."
	Uptake implying some sort of analysis either by isolating the correction received or by incorporating the correct form	T: Why did you. . . ? Response: Why did you <u>fall down on your horse</u>?
Exact repetition	Word for word repetition of T's reformulation, be it complete or reduced	T: What did you eat? Response: What did you eat at McDo?
Noticing of help	Explicit mention that T was trying to help without specifying the nature of the help	The teacher helps us learn when he corrects. It's a good thing to correct the person when he does error. It's good that the T insists for the student to pronounce the question well.
No noticing	Talk of content No answer (line left blank)	I am thinking about sushi. He is a liar.

2.2.1.7 Development Measures

The tests, composed of spot-the-differences and picture description tasks, were completed by all the groups before and immediately after the intervention. The tasks were developed in consultation with the teachers to ensure that they were appropriate for the students' level and were then piloted with a different class of the same proficiency. In the spot-the-differences task (Appendix 2.3,[23] available on the Features tab at www.rowman.com/ISBN/9781498536776), used to elicit questions in the past, student pairs received separate accounts of a fictional character's written biography. Because the accounts differed in ten ways, the students were instructed to ask each other a minimum of ten questions to identify the differences. Each time a question was asked, the questioner wrote it down and his/her partner then answered it; these conversations were also audio-recorded. Two versions (pre-test and post-test) of the biography were developed to counter the test-retest effect.

The picture description activity (Appendix 2.4, available on the Features tab at www.rowman.com/ISBN/9781498536776), designed to elicit the past tense, asked the participants to write a narrative of what happened in a cartoon strip at a specified point in the past (i.e., yesterday, last week). A different cartoon strip was used at each test time. To ensure linguistic uniformity, the learners had to incorporate the provided context-appropriate verbs (10 per strip) in their stories at least once. Of the 20 verbs, four reoccurred across the tests (i.e., enter, tell, leave, and go), nine called for the regular past forms (i.e., enter, point, demand, park, deposit, climb, cross, walk, and stop), and seven called for the irregular forms (i.e., tell, leave, go, put, drive, meet, and come). All the verbs were telic and depicted the accomplishment and achievement verb categories because these call for the use of past tense (Bardovi-Harlig, 1998; Collins, 2007).

To measure changes in the target-like usage, percentage accuracy scores were computed for each target across test times. For the past tense, the total number of verbs accurately supplied in the obligatory contexts was divided by the maximum score of 10 and then multiplied by 100. If the same verb was used more than once, only its initial use was counted to offset overuse. For questions, the number of correctly formed questions was divided by the total number of questions supplied and then multiplied by 100. This was done to account for the different number of questions produced by each learner.

Semi-structured interviews conducted after the intervention asked 20 participants, chosen at random, to reflect on the study as a whole and to comment about the activities used, the red card, and the CF supplied. The interviews, which were audio-recorded, were conducted in small groups and lasted approximately 10 minutes each.

2.2.2 Results

2.2.2.1 The Noticeability of CF

The results indicate that while all groups were able to notice the feedback provided, the learners in both the Prompt ($M = 22.00$) and Mixed ($M = 29.28$) groups were able to notice the teacher's corrective intent more than those in the Recast group ($M = 6.70$). A one-way analysis of variance showed a statistically significant group difference, $F(2, 76) = 12.6$, $p = .01$. Post-hoc Tukey pair-wise comparisons indicated that the Recast group reported significantly less noticing overall than both the Prompt ($p = .006$) and Mixed ($p < .001$) groups. The difference between the Prompt and Mixed groups was not statistically significant ($p = .214$). These differences are illustrated in Figure 2.1.

To determine which of the grammatical features was noticed more overall, a paired-samples t-test was conducted on the noticing scores per target, yielding a statistically significant difference between the past tense noticing scores ($M = 10.11$) and the questions noticing scores ($M = 8.00$), $t(78) = 3.07$, $p = .003$, with the CF on past tense errors being noticed more than that on questions. The mean difference in the noticing scores was 0.47 with a 95% confidence interval ranging from 0.16 to 0.77 (Figure 2.2).

The noticing scores per target were computed and compared in order to determine which of the grammatical features was noticed more across groups. As Table 2.5 shows, CF on errors with the past tense ($n = 121$) was noticed more than that with questions ($n = 84$). This was especially true for

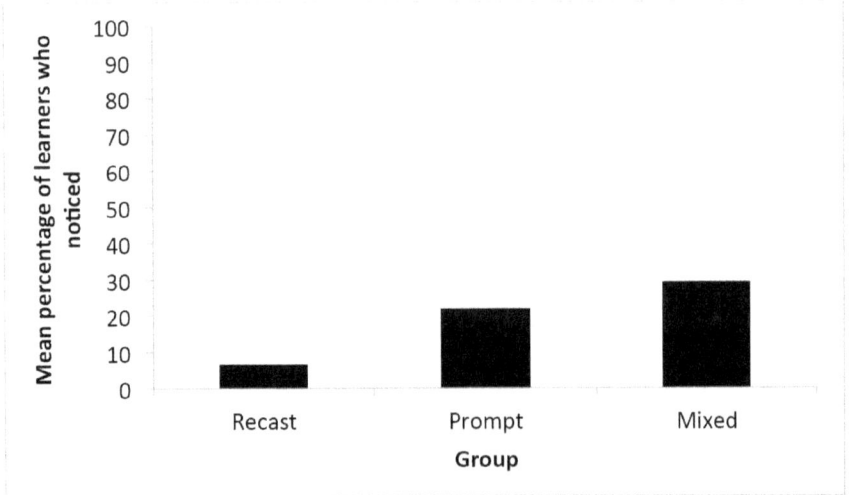

Figure 2.1. Reported noticing means across experimental groups

Noticeability and Effectiveness of Oral Corrective Feedback 69

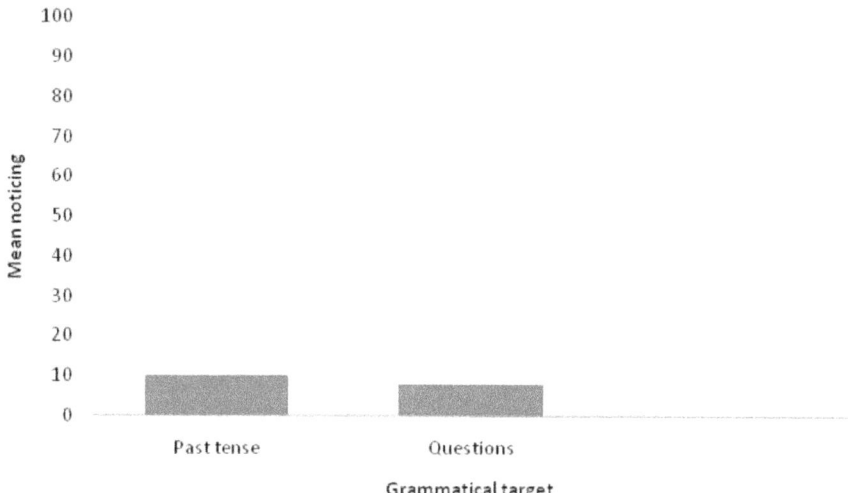

Figure 2.2. Reported noticing means across grammatical targets

Table 2.5. Corrective Feedback Immediate Recall Instances and Learners' Reports of Noticing (Maximum: 100%)

	Noticing					
	Simple Past			Questions		
Group	n	M (%)	SD	n	M (%)	SD
Recast	14	3.47	4.37	12	3.22	4.65
Prompt	35	11.67	11.78	31	10.33	11.85
Mixed—Recast	36	17.39	11.52	24	11.88	14.90
Mixed—Prompt	36			17		
Total	121	10.11	11.02	84	8.00	11.38

the Prompt and Mixed groups, whereas the Recast group reported the least noticing for both targets. Of special interest are the results for the Mixed group because there was an equal number of recasts ($n = 36$) and prompts ($n = 36$) noticed for the past tense errors, but more recasts ($n = 24$) than prompts ($n = 17$) were noticed with the question errors, likely signifying that the presence of prompts may have made the corrective intent of recasts more salient in the classroom.

Separate analyses of variance were conducted for each morphosyntactic feature to explore whether the observed differences in the targets were statistically significant across the experimental groups. There was a statistically significant difference in the noticing of the two morphosyntactic features ($F(2, 76) = 23.8$, $p = .01$ for the past errors, and $F(2, 76) = 6.08$, $p = .004$ for the errors with questions). Post-hoc Tukey HSD comparisons indicated that for the past tense, the Recast group reported significantly less noticing of CF than did the Prompt ($p = .039$) and Mixed ($p < .001$) groups. For questions, the Recast group reported significantly less noticing of CF than did the Mixed group ($p = .003$), but the Prompt group ($p = .090$) did not differ significantly from either the Recast or the Mixed group (Figure 2.3).

In summary, the results showed differences in reported noticing across the groups. Specifically, the Recast group reported less noticing of CF for past tense than did the Prompt and Mixed groups. The Recast group also reported less CF noticing for questions than did the Mixed group. In terms of the grammatical target, past tense was noticed significantly more than questions.

2.2.2.2 L2 Development

To determine how CF promoted the learning of form across the conditions, the groups' accuracy means were computed and compared. As Table 2.6 shows, the post-test scores for past tense were overall higher than those for questions. In terms of group, while the Prompt and Mixed groups' test scores improved for both features, the scores for the Recast group decreased for the two targets.

A paired-samples *t*-test was conducted on the post-test scores for each target to determine which of the grammatical features was learned the most.

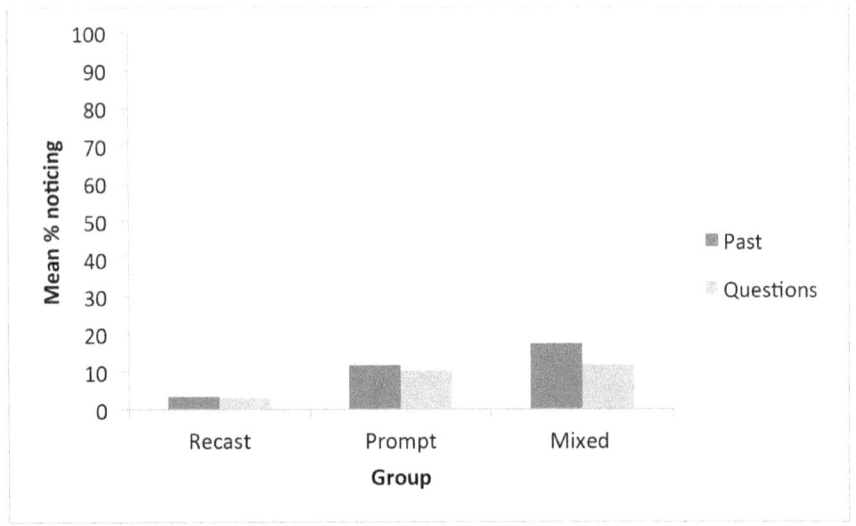

Figure 2.3. Mean percentage target noticing across groups

Table 2.6. Accuracy Means for the Past Tense and Questions Test Scores by Group (Maximum: 100%)

| | | Past Tense | | | | Questions | | | |
| | | Pre-Test | | Post-Test | | Pre-Test | | Post-Test | |
Group	n	M (%)	SD	M (%)	SD	M (%)	SD	M (%)	SD
Recast	31	22.90	31.00	22.26	27.53	15.40	19.59	14.50	18.01
Prompt	25	32.80	36.12	40.40	37.58	11.96	19.18	19.77	26.33
Mixed	23	24.78	26.95	34.34	34.62	12.43	14.46	14.56	24.71
Control	20	19.00	29.72	17.50	25.52	12.19	20.03	13.78	19.26

There was a statistically significant difference between the post-test scores on past tense ($M = 28.70$) and those for questions ($M = 15.70$), $t(98) = 3.82$, $p = .006$ (two-tailed), with the past tense scores being higher than those for questions. The mean difference in the scores was 12.99 with a 95% confidence interval ranging from 6.24 to 19.7 (Figure 2.4).

To assess the impact of the intervention on the participants' scores on the past tense and questions tests across the two time periods, a mixed between/within-subjects analysis of variance was conducted. For the past tense, the difference between the four groups at the pre-test was not significant, $F(3, 95) = .811$, $p = .49$, suggesting that the groups were homogeneous at the onset of the intervention. There was no main effect for group ($F(3, 95) = 1.558$, $p = .205$, partial eta squared = .047) or for time ($F(2, 190) = 4.438$, $p = .10$, partial eta squared = .045). There was no significant Group x Time interaction effect (F

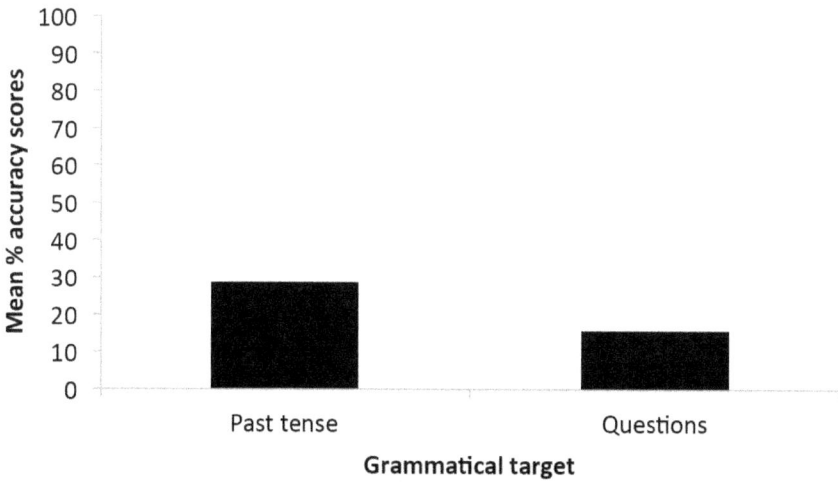

Figure 2.4. Mean percentage accuracy scores across grammatical targets

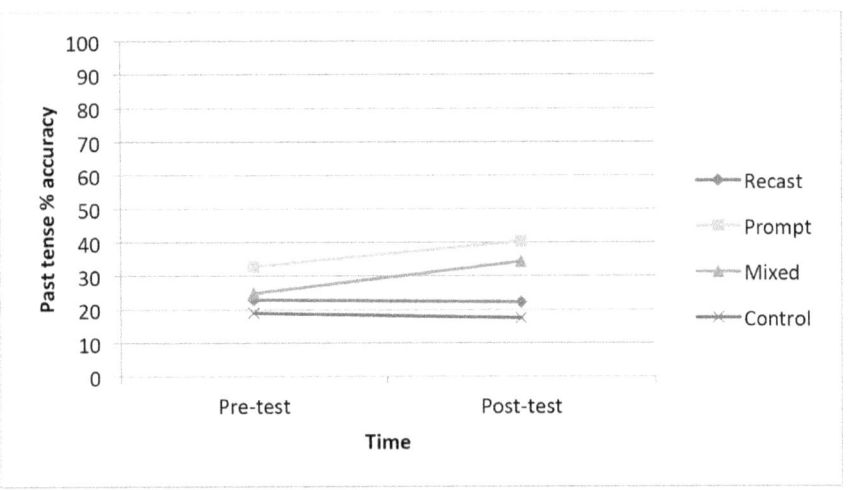

Figure 2.5. Past tense accuracy means across test periods

(6, 190) = 4.342, p =.104, partial eta squared = .121). Figure 2.5 illustrates past tense accuracy means for the pre-test and post-test.

For questions, the four groups were also homogeneous at the pre-test (F (3, 95) = .217, p =.88). There was no main effect for group (F (3, 95) = .530, p =.663, partial eta squared = .016) or time (F (2, 190) = 1.120, p =.329, partial eta squared = .012) and no significant Group x Time interaction effect (F (6, 190) = 2.073, p =.058, partial eta squared = .061) (Figure 2.6).

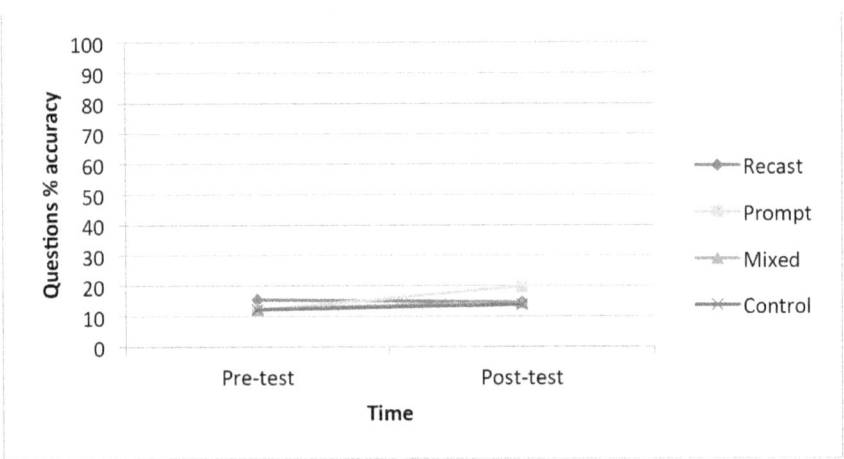

Figure 2.6. Questions accuracy means across test periods

To summarize, the overall accuracy levels for the past tense were statistically more significant than those for questions. In terms of group, however, there were no differences for either of the targets.

2.2.3 Discussion

The purpose of this study was to determine the differential effects of recasts, prompts and a combination of the two on noticing and L2 learning. The results suggest that the learners in the Prompt and Mixed conditions were able to notice significantly more CF overall than those in the Recast group, especially when this feedback targeted errors with the past tense. Furthermore, the Mixed group noticed more feedback on both targets than those in the Recast group; the Prompt group differed from the Recast group only on the noticeability of feedback on questions. As for the learning outcomes, the past tense accuracy levels increased more than those for questions, but the differences between the two targets were not significant across groups.

2.2.3.1 The Noticeability of CF

The superior noticeability of prompts is corroborated by previous research on noticing (Ammar, 2008), which attributed the saliency of prompts to their noticeability. This is because the clue that something is wrong with the form of the utterance and the push to produce the correct form make the corrective intent of a prompt evident to learners. In this study, the Prompt teacher either used gestures, pauses and questions, or supplied metalinguistic information to alert the learners to the error. He then waited for them to self-repair and would not move the lesson along unless it was supplied. These actions made prompts salient, calling on the learners to attend to the form of either their own utterance or that of a peer. For example, to address the error with the past tense (Example 1 below) the teacher used a gesture to indicate that the verb form needed to be in the past and then followed the gesture with a metalinguistic cue ("'take' in the past tense"). Once the student self-corrected, the teacher confirmed the appropriateness of the produced form. In Example 2, the teacher's pause after the question word ("how long") along with the cue ("no 'time'") helped a peer supply the correction of the question error, allowing the original student to successfully repair his/her error. Hence, by highlighting the locus of the error, prompts helped these learners to notice the corrective intent behind the correction, thus satisfying the two basic prerequisites for the effectiveness of CF: locate the locus of the problem and elicit correction (Gass & Varonis, 1994; Schmidt, 1983, 1990).

Example 1

PAST ERROR—"AFTER THAT WE TOOK AIRPLANE"

1. S1: Did you eat Russian speciality?
2. S2: But you know, McDo [McDonalds] is not a Russian speciality?
3. S1: OK
4. T: It is?
5. S2: No!
6. T: No. So, did you eat Russian speciality?
7. S2: No.
8. S1: Why?
9. S2: It's too expensive.
10. S1: So, there you eat nothing?
11. S3: We eat McDo in the airplane.
12. S1: No, there!
13. T: In the airplane you ate McDo?

[Class laughs.]

14. S3: <u>We bought the food and after that we take airplane.</u>
15. T: After that we (gestures the need for the past tense) . . . "take" in the past tense
16. S3: Took.
17. T: Good.

Example 2

QUESTION ERROR—"HOW LONG DID YOU STAY?"

1. S1: Did you visit a museum in China?
2. S2: No.
3. S3: <u>How long time you stay in China?</u>
4. S2: Two hours.
5. T: How long . . .
6. S3: How long did you stay . . .
7. T: Good, how long . . . no "time"
8. S3: How long did you stay in China?
9. T: Beautiful!

The greater CF noticeability in the Mixed group supports the Counterbalance Hypothesis (Lyster & Mori, 2006), which states that a balanced provision of recasts and prompts in a classroom setting may contribute to their effectiveness and their noticeability. The Mixed group teacher provided prompts to elicit the grammar the students already knew and could thus act on. When this was not the case, however, he used recasts to supply the new form and/or to move the lesson along. It can be argued that having been exposed to prompts, the learners came to expect attention to form and that when recasts were then used, the students were more likely to recognize their corrective nature. This was indeed the case here, with the Mixed group noticing more recasts than prompts overall. This difference was especially apparent in the noticing of the grammatical targets, where recasts were noticed more than prompts with questions and noticed at the same rate as prompts for the past tense.

Another explanation for the noticeability of recasts comes from Lyster and Mori's (2006) rationalization that learners are likely to notice and benefit from salient recasts when they are: (1) short and/or are provided with emphasis to highlight the problem, and (2) used with target forms that are above the learners' knowledge (Lyster & Mori, 2006, p. 296). The following examples provide evidence that the perceived recasts were either short in length or provided emphasis of the problem (Example 3) or tackled problems beyond the learners' ability (Example 4).

Example 3

PAST ERROR—"BILL WAS UNDER THE TREE"

1 T: Where was Bill?
2 S1: Bill is under the tree
3 T: WAS under the tree.
4 S1: Bill was under the tree.
5 T: Repeat.
6 S1: Bill was under the tree

Example 4

QUESTION ERROR—"WHEN YOU FELL DOWN, DID YOU BREAK SOMETHING?"

1 S1: When you fell down, did you broke something?
2 T: When you fell down, did you broke something?
3 S1: Break?
4 T: One more time please.
5 S1: When did you fell down?
6 T: When did you fell down?
7 S1: When you fell down, did you broke something?
8 T: When you fell down, did you broke (stresses) something?
9 S1: Yeah. In your ... (inaudible) ... (class laughs)
10 T: OK, slow down ... When you fell down, did you broke (stresses) something?
11 S1: When you fell down, did you broke something?
12 T: Did you break something?
13 S1: Break something.
14 T: OK, one more time.
15 S1: When you fell down did you break something?
16 T: That was great.

The shortness of the recast in Example 3 brings its corrective intent to the forefront, with the learner immediately realizing the problem. Example

4 illustrates the teacher's attempt to have the learner self-correct the error, but realizing that the target form was beyond his/her current proficiency, the teacher supplied a recast, which was clearly noticed and repaired. In this way, this recast is similar to the "corrective recast" used in Doughty and Varela's (1998) study, where the teacher would first repeat the ill-formed utterance, stressing the error, and in the case of no uptake, the teacher would then provide a recast emphasizing the target verb. Hence, it may be argued that the teacher's recast, preceded by error repetition, increased the saliency of the error and encouraged the learner to recognize and correct it. This is in line with Mackey et al.'s (2000) finding that learners who repeat recasts are more likely to appropriately perceive their corrective goal.

While the superior noticeability of CF on past tense errors is in line with the results of Ammar and Sato (2010b), who found PDs and past tense recasts more noticeable than those to the errors in questions, it stands in contrast to Mackey's (2006) results, where CF on questions was noticed more than that on the past tense. One explanation for this may be rooted in the type of past verbs—regular or irregular—that were investigated. The regular forms, which follow the general rule of adding –ed to the base form of the verb, are generally associated with low frequency (Collins, Trofimovich, White, Cardozo, & Horst, 2009), low saliency, low communicative value and high regularity (DeKeyser, 1998; Ellis, 2005). The exemplar-based or irregular verb forms, however, do not follow a clear rule, but are highly salient and frequent in the input (Salaberry, 2000). The frequency of the irregular verbs in this study finds support in the number of such verbs (74.4%) found in the immediate recall instances for the past tense, which originated from the exchanges initiated and carried out by the learners themselves. Because the irregular verbs occurred often, they may have become salient and may have helped the learners notice CF during their attempts to comprehend and communicate messages about the past. This interpretation is supported by Yang and Lyster's (2010) investigation of the CF effectiveness on learners' use of the regular and irregular English past tense verbs, where they reported significant gains for the irregular past verbs (speculated to be more noticeable than the regular past forms).

Additional support for the noticeability of the irregular past tense verbs in this study comes from the post-intervention interviews, where the participants either openly referred to the fact that they noticed feedback on the irregular verb forms (Example 5) or associated the irregular past tense forms with the study of vocabulary (Example 6). In Example 5, the learner clearly noticed feedback on the irregular verb "come" and differentiated between its base and past forms. However, in Example 6, the learner saw the verb "fall" as different from its past tense form "fell," not realizing that the two are connected.

Example 5
I learned the past tense; for example, sometimes I say "I come," but it is supposed to be "I came" because of the past (Anne, Recast group).

Example 6
I learned a lot of vocabulary [during the tasks] that we probably knew but have forgotten because we don't use it. For example, "tomber" [fall] is "fell," but I forgot this (Mary, Recast group).

    Finally, it is reasonable to suggest that tasks which yield production of the target and, at the same time, allow for a focus on form naturally predispose learners to pay attention to what they say and how they say it (Ortega, 2007b).

    Even though the noticeability of feedback on past tense errors was higher, the CF on questions was also noticed. This could be explained by the general frequency of questions in the classroom discourse (Mackey, 2006; Spada & Lightbown, 1999) and questions being a key requirement for the tasks in the study. The difference in the noticeability rates might stem from the complexity of question formation in English and from L1 interference. To form a question, the subject and the question word/auxiliary need to be inverted (syntactic movement) and the subject and the verb must agree in number and tense (morphological agreement). These could make question formation either more salient or harder to understand and, consequently, more difficult to execute. The saliency of questions can be promoted by the use of CF techniques that push learners to recognize the problem of form (Mackey, 2006), which was probably the reason the Mixed and Prompt groups noticed feedback on questions more than the Recast group.

    The L1-L2 difference may have also exacerbated the rate of noticing. Because French forms questions differently and places a limitation on the kind of subject that can be inverted (pronouns) or not (nouns), the francophone learners in this study probably struggled to notice the need to invert the verb with the subject in the English questions, which may have been further restricted by their proficiency level (Hertel, 2003). Since the learners in the Mackey (2006) study were of high-intermediate proficiency, they may have been more attuned to the complexity of the English question formation and, as such, were more likely to pay attention to the form of their questions, a realization that had not become apparent for the high-beginner learners in this investigation. It is also possible that the high-beginner classification assigned to the participants was not a true reflection of their linguistic ability and that, in reality, their proficiency was weaker. Finally, just because the learners did not provide evidence of noticing, it cannot be assumed that they did not notice the provided CF, since the "absence of evidence is not the same thing as evidence of absence" (Mackey, 2006, p. 409).

2.2.3.2 L2 Development

Although there were no statistical differences in the accuracy scores between the groups on the learning of either of the linguistics targets, the overall test scores on the past tense measure were higher than those on questions. This can be attributed to two influences: (1) the different levels of complexity each target represents, and (2) the L1 influence on each. While English questions, unlike the past tense, are arguably easier to learn in terms of form and meaning, it is their inherent subject-verb inversion that often goes unnoticed by learners. The problem is exacerbated further in the way the participants' L1, French, forms questions, i.e., by allowing the declarative word order to be preceded with the question marker "Est-ce que." Furthermore, because the inversion is among the last steps involved in the successful acquisition of the English questions (Pienemann & Johnston, 1987), these high-beginner learners were arguably not ready to benefit from the questions supplied in the input and the feedback on form provided by their teachers.

The past tense, in turn, might have been easier for the participants to improve upon due to the highly irregular verb morphology in French, which may have predisposed them to the irregular past verbs and the rule-governed verb-final *–ed* on the regular past forms in English. The high frequency of the irregular verbs that naturally occurred in the communicative tasks might have also contributed to the higher scores. Furthermore, because the past tense was noticed more, it is reasonable to argue that the test scores on this feature would translate into higher accuracy levels as a result, the same conclusion arrived at by Yang and Lyster (2010). Finally, the use of the telic verbs may have aided the learners on the tests, yielding higher scores for the past tense than for questions.

The lack of differences in the accuracy levels among groups may suggest the need to conduct a delayed post-test since "thinking or processing time may be needed before change can take place" (Mackey et al., 2000, p. 474). In fact, some studies (e.g., Mackay, 1999) have found more development on the delayed post-tests than on the tests carried out immediately after the intervention. In addition to the "thinking time," learners might need multiple exemplars to understand the significance of the feedback provided (Gass, 1997) and to integrate this new information into their interlanguage. Hence, it is possible that an intervention of more than four hours could have allowed for the production of more exemplars and their focused practice. Finally, the developmental measures used might have contributed to the resulting scores in terms of the content, presence of obligatory verbs, and the need to collaborate with another learner on the questions' measure but not on the past tense task.

2.3 CONCLUSION

The results of this study suggest that learners generally notice CF in the language classroom. The noticing rates, however, are contingent on the CF technique used as well as the grammatical feature that the feedback is targeting. The L2 learners studied here were able to notice more feedback that targeted errors with the past tense than with questions. Noticing of the corrective intent behind the teacher's CF was heightened when the teachers used feedback techniques that push learners to self-correct (prompts) alone or in combination with target exemplars (prompts + recasts); the noticing rates for recasts, on the other hand, proved negligible. Yet, the noticing results did not translate into learning gains in that while the overall test scores on the past tense were higher than those on questions, none of the three CF strategies proved to be the cause. What these results point to is a need for additional investigations that not only compare the noticeability of different CF techniques to various grammatical features (with different populations and in different instructional contexts) but that also find ways to increase the noticeability of recasts, arguably, the most common CF type in the language classroom. To explore the latter, Chapter 3 reports on a study that investigated whether training in recasts prior to their provision would make them more noticeable to learners.

Chapter Three

Training Learners to Notice Corrective Feedback

As reported in Chapter 2, Study 1 found that the noticeability of CF is dependent on the grammatical target it addresses (i.e., feedback on past tense errors was noticed more) and that the CF techniques that push learners to self-correct alone (i.e., prompts) or in combination with target exemplars (i.e., prompts + recasts) are more effective than recasts in bringing out the corrective intent of the feedback move. This implies that the corrective properties of recasts do not appear to be easily noticed by learners. However, since recasts are the preferred CF technique of many teachers, helping learners to notice and make use of recasts is an important issue to consider. This chapter argues and tests the premise that one way to make recasts noticeable is by training learners to recognize the corrective intent of recasts. Specifically, the focus here is on Study 2, which examined the impact of the training in recasts prior to their provision on their noticeability and effectiveness. The chapter begins with a discussion of recasts and the challenges associated with their implementation. Then, a review of research on feedback training is provided. Following this, the methodology and findings of Study 2 are presented and discussed.

3.1 BACKGROUND

3.1.1 Recasts

As previously described, recasts—reformulations of learners' ill-formed utterances—have been the primary CF technique investigated for its noticeability and effectiveness in L2 learning. This is due to several factors. First, research on recasts in L1 acquisition has demonstrated developmental gains on certain morphosyntactic features (e.g., present progressive and plurals, Farrar, 1990) made by children exposed to recasts (Farrar, 1990, 1992; Saxton, 1997), which brought about much interest in how this technique might affect SLA. Researchers began studying interactions between native (NS) and non-native (NNS) L2 speakers and found developmental benefits for such interactions (e.g., Doughty, 1994; Mackey 1999; Pica, 1992). Looking to isolate features that benefited these interactions, researchers identified various types of CF, including recasts, which were not only used often in NS-NS, NS-NNS, and NNS-NNS communications, but also seemed to result in language learning (e.g., Long et al., 1998; Mackey & Philp, 1998). Second, from the psycholinguistic perspective, recasts are said to contain two types of linguistic evidence—positive and negative—which are believed to benefit L2 acquisition (Doughty & Varela, 1998; Doughty & Williams, 1998; Long, 1996). Recasts are said to: (1) help learners notice the difference between their original utterance and the target-like reformulation (Long, 1996; Schmidt, 1990, 2001) and (2) free up processing mechanisms by allowing learners to consciously focus on form (VanPatten, 1990, 2004). Finally, pedagogically, recasts are a widely-used corrective technique both in ESL and EFL contexts (e.g., Brown, 2016; Doughty, 1994; Lyster & Ranta, 1997; Panova & Lyster, 2002; Sheen, 2004) and are considered an ideal feedback technique because they are implicit, do not impede on the communicative flow, and simultaneously provide negative and positive evidence by keeping the focus on meaning (Doughty & Williams, 1998; Long, 1996, 2006). This view, however, has been challenged by some researchers, who claim that positive evidence alone is sufficient for L2 learning (Krashen, 1981) and that negative evidence brought about by CF does not only evoke negative reactions in learners, interrupting communicative flow, but may also impede language development altogether (Truscott, 1999).

The types of CF are usually categorized in terms of their implicitness or explicitness. While recasts have often been accorded the implicit tag (Long, 1996; Long & Robinson, 1998), they may be quite explicit (Sheen, 2006) in terms of the context (e.g., Lyster & Mori, 2006; Sheen, 2004), type of instruction in place (Nicholas et al., 2001; Norris & Ortega, 2000; Mackey & Goo, 2007), linguistic target (e.g., Long et al., 1998), learner developmental readiness (e.g., Ammar & Spada, 2006; Mackey & Philp, 1998; Netten, 1991), length and number of changes within the recast (e.g., Philp, 2003) as well as when recasts are combined with other CF techniques (Doughty & Varela, 1998). The same applies to the explicit types of feedback, which usually include prompts[24] and explicit correction, in that they may be implicit when they simply signal the error (e.g., Carroll & Swain, 1993) or include the correct form (Lyster & Ranta, 1997), but more explicit when they provide metalinguistic information (Ellis et al., 2006) and the correct form together (Sheen, 2007).

R. Ellis (2006) offered an alternative way of classifying CF types. His focus was on whether CF is directed at input (i.e., input-providing) or at getting the learner to modify his/her own output (i.e., output-prompting). Because recasts and explicit correction provide correct reformulations of the error, they fall under the input-providing category, whereas prompts belong to the output-prompting type because they do not supply the correction, but, rather, call on the learner, with the help of certain cues (clarification requests, elicitation, metalinguistic clues, and repetition of the error) to self-correct (Lyster, 2002; Lyster & Mori, 2006; Ranta & Lyster, 2007). In terms of the cognitive processing involved, the input-providing feedback types are said to rely on comparisons in the working memory to: (1) help learners notice the difference between their original utterance and the target-like reformulation (Long, 1996; Schmidt, 1990, 2001) and (2) free up processing mechanisms by allowing learners to consciously focus on form (VanPatten, 1990, 2004). The latter reason is of special significance since learners are generally unable to simultaneously focus on both meaning and form (VanPatten, 1990). However, the input-providing CF types are thought to enable the learners to focus on the form and to keep the meaning stable. In fact, VanPatten (1990) showed that when input is made comprehensible, L2 learners are able to focus on the form of the utterance. As for the output-prompting category, the teacher's use of prompts engages learners in the retrieval of the information available to them in their long-term memory in order to self-repair.

Recasts and prompts also vary in terms of the type of evidence they provide. Although recasts are said to provide positive evidence, it is not clear whether they provide negative evidence as well since the learners might not realize the corrective nature of the recast (Nicholas et al., 2001). To determine what aspect of recasts—negative or positive evidence—account for the benefits attributed to recasts in numerous SLA studies, Leeman (2003) designed a laboratory-based study, in which she examined the effects of recasts on the acquisition of number and gender agreement among L2 learners of Spanish. The participants ($n = 74$) were randomly assigned to one control and three experimental groups. The experimental conditions included: (1) recasts, which provided learners with enhanced positive evidence and negative evidence in that the researcher provided a partial recast immediately following the error, (2) negative evidence, which clearly indicated to the learner that the form was incorrect but did not provide a target-like reformulation, and (3) enhanced salience of positive evidence, which did not provide any feedback but the researcher used stress and intonation to make the target form more salient to the learner. The control group (i.e., "unenhanced positive evidence") received no feedback on form and no enhanced positive evidence. It is also important to note that none of the participants was given the opportunity for uptake following instances of feedback. The study employed a pre-test/post-test/ delayed post-test design, with the delayed test being administered one week after the post-test. The treatment included learner-researcher interactions, during which the two engaged in information-gap type activities (i.e., an object-placement task and a catalogue-shopping activity) that created obligatory contexts for the use of noun-adjective agreement. The results revealed that at the immediate post-test both the recast and the enhanced salience groups improved significantly more than the negative evidence and the control groups on the two structures of interest (and this was, despite the lack of significant differences on the pre-test). On the delayed post-test, however, only the enhanced salience group significantly outperformed the control group on the gender agreement structure. These findings were interpreted to show that it is the enhanced salience, and not the implicit negative evidence, that makes recasts effective.

However, the interpretation of the results provided by Leeman should be considered carefully for several reasons. First, this is the only study of its kind in L2 research on CF and as such, no definite conclusions can be made. Second, the fact that enhanced salience was found to make recasts effective does not exclude a potential beneficial role that negative evidence might play in the acquisition of L2 morphemes. This, in fact, was acknowledged by Leeman, who speculated that enhanced salience cannot be considered as the only contributor to the effectiveness of recasts. And finally, the example given for the negative evidence condition (in response to the ill-formed "On the table there's a *red cup", the researcher responded with "Um hmm, but you said a *red cup. What else?", p. 49) is not without problems. One of the issues lies in Leeman's definition of the condition, which was designed with two goals in mind: (1) "to inform the participants of the unacceptability of the original utterance implicitly and (2) to indicate the specific source of the problem" (p. 49). It is unclear how "Um hmm" signals unacceptability of the student's utterance because it can actually be interpreted as a confirmation of the truth value of what was said, as in "yes, there is a cup on the table." Furthermore, the "but you said a *red cup" does not really specify the source of the problem because it could be thought of as a signal that another color should have been mentioned (as in, "the cup is really green, not red"). As such, this example does not inform the learner about the unacceptability of the form or identify the locus of the problem; instead, it can be seen either as confirmation of the meaning of the utterance or as a prompt to supply a different lexical item, making the feedback move rather ambiguous. This ambiguity is exacerbated further by the fact that the participants were not allowed to uptake. Because Leeman's reply in the example above resembles the structure of a prompt in the form of repetition (as defined in Lyster & Ranta, 1997, p. 48), with the exception of the absence of stress, it may be argued that opportunities for uptake should have been made possible because, by definition, prompts require production of output. However, since the participants were not allowed to react to the feedback, it is problematic to claim that the study actually measured the effects of negative evidence.

The effectiveness of recasts, some argue, does not so much depend on the type of evidence they contain (positive, negative or both), but on the learners' perceptions of recasts (e.g., Egi, 2007b; Ellis & Sheen, 2006). To empirically examine whether learners' interpretations of recasts translates into L2 learning, Egi (2007b) investigated the functions (i.e., responses to content, negative evidence, positive evidence, or a combination of positive and negative evidence) L2 learners of Japanese assigned to recasts that they noticed in their interactions with native speakers of the language. The NNS-NS dyads held two conversational sessions to complete picture description and spot-the-difference tasks, during which the NS provided feedback to the NNS on his/her morphosyntactic and lexical errors. To collect instances of noticing, the NNSs engaged in online ($n = 31$) and retrospective ($n = 18$) verbal reports held by the NSs during (immediate reports, cued by two knocks on the table) and immediately after (stimulated recall, facilitated by video clips from the treatment sessions) the interactions. During the verbal recall, the NNSs were prompted to report their thoughts (in English) "without elaboration or reasoning" (Egi, 2007b, p. 256–257). The resulting instances of noticing were then categorized in terms of: (1) the learner noticing (or not noticing) the recast, and (2) the aspect of the recast that was noticed. When the semantic aspect of the recast was noticed, it was classified as "response to content." However, the reports of grammatical form noticing were categorized as either negative (i.e., comments indicating that the NNS recognized that an error had been made and/or that he/she received a recast) or positive evidence (i.e., comments indicating that the NNS noticed the target-like model contained in the recast). And finally, when the learner attended to both types of linguistic evidence (i.e., when the NNS recognized that an error had occurred *and* was corrected by a recast), a "negative + positive evidence" classification was used.

The results revealed that of the 307 recalled recasts, 177 (or 57.65%) received one of the interpretations detailed above (response to content: 16.95%; negative evidence: 35.03%; positive evidence: 19.77%; negative + positive evidence: 28.25%). In terms of the relationship between the NNSs' interpretations of recasts and their L2 development, the results suggest that learners' performance depends on how they interpret recasts. Overall, L2 outcomes improved when the learners recognized recasts as negative and/or positive evidence than when they interpreted them as responses to content. Furthermore, the learners who recognized recasts as positive evidence or "negative

+ positive" evidence showed significantly greater learning gains in the short-term than did those who interpreted them as responses to content. What's more, the recognition of recasts as negative evidence alone did not result in significantly greater learning. As for the impact of noticing in relation to the target linguistic forms, the findings show that lexical items were learned more readily than their morphosyntactic counterparts when the learners noticed positive evidence in recasts. However, noticing of positive and/or negative evidence in recasts did not result in higher gains for morphosyntactic items.

Prompts, on the other hand, provide negative evidence because they cue the locus of the problem and push students to self-correct, which is said to aid learners to juxtapose what they already know and to restructure their interlanguage based on the self-repair process (Lyster, 2002). In fact, when two or more feedback techniques are compared, the one that makes the presence of an error explicit (such as explicit correction and prompts) leads to a markedly improved learner performance than does the one that simply implies it (as recasts often do). This conclusion was first outlined by Norris and Ortega (2000) in their meta-analysis of 49 instructional studies that looked at such pedagogical choices as metalinguistic explanations, input manipulations, and provision of different feedback types. More recently, a meta-analysis of 15 classroom-based studies (Lyster & Saito, 2010) that investigated the pedagogical effectiveness of three types of oral feedback (recasts, prompts, and explicit correction) reiterated the superiority of prompts over recasts in leading to language development. Specifically, the analysis concluded that while the overall presence of feedback (regardless of type) is more advantageous to learning than its absence, prompts are more beneficial than recasts in L2 development:

> CF in a classroom setting may be more effective when its delivery is more pedagogically oriented (i.e., prompts) than conversationally oriented (i.e., recasts). [This is because] learners appear to benefit from the positive evidence available in recasts as well as from the opportunities they provide to infer negative evidence, but these learners seem to benefit even more from the negative evidence available in prompts and from the greater demand they impose for producing modified output (Lyster & Saito, 2010, p. 290).

The effectiveness of recasts and prompts seems to depend on the context in which they are investigated. This is because while classroom studies generally find prompts more effective, laboratory research attributes recasts a facilitative role in L2 development. Havranek (1999), for example, analyzed tapes of language lessons conducted in secondary schools (n = 54) and in university (n = 18), as well as questionnaires completed by the participants[25] to determine the type(s) of feedback the learners recalled and learned from the most. Three feedback conditions were investigated: (1) recasts, (2) recasts + learner repetition, and (3) elicitation of the correct form, followed by a correction and the student repetition of the correction. The results revealed that recasts and recasts + repetition were recalled the least[26] and yielded no significant improvement on the post-test. The elicitation condition, on the other hand, was recalled less than the recasts + elicitation group but led to more post-test improvements than the recasts and recasts + elicitation combined. Hence, despite having been recalled more often, recasts were less effective than elicitation in leading to language learning. This finding is of special interest since the study was conducted in grammar-oriented classes, where learners are conditioned to focus on the form of an utterance, making the identification of recasts as feedback more likely (Ohta, 2000; Sheen, 2004) than in the meaning-oriented contexts (Lyster, 1998a; 2007; Sheen, 2004).

A classroom study conducted in an immersion environment by Lyster (2004), for example, found that prompts were more effective than recasts in facilitating acquisition of grammatical gender among young learners of French (n = 179). Four Form-Focused Instruction (FFI) conditions were investigated: (1) recasts + FFI, (2) prompts + FFI, (3) FFI, and (4) control. To determine the effects of the conditions on the participants' knowledge of the target feature, the learners were asked to complete two written and two oral tasks on three different occasions (pre-test, immediate post-test, and delayed post-test). The results showed that the prompt + FFI condition was the most effective in the four tasks in leading to target acquisition at both post-tests. The recasts + FFI condition was significantly better than the control group on the two written tasks at both post-tests and on the two oral tasks at the delayed post-test. Furthermore, the recasts + FFI group was outperformed by the prompts + FFI condition on the two written measures at the immediate and delayed post-tests.

Similarly, Ammar and Spada (2006) found prompts to be more effective than recasts in the acquisition of the English third person possessive determiners (PDs) *his* and *her* by young French L1 speakers. Three grade six intact intensive ESL classes (n = 64) were assigned to one control and two experimental groups. For a period of four weeks, all the groups received instruction on PDs and participated in 11 practice sessions, during which only the treatment conditions received CF. The participants' knowledge of the target structure was tested immediately prior, immediately after, and four weeks after the instructional period. The results revealed that while prompts were more effective than recasts, learners' proficiency level mediated this effectiveness. Specifically, learners with pre-test scores above 50% (i.e., high-proficiency) benefited equally from both prompts and recasts whereas prompts proved more effective for learners with pre-test scores below 50% (low-proficiency).

Other oft-cited studies that have shown prompts to be more effective than recasts in the classroom setting include Ellis et al. (2006), Loewen and Philp (2006), and Yang and Lyster (2010).

Yet, some have argued (Han, 2008) that in order for recasts to affect morphosyntactic development in the classroom setting, their corrective intent needs to be made salient. This can be done by first having teachers ascertain the meaning the learner is trying to convey and then, having them provide recasts in those instances; this feedback needs to be consistent and focus on one grammatical feature. This was probably the intent of Doughty and Varela's (1998) investigation of the effects of "corrective recasts" versus no feedback on the acquisition of the past tense among 11- to 14-year-old ESL learners (n = 34) attending a compulsory science course. As part of the course, the students were required to produce written and oral reports about the experiments they conducted. While those in the recast condition received feedback on their written and oral reports,[27] the students in the control group did not. The participants' knowledge of the target structure was tested by way of a written and oral task three times: before the intervention, immediately after, and again two months after that. The results showed that on the immediate post-test the recast group attained significant gains on both the oral and written tasks, but that the control group showed no progress on the oral task and a slight, yet significant improvement on the written task. The delayed post-test results, in turn, revealed that while the recast group was able to retain the gains they showed on the oral post-test, the participants' performance on the written measure changed in three ways: (1) the target-like use of the past tense was not maintained, (2) the interlanguage gains decreased, and (3) the non target-like use of the past tense increased. Yet, no change from the immediate to delayed post-test was revealed for the control group.

While these findings led Doughty and Varela to conclude that the use of corrective recasts in content-based classrooms is effective in leading to L2 development, others (Lyster, 1998a; Nicholas et al., 2001) questioned this conclusion, suggesting that the recasts in the study vastly differed from regular recasts. The difference lay in the way the recasts were operationalized and implemented. Doughty and Varela defined "corrective recasts" as both attention-getting and target-form providing. To attract the learner's attention to the presence of an error, the teacher would repeat the ill-formed utterance, stressing the incorrect form. If the learner failed to come up with a correct form following the initial correction (repetition with emphasis), a recast of the correct form would be provided, which the learner was then required to repeat (target-like reformulation). In other words:

> The teacher would repeat a phrase containing an incorrect past verb, putting the error in focus by using stress and rising intonation to prompt the student to

notice the non-targetlike form. Recasts were then used when the student did not attempt any past tense reference at all. In such a recast, the teacher provided the exemplar needed, using falling intonation and, once again, emphasising the verb with added stress (Doughty & Varela, 1998, p. 124).

Furthermore, in terms of implementation, some of the teacher's in-class behaviors (e.g., choral repetition of the correct form, focused attention on the accuracy of the past tense in videotaped oral reports, etc.) could also have been responsible for the learning gains in the recast group since these explicitly signaled the presence of an error. As such, it is difficult to ascertain which variable in these "corrective recasts" aided in the acquisition of the past tense. What is clear, however, is that the effectiveness of recasts can be amplified when they are accompanied by a cue alerting learners that the focus is being placed on the form, and not the meaning, of their utterance (Doughty, 2001). Conversely, recasts with no special focusing element tend to go unnoticed and are unlikely to lead to significant interlanguage changes (Havranek, 1999).

Hence, CF classroom research points to prompts as being more effective than recasts in bringing about learning gains. This is because the corrective intent of prompts is made clear to learners by way of cues and the need to self-repair. Recasts, on the other hand, often go unnoticed by learners because of their frequency in the input (e.g., Farrar, 1990; Morgan, Bonamo & Travis, 1995 for L1 research; Chaudron, 1988; Netten, 1991; Lyster & Ranta, 1997; Lyster, 1998a, 1998b for L2 research) and the functional properties of the technique (Farrar, 1990). In the L1 research, Farrar (1990), for example, identified four roles for recasts: (1) to reformulate a child's utterance (i.e., make a corrective change in the original sentence), (2) to expand on an utterance, (3) to maintain the topic of conversation, and (4) to themselves be the reply to what the child has said. A close examination of the four reveals that recasts, in fact, can be separated in terms of the corrective or non-corrective functions they perform (Farrar, 1992). That is, while roles 2 through 4 signal various contributions to the management of an interaction (i.e., expansion, topic continuation, and reply provision), role 1 speaks solely to its form. Given that all these properties are inherent to recasts, it is difficult to know which of the characteristics actually contribute to learning. The picture gets more complicated with Farrar's (1990) additional finding that corrective recasts are quite infrequent in the mother-child interactions he observed. This is because recasts not only perform multiple functions in naturalistic interactions, but their corrective property in these environments is also utilized the least.

The ambiguity of recasts in the L2 content-based and communicative classrooms was also observed by the early descriptive studies (e.g., Chaudron, 1977, 1988; Fanselow, 1977; Schachter, 1981), which underscored the high frequency of occurrence of recasts in the treatment of oral errors. This frequency, however, was not viewed positively since the teachers in these environments used recasts interchangeably to respond to both meaning and form of their learners' utterances. This, in turn, raised the question of whether or not learners noticed the teachers' modification at all, and if they did, what was their interpretation of it. Schachter (1981) argued that a recast (i.e., paraphrase) could be interpreted as a confirmation of the content rather than as a correction of the form of the utterance. Chaudron (1988) later speculated that a recast can also be "perceived as merely an alternative" (p. 145) to the learner's original utterance. Soon after, Lyster (1998a) observed that in the immersion classrooms, recasts to form as well as the recasts used as "move-ons" (i.e., topic continuation) were as frequent as the non-corrective repetitions provided in response to learners' well-formed utterances. These, he argued, contributed to the ambiguity of recasts and made recognizing the corrective intent behind the provided feedback an arduous task, especially in the content-based environments, where awareness of form takes a back seat to that of meaning (see Sheen, 2004). The difficulty recognizing negative evidence in a recast was further reinforced by the observation that recasts, compared to the other feedback types, yield the least amount of uptake in the content-based L2 classrooms (Lyster & Ranta, 1997).

Yet, recasts have been shown to be effective in the laboratory setting. This was especially the case when there was no control group (e.g., Ishida, 2004) and when recasts were compared with the no-feedback condition (e.g., Han, 2002; Leeman, 2003; McDonough & Mackey, 2006). Investigations that compared recasts to other feedback types either found recasts more effective than the other techniques (Long et al., 1998; Mackey & Philp, 1998) or yielded no differences across the CF types (e.g., McDonough, 2007; Lyster & Izquierdo, 2009). Long, Inagaki and Ortega (1998), for example, conducted two dyadic laboratory studies with learners of Japanese and Spanish to compare the effects of recasts, models, and no feedback. The researchers hypothesized that the learners in the two experimental conditions would significantly outperform those in the control group on their ability to produce the four targets of interest: adjective ordering and fronted locative constructions for the Japanese learners, and object topicalization and adverb placement for the Spanish students. Based on previous L1 research and an earlier study (Mito, 1993), the authors also expected that the learners in the recast (operationalized as "implicit negative feedback") group would show greater gains than those in the models ("pre-emptive positive input") and zero feedback conditions. Twenty-four young learners of Japanese took part in the first study, where they were randomly assigned to four experimental groups and one control group. While the learners in the experimental conditions took part in a communication game, during which they had to describe their actions in the L2, the controls practised the Kanji script. The treatment of errors differed between the recast and models groups in that the recast condition received reformulations in response to errors, while the models group heard prompts, which had to be repeated for the researcher to perform the said action. Surprisingly, the findings did not show any significant differences between the experimental and control conditions, and no differences in the effects between recasts and models.

The lack of differences between the conditions was attributed by Long et al. (1998) to the fact that 20 out of 24 participants had previously studied Japanese and that the pre-test could have jogged their prior knowledge of the targeted structures. The selection of participants for the second study took this shortcoming into consideration and retained only those learners who reported no prior knowledge of the structures of interest. The results revealed that recasts were more effective than models in bringing about short-term gains on the use of adverb placement; this was also true of the two experimental groups in that they showed significant, albeit temporary, benefits over the control group. These results, however, were not confirmed for the object topicalization as no significant differences between the treatments and the control group or between the two treatments were found. The researchers offered three reasons to account for the learners' failure to learn the second target in the Spanish study. First, the adequacy of the instructional tasks was questioned. Second, object topicalization was deemed as more difficult despite the fact that, in accordance with the Pienemann and Johnston (1987) framework, the two features were deemed similar in terms of processing requirements. And finally, the fact that the learners in the models condition were required to repeat the model (i.e., produce output) could have made the focus on form more salient, resulting in similar gains across groups. In spite of these reasons, it may be argued that the treatments delivered under the same circumstances should have accounted for these differences.

Mackey and Philp (1998) investigated the effectiveness of recasts on the acquisition of English questions in the laboratory setting among adult ESL learners (n = 35) in Australia. The participants were randomly assigned to three groups: recast, interactor, and control. In the recast group, the NSs provided the learners with feedback in the form of intensive recasts[28] in response to their ill-formed utterances produced during picture description, story completion, and story sequencing tasks. While the interactor group participated in the same tasks but did not receive feedback, the control group only took part in the tests. L2 development was measured by way of spot-the-differences tasks, where by asking questions, the participants had to find ten differences between his/her card and that of the NS. The researchers hypothesized that intensive recasts provided in response to ill-formed questions during an interaction would propel the learner's existing knowledge of the structure to a more advanced level than during an interaction without recasts. Since the developmental level of the learners in relation to the three different conditions of the study was a variable of interest, the 35 participants were classified according to their developmental readiness to learn the word order of questions. This resulted in two groups—'readies' and 'unreadies.' The results revealed that if the participants were at a higher stage of question development ("readies"), they were more likely to benefit from recasts than their less advanced counterparts ("unreadies"), for whom the presence or absence of recasts in interaction seemed to make little difference. This led the researchers to conclude that the corrective nature of the recast is more likely to be perceived and learned from by those learners who are developmentally ready.

Still, recent laboratory studies have also failed to differentiate the effectiveness of recasts and prompts. McDonough (2007), for example, compared the effectiveness of recasts to clarification requests on the learning of English simple past verbs (achievement and accomplishment) among Thai L1 university students (n = 106) enrolled in a bachelor's degree program in English. The premise was to compare the effectiveness of two seemingly implicit techniques that differ in the elicitation of learner responses, as recasts usually do not elicit learners' responses, but clarification requests push learners to modify their answers (pp. 323–324). The NS—NNS dyads engaged in communicative activities designed to elicit past tense verbs. The NSs provided one type of feedback (recasts or clarification requests) during the treatment tasks; the NNSs were randomly assigned to the feedback groups. Learning was measured by using the pre-test/post-test design by means of one-way information gap tasks. The results showed that both recasts and clarification requests were effective in bringing about the simple past verbs. Similarly, in the classroom context, Ammar and Sato (2010b) found explicit recasts more beneficial than the implicit recasts in the learning of the past tense, questions, and the third person possessive determiners.

Lyster and Izquierdo (2009), in turn, investigated adult L2 learners' (n = 25) acquisition of the French grammatical gender in an intermediate level French as a Second Language class at an English-medium university. For a period of two weeks, all the participants were exposed to a three-hour FFI, after which they took a computerized binary-choice test (that served as a pretest). Based on the results of the pre-test, they were assigned to either a recast (n = 14) or a prompt (n = 11) group. In dyadic interactions with a near-native speaker of French, the participants engaged in object-identification, picture description, and riddles tasks. Language development was measured by way of the binary-choice test, reaction-time measures, as well as the object-identification and picture description activities. The results indicate that the two groups improved significantly over time on accuracy and reaction-time scores, suggesting that the feedback type did not make a difference in the learning outcomes. The researchers explained the findings by attributing different roles for the two CF types in L2 development. Specifically, repeated exposure to recasts exposes learners to the positive evidence available in recasts and allows them to infer negative evidence within the recasts by engaging in dyadic interactions. Prompts, in turn, allow learners to draw on the repeated exposure to negative evidence within them as well as to produce modified output.

The effectiveness of recasts demonstrated in the early laboratory studies compared to the classroom results could be explained in a number of ways. First, the controlled nature of the laboratory may make any target feature appear more prominent to the participants, even if they are asked to partake in a communicative task (Lyster, 1998a; Nicholas et al., 2001; Spada, 1997). Second, unlike the classroom, the target feature is often isolated in the laboratory setting, making it more noticeable (Lyster, 1998a; Spada, 1997). Yet, even the classroom can influence recasts effectiveness in that the corrective intent of recasts may be more apparent to learners in primarily form-focused settings (Lyster & Mori, 2006). Third, the researcher-participant interactions may help learners recognize that (a) the researcher's reactions to the learner's productions are a form of feedback, and (b) that this feedback is corrective in nature.[29] Fourth, interactional feedback research (e.g., Egi, 2007a; Iwashita, 2001; Mackey & Philp, 1998) has often conflated recasts (input-providing CF type) with clarification requests (output-promoting feedback), making it difficult to ascertain which of the two affects learning. Mackey and Philp (1998) reported that in some cases recasts can be "part of negotiation sequences and function as confirmation checks" (p. 342), a statement reiterated by Loewen and Philp (2006), in that "recasts in the context of conversation are often part of negotiation sequences and function as confirmation checks" (p. 540). The lack of categorical definitions for recasts and negotiation sequences (which often include confirmations or clarification requests, Iwashita, 2001; Mackey & Philp, 1998) moved Lyster and Saito (2010) to exclude many studies on interaction (e.g., Iwashita, 2003; Mackey & Philp, 1998; Oliver, 2000) from their meta-analysis of studies that investigated the effects of oral CF on target language development. Instead, they focused on the investigations that used clearly defined recast, explicit correction, and prompt categories. Fifth, Ellis (2015) argued that because the "prompt" category includes four strategies (elicitation, repetition of error, clarification requests, and metalinguistic cues) compared to the single one of recasts, "it is possible that the greater effect found for prompts is simply because many strategies are more effective than one" (p. 162). Finally, because prompts include both implicit and explicit strategies, whereas recasts are primarily implicit, "it is possible that [prompts] are more effective because they are more salient" (ibid).

However, the fact that the recent laboratory studies have failed to differentiate the effectiveness of CF techniques suggests that the input-providing and output-prompting feedback types differ in the type of learning opportunities they afford (Lyster & Izquierdo, 2009; Lyster & Saito, 2010). This, along with the type of evidence each type provides, may also be the reason why learners benefit more from prompts than from recasts in the classroom. Thus, prompts, since they provide learners with instances of negative evidence, cue the locus of the problem, and push students to self-correct, seem to be more effective than recasts alone in leading to learning in the classroom. Recasts, in turn, provide positive evidence and opportunities to infer negative evidence, the difficulty of which may depend on the context (laboratory versus classroom), instruction in place (Lyster & Mori, 2006), and a number of individual learner differences (e.g., Mackey et al., 2002; Trofimovich et al., 2007; Ammar, 2008; Ammar & Sato, 2010). One thing remains clear: when two or more feedback techniques are compared, the one that makes the presence of an error explicit and elicits the correct form from the learner leads to a markedly improved learner performance than does the one that simply implies it (as recasts often do). This conclusion was first outlined by Norris and Ortega (2000) in their meta-analysis of 49 instructional studies that looked at such pedagogical choices as metalinguistic explanations, input manipulations, and provision of different feedback types. More recently, Lyster and Saito's (2010) meta-analysis of 15 classroom-based studies that investigated the pedagogical effectiveness of three types of oral feedback (recasts, prompts and explicit correction) reiterated the superiority of prompts over recasts in leading to language development. Even so, the ongoing debate about which type of CF is most effective (e.g., Goo & Mackey, 2013; Lyster & Ranta, 2013), is according to Ellis (2015), "somewhat unnecessary" (p. 163) since "learners benefit most when they receive a mixture of these two types of CF" (ibid) and "combinations of CF types [. . .] more closely resemble teachers' practices in classroom settings" (Lyster et al., 2013, p. 30). This sentiment finds support in Study 1, which demonstrated superior noticeability of the mixed (recasts + prompts) CF condition.

3.1.2 Training Learners to Notice Recasts: Rationale

The effectiveness of recasts seems to depend on how salient they are in the input and on the opportunities they provide learners to infer the corrective intent (see Chapter 2 for research on the noticeability of CF). These opportunities are often limited by the error type, length and explicitness of a recast, as well as various learner-internal factors (e.g., proficiency level, working memory, attention switching ability). Furthermore, though recasts dominate language classrooms, their noticeability is challenged by the extensive cognitive processing they require. Specifically, the learner must: (1) recognize that he/she made an error, (2) retain his/her incorrect utterance in memory long enough to compare it with the teacher's reformulation, (3) identify the type of error made, and (4) correctly pinpoint the error's location—all within a conversational turn. What is needed, then, is an investigation into the role and utility of CF training for L2 learners to help them with the task of noticing. Such training is necessary for several reasons.

First, training of any kind strives to "help learners make more effective use of the learning opportunities they encounter and encourage learner autonomy" (Hall, 2011, p. 248) by identifying the learning strategies that suit individual learners' preferences and augment learning (Sinclair & Ellis, 1992). Strategy instruction that is overt, contextualized, and related to students' specific problems is considered effective, especially when the strategies are incorporated into class materials on a regular basis (Gregersen & MacIntyre, 2014). While CF can be seen as a strategy to raise learner awareness about form-related issues within classroom exchanges, it is not always overt, perceived as overt, or regular in the language classroom. Training learners to recognize the corrective intent of the teacher's CF may lead to learning, but currently there is limited evidence to support this. Second, to date, L2 research on learner training has mostly focused on peer CF, where learners are taught how to collaborate and provide each other with CF (Sato, 2013; Sato & Ballinger, 2012; Sato & Lyster, 2012). Yet, little research has considered training learners to recognize teacher CF. In fact, the only study that has attempted such training involved young learners (Bouffard & Sarkar, 2008), necessitating research with adult learners. Third, recasts are used the most in both second and foreign language contexts (Lyster & Ranta, 1997; Lyster, 1998a, 1998b; Sheen, 2004) but generate the least amount of uptake and successful repair. When recasts are made explicit, however, they yield higher levels of uptake than do implicit recasts (Lyster, 1998a; Nassaji, 2009; Sheen, 2006). Yet, it is not clear whether training in recasts impacts the amount of uptake generated, and if this amount, in turn, affects the learning that takes place. Clarifying this issue is of special value to the language classroom since this is where the "real" language learners and teachers operate. Fourth, the infrequency of uptake in response to recasts may be due to the ambiguity of the recasts. This ambiguity is especially evident in language immersion and communicative classrooms (Chaudron, 1977), where teachers use recasts to respond to both the meaning and the form of the learners' utterances (Lyster, 1998a). For example, if in response to a learner's "I go to the movies yesterday," the teacher recasts with

"Oh, you <u>went</u> to the movies yesterday. <u>What did you see</u>?" the learner (if he/she notices the recast at all) will be left wondering if the teacher was simply interested in the title of the movie (meaning) or was correcting the verb tense (form). CF training may demonstrate if learners are able to identify recasts that focus on the form of an utterance. Fifth, instructional context plays a role in the amount of uptake and repair generated following recasts (Sheen, 2004; Oliver, 2000). For example, Sheen (2004) found that Korean EFL students and New Zealand ESL students reacted to their teachers' recasts more often than learners in the Canadian ESL and French immersion contexts. This was because in the former form-oriented contexts the learners expected attention to form in the language class and were attuned to intent of the CF. Conversely, in the more meaning-oriented Canadian classrooms, CF is more implicit, making it difficult for learners to recognize the corrective properties of recasts. It is, however, not known whether CF training may affect the rate of uptake generated in the more meaning-oriented Canadian classrooms. Finally, in terms of the cognitive processing involved, recasts are said to rely on comparisons in the working memory to (1) help learners notice the difference between their original utterance and the target-like reformulation (Long, 1996; Schmidt, 1990; 2001) and (2) free up processing mechanisms by allowing learners to consciously focus on form (VanPatten, 1990, 2004). Since learners are generally unable to simultaneously focus on both meaning and form, it is possible that training in recasts may enable them to focus more on the form, rather than the meaning, which may, in turn, result in opportunities to acquire new or modify their existing knowledge of the L2 (Carroll & Swain, 1993; Doughty & Varela, 1998; Mackey, 2006).

If such training is effective, then learners will be able to do any or all of the following: (1) verbally respond to the provided CF (as evidenced by increased uptake—student's immediate reaction to the teacher's feedback), (2) repair the errors, (3) show immediate and long-term learning gains, and (4) verbalize the grammatical analysis they engaged in as the result of the CF training. Before putting these claims to the test (in Study 2), a review of research that has investigated the effectiveness of feedback training needs to be considered.

3.1.3 Research on Feedback Training

Research on feedback training has primarily focused on three broad areas of investigation: (1) the effect of feedback training on learner and teacher beliefs about CF, (2) the link between teachers' prior education and teaching practice on their CF provision, and (3) the impact of feedback training on learners' willingness to supply each other with CF during collaborative tasks. While the first two foci are beyond the focus of this review (but see Kartchava, in press; Nassaji, 2016), a discussion of one related study is in order. Specifically, Sato (2013) examined the effect of feedback training on learners' attitudes towards peer interaction and peer CF provision. The same population (n = 167) as that described for Sato and Lyster (2012) below, completed a beliefs questionnaire before and after training, with some learners (n = 36) also being interviewed. The results indicated that while prior to the training learners were in general agreement about the importance of peer interaction and utility of peer CF, the trained peers not only became more willing to provide their peers with CF but also began to see their peers as linguistic resources to draw on, not merely as other "bodies" in the class. This finding points to an important role that training in general and feedback training in particular can play in facilitating L2 development.

Much of the research investigating feedback training has focused on training L2 peers to provide each other with CF. It is argued that learner interaction not only promotes collaboration in solving communicative breakdowns and co-constructing knowledge, but that the effectiveness of the processes involved can also be amplified through priming and training (Sato & Ballinger, 2016). CF is seen as one of these processes since provision and receipt of form-focused information from a peer may engage both learners in noticing what they know and don't know as well as point to gaps in their ability to communicate in the L2, prompting a re-examination of the existing hypothesis about the L2 (Ammar & Spada, 2006; Lyster, 2004; Ohta, 2001; Swain, 1985, 1995, 2005). Invoking Levelt's (1983) perceptual loop theory, Saito and Lyster (2012) have also argued that simultaneous monitoring of one's own output and analysis of another speaker's input, which is so prevalent in peer interaction, contributes to CF effectiveness. Yet, despite these arguments, little research on training learners to provide feedback to each other and the effects of that training on L2 learning has been carried out to date (e.g., Fujii, Mackey, & Ziegler, 2016; Sato & Ballinger, 2012; Sato & Lyster, 2012).

Sato and Lyster (2012) were perhaps the first to delve into the topic area. Working with four groups (n = 167) of Japanese university-level learners of English, the researchers explicitly taught two of the groups to provide each other with CF during meaning-focused tasks. While one of these groups was trained to use recasts as the CF technique (n = 46), the other employed prompts (n = 41). The remaining two groups either engaged in completing the communicative tasks without any focus on CF (peer-interaction-only group, n = 42) or did neither, serving as the control group (n = 32). L2 development was assessed for all the participants at the beginning and again, at the end of the semester. One of the tasks, administered at both test times, was for learners to individually record (working in a language lab) a description of events depicted in a picture. The other task, carried out at the end of the course, was a decision-making activity, during which learners working in pairs were instructed to agree on a gift they would give to a famous person (e.g., the prime minister of Japan).

The CF training (administered to the recasts and prompts groups only) lasted approximately 30 minutes (over a 3-week period) and followed three phases: modeling, practice, and use-in-context. In the modeling phase, two instructors team-teaching the English course participated in a role-play, during which one teacher made errors and the other supplied CF using one of the corrective strategies (i.e., recasts or prompts); the role-play followed the same format as the student role-plays would. The CF responses were either in the form of recasts or prompts, depending on the group where the demonstration was taking place. The recast group was told to supply a correct reformulation of an erroneous utterance (albeit recasts of varied degrees of explicitness were demonstrated in the teacher role-plays) whereas the prompt group was instructed to either use clarification requests or metalinguistic feedback "to parallel possible variation in the explicitness of recasts" (Sato & Lyster, 2012, p. 602). To practice CF provision, learners working in groups of three were instructed to engage in a role play for a total of 180 minutes (20 minutes during nine in-class sessions each). Each student was given the role of a speaker, observer, or feedback provider as well as a different scenario and a list of sentences with errors to include in the role plays the speakers would create. During the story telling, the feedback provider was to detect the errors and correct them. The observer, in turn, was to keep track of the errors that were detected and/or corrected as well as those that were not. In the last phase, the learners engaged in a separate pair information-exchange activity, during which they changed partners several times, relayed the information received from the previous partner to the new one in the same amount of time, and provided CF. The authors claim that despite the decontextualized nature of the activity and frequent focus on form, "students' attention was primarily drawn to meaning [. . .] by providing them with authentic visual materials and embedding an information-exchange element" (ibid, p. 603). The results showed that the CF trained learners improved both in accuracy and fluency and that the interaction-only group performed better overall than did the controls. Furthermore, while both CF trained groups provided more feedback than the other two groups, the recast group corrected more than the prompt group. This study provides positive evidence for the effects of CF training on learners' ability to process and learn from the supplied feedback. It also points out that it was instruction and not naturalistic exposure to L2 that resulted in the reported learning.

Another study that trained learners to provide CF to each other in the context of classroom instruction is that of Fujii, Mackey, and Ziegler (2016). Two groups of low-intermediate learners drawn from intact EFL classes in Japan (N = 39) completed two types of information-gap tasks (spot-the-differences and problem-solving tasks) at the beginning and at the end of the study. One of the groups (treatment group, n = 23) also received a four-part "metacognitive instruction session," whose aim was to highlight the importance of CF and to train learners to provide it to their peers. The session began with a discussion on the benefits of feedback in the development of accuracy and provided video examples of effective teacher-learner interactions. The learners were then presented with examples of clarification requests ("I'm sorry, I don't understand"), confirmation checks ("So, you mean . . ."), and recasts as "useful phrases" to employ in determining the interlocutor's intended meaning. The final phase included the opportunity for the whole class and learner-pairs to practice the use of CF in interaction. Working on a spot-the-differences task as a class, the teacher modeled ways in which learners could initiate negotiation and employ CF moves during a similar task they would engage in as pairs following the demonstration. The treatment group also completed an exit questionnaire to share their perceptions of the training received. The results showed that the treatment group employed more CF than the controls (n = 16) and that there were significant differences in the gain scores between the groups. Furthermore, the exit questionnaires indicated the learners' appreciation for the concepts brought forward in the training and pointed to their increased understanding of the benefits of CF.

Similarly, Sato and Ballinger (2012) investigated whether instruction in CF provision would have a positive effect on L2 learners' ability to attend to accuracy in their own and peer's output during collaborative tasks. Working with different instructional contexts—university-level English classes in Japan (n = 129) and two elementary-level French immersion classes in Canada—the researchers designed two types of CF training. While the Japanese training focused exclusively on the peer provision of recasts or prompts and included CF-related information and practice that lasted for a period of ten weeks (see the description of Saito & Lyster, 2012, above), the Canadian training lasted seven weeks and focused on teaching learners a set of strategies designed to: (1) increase L2 interactions, (2) facilitate learners recognition of the learning opportunities present in peer interactions, and (3) to demonstrate how to seek and give language-related assistance. Role plays, games, and discussions were at the core of strategy instruction, which lasted approximately 6 hours in both English and French, and included demonstrations of "both good and bad methods" (Sato & Ballinger, 2012, p. 163). The CF portion (focus 3) emphasized strategies for "noticing that a partner needs language help" and "giving and receiving CF" (p. 164). In addition to the role plays, the learners were also exposed to a series of cartoons on "polite and impolite methods of giving and receiving CF" (ibid) and participated in discussions on the more effective CF strategies. Students were paired with a partner according to their language dominance in that English-dominant students were paired with their French-dominant counterparts.

The results for the Japanese context show that over the course of the academic term only the trained learners were able to increase their awareness of L2 form (in meaning-focused tasks), which was evidenced by their increased use of CF. The analysis of interaction between four student pairs in the immersion context, however, show that CF provision (i.e., instances in which learners provided CF within the on-task, partner focused turns, p. 168) was uneven and often depended on the level of engagement (operationalized as the percentage of collaborative conversation turns calculated by dividing the number of collaborative turns by the number of overall turns, p. 165) that each partner brought to the task. That is, if the level of engagement was on par, both partners provided comparable amounts of CF; yet, a qualitative analysis of CF events showed that learners who provided more CF engaged with the task less, a surprising finding that was attributed to the amount of respect one partner felt towards the other partner's linguistic resources. This is to say that learners who provided more CF did not regard their partners as learning resources (as was evidenced by their "emphatically derisive or argumentative tone of voice" when delivering CF and indifference about the partner's understanding of or engagement with the supplied CF, p. 169) and that the latter, in turn, sensing their partner's negative attitudes, did not provide much CF assuming that its legitimacy may be questioned, or worse, the CF may be ignored altogether (resulting in wasted effort). In light of this, the authors stress the importance of creating a supportive classroom environment and nurturing of feelings of trust and respect between partners when engaging in pair/group work (see Sato, 2017, for discussion on the social dynamics of peer CF). After all, the partners in the most collaborative pair not only supplied CF at equal rates, but also reacted to the provided CF with uptake, signaling their willingness to accept and learn from the partner's CF. This is an important point since "unlike CF from teachers, reception of peer CF may not necessarily promise a positive developmental outcome, and a collaborative mindset between partners is the complex factor that may affect the outcome" (Sato & Ballinger, 2012, p. 172). Hence, taken together, these findings suggest that while training learners to provide CF can raise their L2 awareness (Japanese context), for the feedback to be effective, learners should be willing to collaborate and value each other's linguistic contributions (Canadian context).

Looking at the issue of training from a different vantage point, Kim (2013) considered the effect of pre-task modeling on EFL Korean middle school learners' (n = 45) L2 development as well as their ability to attend to errors in question formation during task planning and task performance. While L2 development was operationalized as stage increases (according to Pienemenn and Johnston's (1987) developmental sequences for question formation) between the pre and post tests, the learners' attention to form was evidenced by language-related episodes (LRE), during which the students vocalized or questioned their linguistic choices as well as corrected themselves and/or other learners. The students were randomly assigned to either the modeling (n = 21) or no modeling (n = 24) group. While both groups carried out three communicative tasks and engaged in pre-task planning for each with peers, only the modeling group watched a (different) video before carrying each task. Each video lasted two minutes and provided examples of LREs as well as ways to engage in collaborative pair work, where both partners were engaged with the task by asking questions, sharing ideas, and providing feedback in the form of explicit correction and recasts. The results showed that the modeling group produced more LREs than the no modeling group during both the planning and carrying out of the tasks. Furthermore, 76% of the learners in the modeling group advanced to a higher stage of question development, compared to 46% of those in the no modeling group. These findings support Sato and Lyster's (2012) results, suggesting that task modeling may be an effective tool "to raise learners' awareness about the *whys, whats,* and *hows* of attention to form during both task planning time and task performance so that [learners] can understand the benefits of task-based interactional processes and how to engage in them" (Kim, 2013, p. 25, original emphasis).

The findings unearthed in peer training research notwithstanding, it is important to note that "learner feedback is fundamentally different from teacher CF because it does not (or cannot) necessarily contain the pedagogical intent to assist language development of another learner" (Sato & Ballinger, 2012, p. 159). As such, research needs to consider ways to amplify teacher's CF practices. The author knows of only one study that has attempted to train learners to become aware of the focus of the CF provided in the classroom. Working with a class of 8- to 9-year-old (Grade 3) French immersion students (n = 43), Bouffard and Sarkar (2008) devised a feedback training to help the learners to notice and repair their lexical, phonological, and grammatical errors. The data came from 23 video-recorded communicative in-class activities (such as project presentations and storytelling), during which the teacher supplied feedback in the form of prompts (elicitation, repetition, and metalinguistic cues). In total, 287 episodes of the error-feedback-repair format (one error per episode) were first isolated (167 minutes in total) by the teacher and then presented to groups of four to seven learners (n = 38) for discussion. During the sessions, the teacher guided the students in "think-aloud explorations" to notice errors, identify their locus/nature, and repair them to stimulate collaborative analysis. Data analysis revealed three levels of focus on form: (1) noticing—when learners located the error or repaired it, (2) language awareness—when the nature or locus of the error was located, and (3) analysis—when learners engaged in grammatical analysis of an error. The analysis also showed notable improvement in the students' ability to discuss and analyze errors. Specifically, the learners became not only more aware of the processes underlying the sampled errors, but also developed a metalanguage by means of which they could articulate the source of an error and analyze its repair; what's more, "think-aloud explorations by stronger learners were learning opportunities for weaker learners" (p. 20). However, although this study supports the notion that teachers can guide (even young) learners to notice errors in the classroom context, absence of a comparison group precludes the conclusion that such training is effective. Furthermore, the fact that prompts (whose corrective intent is more explicit) were used to alert learners to the presence of an error and the learners were given opportunities to reflect on individual errors does not mean that all classroom-based training may yield similar results. What is needed then is an investigation of a classroom-based feedback training that would help learners to recognize the corrective intent of implicit CF types supplied by teachers during meaning-based tasks.

3.2 EVIDENCE: KARTCHAVA'S EXPERIMENTAL STUDY 2

As mentioned previously (Chapter 2), the extent to which learners are able to notice CF has received some attention, but it is still not clear which corrective techniques are noticed more. Whereas prompts are deemed more noticeable, recasts are often noticed less. This was the case in Study 1 that showed learners noticing the corrective intent of prompts alone and in combination with recasts more often than when recasts were provided on their own. Yet, the frequency of recasts in the world classrooms warrants an investigation into how their corrective properties may be made more apparent to learners. Study 2 investigated whether training in recasts prior to their provision would make them more noticeable, yielding increased uptake and larger gains on the post-intervention scores. The following research question guided the study: Does feedback training promote noticing and learning of L2 norms in the L2 classroom?

3.2.1 Method

3.2.1.1 Participants

One ESL teacher and 62 francophone college students participated in this study. The students came from the same college as the ones profiled in Study 1. They were high beginners, with a mean age of 20.75. While many spoke

Table 3.1. Group Distribution

Group	Teacher	n
Recasts only	Albert	20
Recasts + Feedback training	Albert	24
Control	Kartchava	18

more than one language (language mean: 2), the majority (78.8%) reported French as their mother tongue. The classes met once a week for three hours, two of which were spent in the classroom and one in the language laboratory (see Section 2.2.1.1 in Chapter 2 for a detailed description of the context). Prior to the study, the participants were exposed to ESL instruction for three years in primary school (~120 hours) and five years in high school (~670 hours). Albert, the same instructor observed to naturally provide CF in the form of recasts in Study 1, was the teacher here. Two of his intact classes were randomly assigned to either a "recast-only" or "recasts + training" experimental group. Since it was not possible to find another teacher from the same college who provided no feedback, Kartchava taught the control group during the communicative activity described below and was the one to provide the feedback training. Table 3.1 shows the group distribution.

3.2.1.2 Feedback Conditions

Recasts were operationalized as a teacher's reformulation of the learner's incorrect utterance. The teacher was instructed not to comment on the grammaticality of the students' incorrect utterances or push learners to correct their ungrammatical utterances. Instead, the teacher could react with a full, partial, interrogative, or integrated reformulation (see examples below). In response to a student's utterance *He go to the movies yesterday*, any of the following approaches could be adopted:

Full reformulation: Okay. He went to the movies yesterday.
Partial reformulation: (He) Went
Interrogative reformulation: Where did you say he went yesterday?
Integrated reformulation: He went to the movies yesterday. Did he go alone or with someone?

3.2.1.3 Linguistic Target

The past tense was chosen as the linguistic target because it: (1) is problematic for ESL learners, regardless of L1; (2) represents a level of complexity (DeKeyser, 1998, 2005); (3) is subject to L1 interference (Ammar, Sato & Kartchava, 2010; Collins, 2002); (4) occurs frequently in the input (Doughty

& Varela, 1998), which facilitates its elicitation during communicative tasks (McDonough, 2007); and (5) has been shown to be a good candidate for learner improvement when it is targeted with CF (Doughty & Varela, 1998; Ellis et al., 2006; McDonough, 2007; Yang & Lyster, 2010). Research has also shown that the noticing of CF leads to language development, though it largely depends on the technique employed and on the nature of the error (Mackey et al., 2000; Ammar, 2008; Ammar & Sato 2010a).

3.2.1.4 Development Measures

The tests, composed of a picture description task, were completed by all the groups before and immediately after the intervention. The tasks were developed in consultation with the teacher to ensure that they were appropriate for the students' level and were similar in format to those used in Kartchava's previous research. The picture description activity, designed to elicit the past tense, asked the participants to write a narrative of what happened in a cartoon strip at a specified point in the past (i.e., last week). A different cartoon strip was used at each test time. To ensure linguistic uniformity, the learners had to incorporate the provided context-appropriate verbs (12 per strip) in their stories at least once. The same 12 verbs were used across the two tests. Of the 12 verbs, five called for the regular past forms (i.e., pack, walk, watch, return, and arrest), and seven called for the irregular forms (i.e., see, take, swim, meet, eat, sleep, and buy). All the verbs were telic and depicted the accomplishment and achievement verb categories because these call for the use of past tense (Bardovi-Harlig, 1998; Collins, 2007).

To measure changes in the target-like usage, percentage accuracy scores were computed. Specifically, the total number of verbs accurately supplied in the obligatory contexts was divided by the maximum score of 12 and then multiplied by 100. If the same verb was used more than once, only its initial use was counted to offset overuse.

3.2.1.5 Feedback Training

The three-part feedback training (explanation, examples, intervention) was delivered by Kartchava in English, with the teacher (Albert) present. In Phase 1, the students were shown two video clips (two minutes in length) of an English teacher correcting errors made by students in an ESL class. Each video contained one error and was of the error-feedback-repair pattern. The videos came from the data collected for Study 1 and focused on the use of grammatical targets other than the past tense. The students in the videos and the ones watching them came from comparable populations in that they were of the same linguistic background (French L1), lived in the same geographic location (Montreal, Quebec), attended the same college, and were of a similar proficiency in English (high beginners). This was done to maintain ecological validity as well as to help learners relate to the task. After viewing each video, the students were asked to reflect on what they saw first in pairs and then again, as a whole class. The following questions were used to prompt the reflection: "What happened in the video?," "What did the teacher do?," "What did the student(s) do?" After the discussion, the class was informed that an error was made by the student in the video and that the teacher corrected it. The recast used to alert the learner to the error was highlighted (verbally and on the accompanying PowerPoint slide) and alternative corrective strategies within the same CF type (i.e., other recast types) were provided (Example 1).

Example 1
Error: My best friend, Anne, *like* movies and *want* to watch the new James Bond film this weekend.
Teacher's correction: Oh, your friend Anne likes movies and wants to watch the new JB film.

Alternative CF moves:
a. Anne likes movies and wants to watch the James Bond film?
b. Anne likes movies and wants to watch the new JB movie. Has she watched other JB movies?
c. Likes; Wants

For additional practice (Phase 2), the students were presented with three other decontextualized erroneous sentences and asked to identify the errors and suggest ways to correct them, using recasts. The errors were particular to francophone learners of English and focused on the 3rd person singular (Sentence 1), the plural –s (Sentence 2), and possessive determiners (Sentence 3).

1. I *have* 16 years old.
2. I have many *friend*.
3. Bob wants to come with us, but Anne says that she will not pay for *her* ticket again.

Following this, the students were told that they would engage in a communicative task, during which the teacher would supply correction (Phase 3—Intervention). The types of correction would be similar to the ones demonstrated in the videos and discussed afterwards (see "Alternative CF moves" in Example 1 and the Feedback conditions section). The one-hour practice activity was a communicative task designed to promote the use of the past tense (adapted from Gatbonton, 1994). The students worked in groups to create accounts of their whereabouts (activity 1), which were then questioned by the whole class.

CF was provided during the student-fronted portion of the activity, which lasted 20-30 minutes. No instruction on the linguistic target was provided beforehand. While all three groups participated in the communicative task, only the recast groups (recast only and recasts + training) received feedback. The recast + training group was the only one to receive feedback training.

3.2.1.6 Noticing Measures

Noticing was measured with uptake, which was operationalized in line with Lyster and Ranta's (1997) definition that focused on the learner's immediate reaction following feedback. While the use of uptake as a measure of noticing may be problematic (Leeman, 2007), it provides evidence that the CF has been perceived by the learner (Lyster & Ranta, 1997; Ohta, 2000; Sheen, 2006). Moreover, uptake that includes instances of repair evidences modified output (Nassaji, 2016). The true effect of uptake in this study, however, was not in the rate of uptake but in its quality. The student-fronted portions of the activity carried out during the communicative task in the two CF groups were analyzed for instances of uptake. Specifically, 25:09 minutes were analyzed for the recasts only group and 28:52 minutes for the recasts + training group. Instances of uptake (see Chapter 1 for information about the uptake measure) were classified into "repair" and "needs repair" (Example 2); instances of repair were further classified into the "repetition" (Example 3) and "incorporation" (Example 4) types. While the repetition type of repair entails a learner repeating the teacher's feedback, the incorporation repair has the learner repeat the correction, incorporating it into a longer utterance.

Example 2
Student: Me? I drink some water.
Teacher: I drank
Student: *I drunk some water [Needs Repair]
Teacher: I drank
Student: Yeap.

Example 3
Student: *We go to Buffalo.
Teacher: You went to Buffalo.
Student: We went to Buffalo. [Repair—Repetition]

Example 4
Student: We do? *I drink
Teacher: I drank
Student: I drank rum and coke. [Repair—Incorporation]

3.2.1.7 Exit Interviews

Semi-structured interviews were conducted with the three groups after the intervention. A total of seven student-volunteers (two learners from the recast group, three from the recasts + training group, and two from the control group) met with the researcher one-on-one to reflect on the study as a whole and to comment about the activities used. The recast groups were questioned on the CF supplied and the CF noticing achieved. The recast + training group was also asked about their perceptions of the feedback training received. The interviews were audio-recorded and lasted approximately 10 minutes each. They were analyzed qualitatively for additional evidence of noticing, L2 development, and attitudes towards the feedback training.

3.2.2 Results

3.2.2.1 The Noticeability of CF

The results indicate that both experimental groups produced uptake despite the differences in the total number of CF episodes. As Table 3.2 shows, the recast group produced 21 past tense errors and reacted to the teacher's CF 7 times (33%), 5 of which resulted in repair and 2 in needs of repair. The recasts + training group, in turn, produced fewer past tense errors overall but reacted to the same number of CF instances as the recasts group. Specifically, out of 13 errors, 7 were reacted to (53.8%), with 6 being repaired and 1 requiring additional repair.

3.2.2.2 L2 Development

To determine how CF promoted the learning of form across the conditions, the groups' accuracy means were computed and compared across test times. As Table 3.3 shows, there was an increase on the post-test for the three groups. A repeated measures analyses of variance was conducted to explore whether the observed means were statistically significant across the experimental groups. There was no significant Group x Time interaction effect, $F(2,136) = .297$, $p = .744$, and no main effect for group or time. Hence, no statistically significant differences in the scores of the three groups were

Table 3.2. Noticing Raw Counts

Group	Past Tense Errors Made	Uptake	Repair	Needs Repair
Recasts	21	7 (33%)	5	2
Recasts + Feedback training	13	7 (53.8%)	6	1

Table 3.3. Accuracy Means for the Past Tense by Group (Maximum: 100%)

Group	n	Pre-Test M (%)	Pre-Test SD	Post-Test M (%)	Post-Test SD
Recasts	20	47.08	29.03	53.75	21.2
Recasts + Feedback training	24	54.16	27.8	55.9	31.9
Control	18	27.47	23.21	37.34	25.77
Total	62	42.01	28.68	48.24	27.88

found, suggesting that the intervention did not result in learning gains for any of the groups. Figure 3.1 illustrates past tense accuracy means for the pre-test and post-test.

To control for differences in the pre-test scores, the pre-test scores were adjusted using one-way ANCOVA (Table 3.4). The independent variable was the group and the dependent variable consisted of scores on the developmental measure. Participants' scores on the pre-test were used as the covariate in this analysis. After adjusting for the pre-test scores, no significant differences between the three groups on post-test scores, $F(2, 58) = .127, p = .881$, partial eta squared .004, were found.

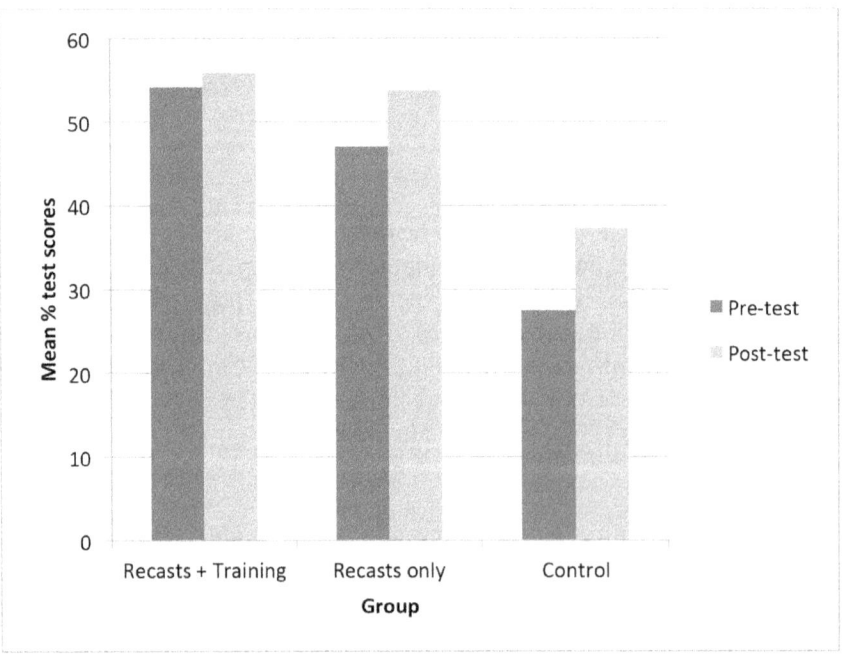

Figure 3.1. Past tense accuracy means across groups

Table 3.4. Estimated Post-Test Accuracy Means for the Past Tense by Group (Maximum: 100%)

		Pre-Test		Post-Test	
Group	n	M (%)	SD	M (%)	SD
Recasts	20	47.08	29.03	53.17	21.2
Recasts + Feedback training	24	54.16	27.8	52.8	31.9
Control	18	27.47	23.21	49.18	25.77
Total	62	42.01	28.68	48.24	27.88

To sum up, there were no differences in the learning gains for any of the three groups. In terms of noticing, however, both CF groups produced uptake in reaction to feedback. Yet, despite the same uptake totals, the trained group showed a higher percentage of uptake (albeit on a smaller number of errors) compared to the recast only group.

3.2.3 Discussion

This pilot study investigated whether training in recasts prior to their provision would make them more noticeable, yielding increased uptake and larger gains on the post-intervention scores. While three groups ("recasts + training," "recasts only," and "control") of learners participated in a whole-class communicative task, recasts were provided to only two groups in response to their errors with the past tense, with one of the two groups receiving recast training prior to the task. The results show that the learners who received recast training made fewer errors overall, had a higher CF-uptake ratio, and produced one more instance of repair than their "recasts-only" counterparts. Yet, there were no differences in the learning outcomes for any of the groups.

3.2.3.1 The Noticeability of CF

The results indicate that despite the training, both treatment groups produced uptake. It is argued, however, that the quality of that uptake was different. The trained group produced fewer target-related errors (n = 13) overall and repaired 54% of them; the recasts-only group, in turn, produced proportionally more errors (n = 21), having repaired 33% of the total. Furthermore, the trained group produced a total of 6 instances of repair compared to 5 instances in the recasts-only group. It may be argued that the trained group noticed more feedback because their attention to the corrective focus of recasts was pre-empted prior to the task (through the feedback training) and was solidified during the task completion. The training helped learners to discover the role of CF in the L2 learning classroom and to reflect on its benefits, suggesting that even a brief CF instruction like the one provided here can assist learners in becoming informed "consumers" of the teacher-supplied CF. This conclusion finds support in Bouffard and Sarkar (2008) as well as research on peer CF that has empirically shown positive effects of training on the learners' ability to become effective providers of CF (Fujii et al., 2016; Sato & Ballinger, 2012; Sato & Lyster, 2012). Knowing that feedback would be provided during the communicative task allowed the "trained" learners to attend to the accuracy of their output (which is indicative of the low number of errors overall) and to pay special attention to the provided recasts, the saliency of which was highlighted in the training (Excerpt 1); Excerpt 1, in particular, suggests an experimental effect.

Excerpt 1
[Was the training helpful?] *In some way yes, because you are trying to make an effort about how you are going to talk and the teacher, you will know that the teacher will correct you and you will try to not leave him correct you so you will do your best that you can, but if we didn't know that, it would be a little bit harder and maybe we could be, like, <u>disappointed why is he always correcting me or something</u>? [. . . having been told that I would be corrected] was helpful. . . . It made me aware of how we should react while we are talking.*

The task itself could have also contributed to the learners' noticing of recasts. By the virtue of its design, the task made the use of the past tense genuinely repetitive and inevitable for the discussions of past events. This, in turn, allowed learners to maintain the meaning constant and attend to the accuracy of their output. This is probably why the trained group became aware of the target of the supplied feedback (Excerpt 2 and Excerpt 3).

Excerpt 2
I noticed that the teacher was correcting some of the grammar. Um, past tense and present tense, but mostly. . . . Past. Like people say "I go," but it's "I went" or stuff like that.

Excerpt 3
After two, two, groups, when they pass, I notice that he was, because I was paying attention about what the person in front was talking about. . . . And when he say, like let's say a verb in the present tense, the teacher automatically, he say, he corrected him into the past tense.

However, the task did not seem to have the same effect on the learners in the recast-only group, who were unsure about the goal of the teacher's verbal reactions (Excerpt 4). It was only with the researcher's prompting during an exit interview that the student appeared to realize the teacher's intention to provide corrective information and this despite the learner having been able to identify the target of the feedback. This points to the fact that absence of uptake does not imply absence of noticing in that the learners may have been aware of the errors they were making but did not feel it necessary/appropriate to act on this understanding. This was the case in Mackey and Philp's (1998) study, where they found that even when learners did not produce immediate uptake, their test scores evidenced learning gains. Similarly, investigating the relationship between noticing and learning, Kartchava and Ammar (2013) found evidence that even when learners did not report noticing, their test scores increased or decreased; there were also cases when the reverse was true—learners reported noticing, but this either did not affect or produced a decrease in their test scores. Finally, Yoshida (2010) provided evidence of learners' responding to feedback despite their reported non-noticing of the supplied CF. In the context of the present study, simple repetition of the recasts did not mean that the teacher's feedback was noticed, understood, or incorporated (Gass, 1997). It may simply imply that "mimicking" (Gass, 2003, p. 236) devoid of analysis took place. Because of the larger instances of error and proportionally fewer uptake occurrences, it is possible that the recasts-only group engaged in this type of repetition. Still, the act of repeating recasts has been shown to help learners acknowledge the corrective focus of recasts (Mackey et al., 2000). This was especially the case when learners repeated feedback, incorporating it into a new utterance (Nassaji, 2011b).

Excerpt 4
Researcher: Did you notice the teacher doing something, did the teacher do anything when the stories were being presented?
Student: *I think he was filming. Or . . . Well, there was a camera in the class.*
R: Did you notice him correct?
S: *No, I didn't see that.*
R: Did you hear him correct?
S: *Me, I was too focused on the story . . .*
R: Just focused on the story. . . . OK. So you didn't feel that he was correcting? Do you know the tense that you were using?
S: *The past tense?*
R: The past tense. How do you feel about it? Do you feel comfortable about using it?
S: *Yeah, close, close enough.*

The recasts-only group produced less uptake in terms of percentages (33%) than the trained group (54%). One of the reasons for this might be that recasts, unlike prompts, often do not provide learners with an opportunity to respond. That is, prompts signal the need for a response and provide learners with *time* in which to tackle the correction received and attempt multiple repairs, the process supported with additional input from the teacher and/or other students. Recasts, on the other hand, do not require a reaction from the learner, impeding the need to notice their corrective nature (Nicholas et al., 2001), and are often seen by teachers as a way to move the conversation/lesson forward (Lyster, 1998a). This is exacerbated by the fact that recasts are initiated and completed by the teacher, precluding the need for learners to work out accuracy issues themselves (Panova & Lyster, 2002). Hence, since, as Excerpt 4 shows, the recast-only students were generally unaware of the corrective intent behind the teacher's feedback and were not required to respond to the CF, their reaction to feedback was limited.

Another reason for the uptake results may lie in learner individual differences. The noticeability and effectiveness of recasts has been shown to depend on learners' individual abilities to process recasts and draw on the learner-internal and context-specific clues. That is, learners of advanced analytical ability, proficiency, and attention span tend to benefit from recasts (e.g., Ammar & Spada, 2006; Philp, 2003; Trofimovich et al., 2007). Yet, such affective variables as anxiety, willingness to communicate, self-esteem, and beliefs may also affect learners' ability to learn from exposure to recasts. For example, if a learner does not believe in the value of feedback, he/she may not be attuned to the teacher's corrective practices, choosing to ignore them altogether or avoid feedback-related practice. Conversely, learners who value feedback may be more willing to engage in such practice, requesting more corrective focus and even deciding on the technique(s) that may work best for them in particular (e.g., Kartchava & Ammar, 2014b—Study 3). Furthermore, instructional context, experience with feedback, and tasks that engage learners in free-style communication may affect how learners perceive recasts or what actions they choose to take to improve their L2 knowledge. Interviews with the recasts-only group showed that for many this was the first time they had received CF or realized that the teacher was correcting their oral production (as the feedback they knew previously was that given to their writing) and in this way; what's more, they found attention to form helpful overall (Excerpt 5). This suggests that if given the opportunity and additional exposure to feedback, these learners may become more active in seeking out occasions to focus on accuracy and develop opinions on strategies that resonate with their approaches to L2 learning.

Excerpt 5
Researcher: Was this the first time that you were corrected in this way?

Student: *Yes, because other teachers would just let us talk even if we made errors . . .*
R: Was the correction helpful?
S: *Yes, especially when we were in front of the class—we knew that if we made a mistake, the teacher would correct us . . .*
R: So, you have never been corrected until now?
S: *Well, the teachers would tell us «don't do this» or «don't say that», but that was mostly in writing*

Finally, the fact that recasts were the only feedback strategy that targeted one grammatical feature may explain the small differences in uptake results. Theoretically, feedback that is provided intensively (i.e., targeting one pre-selected feature, Nassaji, 2017) has been said to be more effective than extensive feedback that targets many features at once (Ellis & Sheen, 2006; Hawkes & Nassaji, 2016). It is argued that intensive feedback is more effective because it helps learners to focus on one feature at length. Recasts, in particular, are "more likely to be effective when [they are] targeted at only one or few features" (Doughty, 2001, p. 255). It then stands to reason that since both treatment groups were exposed to the same CF strategy that was used to treat one target feature intensively, the groups were afforded the same opportunities to react to feedback. Yet, it is not clear whether extensive recasting would have resulted in a different outcome—this is an important point to consider in light of the positive evidence for extensive feedback (Loewen, 2005; Nassaji, 2009, 2017).

3.2.3.2 L2 Development

Even though the past tense was the only target in the intervention, there were no statistical differences in the accuracy scores between the groups on the post-test. This may be due to a number of reasons. First, the intervention was one-hour long, which may not be enough for any significant change to take place. As such, a delayed post-test conducted at a later point during the term could have provided a different, more robust measure of learning. This is because delayed post-tests have been shown to bring out more developmental change than immediate post-tests (Li, 2013; Mackey, 1999; Mackey & Goo, 2007). Furthermore, to enable change, learners may need opportunities for additional exposure to target-filled input (Gass, 1997) and more "thinking or processing time" (Mackey et al., 2000, p. 474) to integrate it into their developing L2 knowledge. Second, the effectiveness of feedback often depends on a number of learner-internal factors that may include both cognitive (working memory, Goo, 2012; Mackey et al., 2002; attention control and analytic ability, Trofimovich et al., 2007; aptitude, Li, 2013; Sheen, 2007; developmental readiness, Mackey & Philp, 1998; proficiency, Ammar & Spada, 2006) and affective variables (anxiety, Sheen, 2008; beliefs, Sheen, 2007). Recasts have been shown to be more beneficial for learners who are developmentally more advanced (Mackey & Philp, 1998) and of higher proficiency level (Ammar & Spada, 2006) than their counterparts. Because learners in this study were of the same low proficiency (based on their course placement) and arguably, at the lower developmental level, the recasts supplied proved ineffective at yielding a noticeable change in the test scores.

Third, despite the feedback having been focused on one single structure, it may be that the classroom context affected the effectiveness of recasts. That is, research has shown more success for recasts in the laboratory setting (e.g., Han, 2002; Mackey & Philp, 1998; McDonough & Mackey, 2006), where learners engage in dyadic interactions that are individualized, intensive, and learner-focused (Nicholas et al., 2001). Still, high frequency of the past tense verbs in the input and the likeness of the English past tense morphology (for both regular and irregular past verbs) to its highly irregular French counterpart could have helped the participants improve their knowledge of the feature (Kartchava & Ammar, 2014a—Study 1; Yang & Lyster, 2010). Fourth, the effectiveness of the picture description task as a measure of the participants' knowledge of the past tense may have been limited. That is, due to a number of logistical challenges, the students were asked to complete the task in writing. Yet, several meta-analyses have found recasts to be more effective on oral rather than written measures (Lyster & Saito, 2010; Mackey & Goo, 2007). This is because the mode by which CF is delivered, some argue, should match that of the test measure to allow for transfer of learning (Ellis, 2008; Lightbown, 2008). Finally, learners in the recast-only group may have experienced difficulty in perceiving the corrective nature of recasts since they targeted a morphosyntactic feature. This is because recasts are more likely to be perceived as corrective when they address lexical or phonological errors than when they target grammatical errors (Egi, 2007a; Mackey et al., 2000).

3.3 CONCLUSION

This study examined the effectiveness of feedback training on learner's ability to notice and benefit from recasts provided intensively during a whole-class communicative task. In the rationale for the study it was argued that if the training is effective, learners would be able to do any or all of the following: (1) verbally respond to the provided CF, (2) repair the errors, (3) show immediate and long-term learning gains, and (4) verbalize the grammatical analysis they engaged in as the result of the CF training. The results show that the treatment groups were able to do points 1 and 2 but were unsuccessful in achieving immediate learning gains in point 3 (N. B.: long-term learning gains were not measured); point 4 was partially realized in the exit interviews. The feedback training, however, did have an impact on the trained group's behavior and noticing outcomes. Still, the training did not appear to yield any learning differences. One of the limitations of the study is its inability to provide the participants with an opportunity to verbalize grammatical analyses they engaged in to process the feedback; clearly, the few responses probed during the interviews are not enough, and future research would benefit from a more extensive focus on this topic. Furthermore, the short training (10 minutes) and practice session (one hour) preclude any definitive conclusions from being made. It can, however, be said that this pilot study has provided an indication that training learners to notice feedback might bring benefits to their ability to recognize corrective intent of recasts, especially in content-based classrooms. More research investigating this question with different populations, (training, noticing, developmental) instruments, and in varied classroom-based contexts is needed. Because learner differences have been suggested as one of the reasons for the noticing results reported here, the impact of learner beliefs on the noticeability and effectiveness of feedback is examined in the next chapter (Chapter 4).

Chapter Four

Learner Beliefs and Corrective Feedback

While training learners to notice CF was shown to be partially effective in Chapter 3, it is now important to consider the impact of individual differences (IDs) on learners' ability to recognize the corrective intent of feedback. A number of IDs such as intelligence, aptitude, motivation, risk taking, anxiety, strategy use, self-regulation, proficiency, and beliefs have been investigated in relation to the influence they may have on one's language learning success (e.g., Cotterall, 1999; Horwitz, 1990; Peacock, 1999; Siebert, 2003; Tanaka & Ellis, 2003; Wenden, 1991, 1999; Yang, 1999). Together these investigations point to a link between personal variables and learners' ultimate attainment in the L2. Moreover, individual factors are thought to predict how successful the task of language learning may become (Breen, 2001; Dörnyei, 2005; Fox, 1993; Gardner & MacIntyre, 1992; Horwitz, 1985, 1999; Sawyer & Ranta, 2001; Tanaka, 2004). What is not known, however, is the effect of IDs on the processes of L2 acquisition and their influence on learners' ability to process language instruction (Sheen, 2011). Since CF is a factor in FFI and is concerned with facilitation of learners' noticing of the difference between their incorrect utterance and the target form, understanding the impact that IDs may have on the processing of feedback is of value.

This chapter will describe a study that investigated the impact of learner beliefs, a "significant learner characteristic to take into account when explaining learning outcomes" (Dörnyei & Ryan, 2015, p. 187), on learners' ability to notice and benefit from the feedback they received in an L2 classroom. Investigations of this ID are especially important in relation to CF since: (1) learner beliefs is one of two affective IDs (anxiety being the other) that have been investigated in terms of CF effectiveness, but not its noticeability, (2) the number of such investigations is very limited (Li, 2017), and (3) despite beliefs being an important predictor of L2 development, their impact on leaners' in-class actions (such as noticing and learning from the supplied CF) and consequently, general L2 success is unclear. Understanding how students view instruction and what elements they consider imperative to its effectiveness stands to benefit the learners themselves as well as to inform teachers' practice in general and specifically in regard to CF. The chapter begins with a discussion of the various views that have been adopted in defining beliefs, followed by an outline of the different types of beliefs and their possible sources. Then, a review of investigations that studied the impact of beliefs on language learning in general and beliefs about CF in particular is presented. Following this, my study, originally published in *TESOL Quarterly* (Kartchava & Ammar, 2014b[30]), is replicated. The chapter concludes with a consideration of pedagogical implications that the results of this investigation may have for the language classroom.

4.1 BACKGROUND

4.1.1 Defining Learner Beliefs

In his 2005 publication on the main variables that affect and define the psychology of the language learner, Dörnyei hesitated to label learner beliefs as an individual variable, claiming that due to their dynamic, situated, and non trait-like nature, this classification was unwarranted. Dörnyei (2005) claimed that "ID constructs refer to dimensions of enduring personal characteristics that are assumed to apply to everybody and on which people differ by degree" (p. 4). In light of the burgeoning research on the topic of IDs, in the second edition of the volume ten years later Dörnyei and Ryan (2015) posited that their original definition of an ID needed to be redefined, and with it, their notion of beliefs as having to be an established, state-like factor. Not only do they now praise the dynamic and situated nature of beliefs, they see them as potentially "the most versatile of all the learner characteristics" and call for continued research to help explain such established IDs as motivation, aptitude, and affect (ibid, p. 191). After all, it is precisely because learner beliefs are "personal convictions about various facets of SLA" that studying them may illuminate our understanding of "the narrative accounts that people create about themselves to organize and understand their L2 Learning Experiences" (ibid, p. 192).

To enable research into any variable, it first needs to be operationalized. In the case of beliefs, this has proven to be a complex task, with the literature on the subject producing a variety of definitions. Cognitive psychology, for example, defines "beliefs" as representations of a reality that guide thought and behavior (Abselson, 1979; Anderson, 1985). Beliefs are said to contain a cognitive component, an emotional component, and a behavioral component—that is, they influence what one knows, feels, and does (Rokeach, 1968). The French-medium educational literature, in turn, views beliefs as having four facets: (1) representation (*la représentation*), (2) attitude (*l'attitude*), (3) perception (*la perception*), and (4) belief (*la croyance*). "Representation," according to Biron (1991), involves interpretation or reorganization of a certain reality in accordance with personal beliefs (Leif, 1987). "Attitude," in turn, is the result of feelings, desires, and emotions one may possess about an object or situation; it ("attitude") influences individual perceptions and behavior (Thurstone & Chave, 1980). Dörnyei (2005) differentiated between "beliefs" and "attitudes" on the premise that the latter is "deeply embedded and can be rooted back in our past" whereas beliefs "have a stronger factual support" (p. 214) and can change. Wenden (1999), in turn, equated beliefs to attitudes by drawing a parallel between *metacognitive knowledge*—the portion of a learner's knowledge base that consists of what he/she knows about learning—and learner beliefs, arguing that the latter are distinct from the former in that they reflected the values one adhered to and as such, are more persistent. Finally, "perception" represents "the process by which any person or group of people becomes aware of the objects which are presented to them or the events which occur" (Gagné, 1979, p. 25).[31] In fact, any human perception is influenced by beliefs that impact the ways in which events are understood and acted upon (Nisbett & Ross, 1980).

Research on learner beliefs in SLA has been primarily based on the cognitivist assumption that learners' attitudes and behaviors are shaped by mental representations about the nature of language and language learning (Barcelos, 2003; Benson & Lor, 1999; Wenden, 1998, 1999). In this view, beliefs are a subset of the metacognitive knowledge in that they are stable but may differ from one learner to another because they are value-related and tenaciously held (Wenden, 1999). If, for example, a learner believes that the best way to learn a language is through the study of rules and rote memorization of language parts, he/she will likely embrace vocabulary and grammar learning as well as be open to systematic analysis, memorization, and practice drills of the target language. Should the learner believe, however, that learning a language is best achieved through natural exposure to it, he/she will hold positive attitudes towards communication with the speakers of the language, adopting a range of social and communication strategies (Benson & Lor, 1999). Recent investigations, however, have challenged the assumption of beliefs as a stable construct, suggesting that beliefs can change over time and under different circumstances (Amuzie & Winke, 2009; Barcelos, 2003; Tanaka & Ellis, 2003). In light of this, Barcelos and Kalaja (2011) proposed a new vision of beliefs as situation-driven, fluctuating, complex, ideologically determined, and intrinsically related to such affective constructs as concept of self, as well as influenced by self-reflection and interactions with other people (pp. 285–286). This definition has recently been expanded even further to highlight the emotional effect of beliefs on cognition and construction of identities (Barcelos, 2015). In this view, strong emotional attachment to certain beliefs makes them less susceptible to change. Yet, because change is possible, Barcelos calls for an increased sensitivity to "the sorts of emotions that are constructed in the interaction within the classroom and inside schools, and in the discourses and practices in the classroom" (p. 316).

4.1.2 Types of Beliefs

Investigations into learner beliefs have primarily focused on the types of beliefs learners hold and their possible underlying sources. Several approaches have been used to study beliefs, including the (1) normative, (2) metacognitive, (3) contextual, and (4) indirect methods. The normative approach presupposes that beliefs are general and fixed, and thus can be studied through the use of Likert-style questionnaires. While similar to the normative approach in that it assumes that beliefs are stable and "statable" (Wenden, 1986, 1987, 1999, 2001), the metacognitive method, in turn, views beliefs as "theories in action" (Benson & Lor, 1999; Wenden, 1986 & elsewhere). This is because learners are prompted to observe their cognitive processes and articulate beliefs by way of semi-structured interviews and/or self-reports. One of the benefits of this approach is that "learners become aware of their learning styles, strategies and beliefs that could lead them to improve their own learning processes" (Bernat & Gvozdenko, 2005, p. 6) in a variety of contexts. In contrast, the contextual approach rejects the idea that beliefs are trait-like, claiming that because beliefs are context-dependent they need to be examined by a variety of data types and means of data analyses (Barcelos, 2003; White, 1999). Finally, the indirect approach views learner beliefs as "covert" and employs metaphor analysis to uncover them (e.g., Kramsch, 2003).

Horwitz[32] (1985, 1987, 1988) is credited as being the first researcher to investigate the relationship between learner beliefs and L2 outcomes.

Her original Beliefs About Language Learning Inventory (BALLI) probed students' beliefs about: (1) the difficulty of language learning, (2) foreign language aptitude, (3) the nature of language learning, (4) language learning and communication strategies, as well as (5) motivation and expectations. A more recent version of the questionnaire (Horwitz, 2015), in addition to the original 34 statements, now includes 10 new statements about native-speaking teachers, learner autonomy, and standardized language tests. Horwitz' program of research has consistently shown that learners across linguistic and cultural backgrounds converge in their views on language learning. There is, however, evidence that learners perceive language learning (and learning of specific subjects) differently from learning in general (Mori, 1999). What's more, within language learning, students have also been shown to differentiate between the various segments inherent to the study of language. Loewen et al. (2009), for example, demonstrated that learners view grammar instruction and CF as distinct categories, calling on future research to consider this differentiation.

4.1.3 Sources of Beliefs

Research on belief sources has investigated the impact of learners' personalities, past language learning experiences, culture, and instructional context. While several studies in psychology have suggested that personality traits are strongly related to beliefs, little SLA research has actually considered the link, with "recent years [having] been a particularly barren time for research into the relationship between personality and SLA" (Dörnyei & Ryan, 2015, p. 34). Still, the respondents ($n = 54$) in Alexander and Dochy's (1995) study felt that personality was the key factor in shaping beliefs and was directly responsible for their willingness to question and reflect on their beliefs. The researchers recruited adult participants who were asked to share: (1) their personal theories of knowledge and beliefs, (2) factors that they felt shaped these beliefs, and (3) the stability they perceived these beliefs to have. The analysis of the personal theories identified 101 beliefs, which were classified into five categories: (1) information/knowledge, (2) education/experience, (3) personality, (4) nature of beliefs, and (5) other. One in five responses (21%) fell under the "personality" category, suggesting that the participants saw it as an important variable in the construction of beliefs and the one that could determine whether or not beliefs could be altered. The stability of beliefs carries an added importance in the study of personality on language learning. There is some evidence that "conscientiousness" and "extraversion," two of the five dimensions in the "Big Five" personality paradigm,[33] correlate with academic achievement. Conscientiousness, which subsumes a hard-working, persevering, and self-disciplined learner, has produced positive associations with learning while extraversion, which is associated with highly sociable, gregarious, active, passionate, and talkative students, has resulted in a negative relationship between personality and learning "because of introverts' greater ability to consolidate learning, lower distractibility, and better study habits" (Dörnyei & Ryan, 2015, pp. 25–26). Yet, even when a relationship between personality and learning is reported, the maximum variance in academic performance that personality can account for is no more than 15% (Dörnyei & Ryan, 2015).

The situation is quite different, however, when it comes to the effect of past learning experiences and contextual differences on learner beliefs. Several L2 scholars (Almarza, 1996; Horowitz, 1985; Kern, 1995; Little & Singleton, 1990) have provided evidence that "student beliefs about language learning [can] originate from their L2 learning experiences" (Peacock, 2001, p. 187). Little and Singleton (1990), for example, reported on a study where undergraduate and graduate students of foreign languages in Ireland were surveyed about their views on language learning. The results demonstrated a strong impact of past instructional experiences on learners' beliefs about language learning. This was evident in the type of activities they preferred to practice in the classroom. That is, they felt that oral repetition and writing activities were more beneficial to language learning than those that focused on listening and reading. The authors claimed that "past experience, both of education in general and language learning in particular, played a major role in shaping attitudes to language learning" (ibid, p. 14).

Past language learning experiences were also suggested as reasons for the reported beliefs about CF among the Canadian (francophone) and Russian learners of English described in Kartchava (2016). Using a 40-item questionnaire, the two groups were surveyed about their preferences for CF in general and specific CF types. The findings showed that regardless of the context, the learners' views appeared to be shaped by their past experiences with CF and how autonomous they were allowed/encouraged to be in their learning. That is, learners with little experience in autonomous learning were more likely to rely on the teacher for any information about their achieved and to-be-achieved L2 learning. Similarly, provision or absence of CF during one's language learning journey could also affect learners' CF views. Furthermore, extensive experience with language learning and higher L2 proficiency translated into positive views of CF overall as well as allowed speakers of several languages in the Russian sample to have an opinion about the amount and type of errors that would benefit from CF the most.

Similarly, past and present language learning experiences were said to be the reason learners of English and other languages studying in the U.S.

reported divergent views on the importance of grammar teaching and CF (Loewen et al., 2009). That is, English L2 learners stated a strong dislike for attention to accuracy whereas English L1 foreign language learners viewed the corrective focus much more favorably. It was argued that English L2 learners' present circumstances of living in the L2 were instrumental in pushing them to seek communicative opportunities that were sorely absent in their past L2 learning experiences filled with intensive attention to accuracy. The learners of foreign languages, on the other hand, saw a need for accuracy-driven instruction in an environment devoid of genuinely authentic foreign language communication.

Culture has also been suggested to play a role in the type of beliefs learners bring to the task of language learning (Alexander & Dochy, 1995; Prudie, Hattie, & Douglas, 1996; Truitt, 1995; Tumposky, 1991). For example, Prudie et al. (1996) found that Australian and Japanese learners differed in their perceptions of what constituted learning. This claim, however, has still to be substantiated, since a number of studies have failed to establish a clear link between culture and learner beliefs (Horwitz, 1999; Kartchava, 2016; Schulz, 2001; Tumposky, 1991). Tumposky (1991), for instance, suggested that culture played a secondary role in the beliefs of Soviet and American students and that previous experience and learning style were likely to affect beliefs much more than the cultural differences (p. 62). Similarly, in her comprehensive review of cross-cultural beliefs literature, Horwitz (1999) concluded that there was not enough evidence to show that "beliefs about language learning vary by cultural group. Rather, the results point to the possibility that within-group differences [. . .] likely account for as much variation as the cultural differences" (p. 575). This conclusion is supported by Kartchava's (2016) study, where the participants' different cultural (French Canada versus central Russia) and instructional (second versus foreign language) contexts did not affect their belief in the importance and need for CF in the language classroom; the differences primarily stemmed from the learners' individual differences (such as gender, number of languages spoken, and L2 proficiency) whose effects were often independent of a given cultural/instructional setting. Yet, in her investigation of teacher and learner attitudes toward the role of explicit grammar study and CF in foreign language learning, Schulz (2001) detected a few cultural differences between the Colombian and American learners in that the students in the former context expected teachers to provide slightly more feedback to form (97%) than those in the latter setting (90%). The teachers, however, regardless of the context, disagreed with their students on the benefits of grammar study and error correction. Specifically, the teachers appeared to be unaware of the value their students placed on receiving feedback in the classroom and the extent to which the students relied on grammar rules during language production.

4.1.4 Beliefs about Language Learning

Studies that have investigated the relationship between beliefs and language learning do not clearly indicate that beliefs directly affect what is learned. What they do show, however, is that the amount of achieved learning is largely dependent on the actions learners take to improve their knowledge of the target language and not solely on what they believe about language learning (Abraham & Vann, 1987; Ellis, 2008b; Mori, 1999; Tanaka, 2004; Zhong, 2008). The effectiveness of these actions may vary depending upon the situational, cultural, and personal constraints learners experience at a given point in time. As such, the degree to which beliefs affect learning is mediated by a learner's ability and readiness to act on his/her beliefs.

Zhong's (2008) case study, described in Ellis (2008b), of a Chinese migrant ESL learner, Lin, who lived in New Zealand for a period of ten weeks, is an example of a language learner who recognized and acted on her beliefs about language learning. The study aimed to investigate the developments in learner beliefs and the relationship between beliefs and learning. To fulfill the first goal, two interviews (one at the beginning and the other, at the end of the study period) and three classroom observations followed by stimulated recall sessions, during which the learner was asked to comment on selected episodes taken from the lessons, were carried out. To determine changes in proficiency, the learner took the Oxford Quick Placement Test as well as the Nation's vocabulary level tests and was asked to record a narrative at the beginning, and again at the end of the study. In terms of changes in beliefs, Lin seemed to become more secure in her ability to learn English and to manage this learning on her own (i.e., beliefs about self-efficacy). The learner chose to keep a vocabulary book, sit next to non-Chinese students in class, communicate in English outside of class, and to constantly monitor her own progress, which assured an increase in her vocabulary knowledge and communicative proficiency. However, her decision to accord accuracy less importance over time resulted in a decrease in her ability to produce an error-free and complexity-rich oral narrative at the end of the investigation.

Another example of a strong link between beliefs and language learning comes from Abraham and Vann's (1987) study of two learners, Gerardo and Pedro. Both learners believed in the importance of language practice in and outside the classroom as well as the need for error correction. Unlike Pedro, however, Gerardo believed in the importance of grammar knowledge and the need to get to the bottom of what was being communicated. In the end, Gerardo's Test of English as a Foreign Language (TOEFL) score was much higher than that of Pedro's (523 and 473, respectively), but Pedro's total on the test of spoken English superseded Gerardo's result. This suggests that different views about language learning and learners' engagement in the process may affect the learning outcomes. Loewen et al.'s (2009) descriptive study, arguably, points to a similar conclusion.

Mori's (1999) study also found that learner beliefs about language learning were largely task-specific and depended upon the perception of one's own learning ability. In other words, those learners who saw language learning as attainable and dependent on one's effort were more likely to display higher levels of achievement than those who did not.

Finally, Tanaka's (2004) study considered learner views on their language ability and the role context plays in their learning success. Tanaka examined the change in beliefs among Japanese learners of English ($n = 132$) when they went to New Zealand on a study abroad program. The participants were asked to complete a questionnaire, which contained 27 Likert-scale items and measured beliefs about analytical and experimental learning as well as such affective factors as self-assessment of achieved learning and anxiety. In addition to the questionnaire, some learners were interviewed at the end of this 12-week study, and five were asked to keep a journal about their English learning experiences throughout the study. The results revealed that while the questionnaire responses did not yield significant change in beliefs, the interviews and journals showed several transformations. For example, upon arrival in New Zealand, the majority of the participants felt dissatisfaction with their English ability and blamed it on the English language education they received in Japan. However, by the end of the study, their views shifted from criticizing the Japanese educational system to the realization that language learning is a long and difficult process, and that they, as learners, needed to become more active in their language learning.

4.1.5 Beliefs about CF

Only two affective variables, anxiety and learner beliefs, have been investigated in relation to CF effectiveness, but not to its noticeability (Sheen, 2008, 2011). These two variables, along with analytical ability (a cognitive factor), were examined in relation to both oral and written feedback. The results showed that while all three factors mediated the effectiveness of different types of CF, their impact depended on the feedback delivery mode and on the specific CF type. Of the affective factors, anxiety proved to be a variable in oral feedback, but did not play a role in written feedback. Learner attitudes towards CF, on the other hand, figured much more in the case of written than oral feedback. These attitudes measured the degree to which the participants were willing to accept feedback and whether they saw it as helpful and important. Their perceptions towards grammatical accuracy were also investigated. In terms of CF type, learners with lower anxiety outperformed those with higher anxiety in the case of oral metalinguistic CF (operationalized as the teacher's provision of the correct form following the error, together with a metalinguistic explanation, Sheen, 2011), but anxiety was not a factor in the effectiveness of oral recasts (defined as "a teacher's reformulations of a student's erroneous utterance, without changing the meaning of the student's original utterance in the context of a communicative activity," Sheen, 2011, p. 62). Similarly, learner attitudes mediated gain scores for the learners in the oral metalinguistic group, but not for those in the oral recast group. These findings suggest that affective variables influence the effectiveness of CF in the classroom, but it is still not clear whether they impact the noticeability of oral feedback. As such, more research is needed to determine whether or not the noticeability and benefits of feedback are dependent on differences in learner beliefs about corrective feedback.

Furthermore, this research may benefit from tools that explore learner views about CF more broadly. That is, Kartchava (2016) argues that, to date, studies that have used questionnaires to probe learner beliefs about CF have allocated the concept a very limited attention. Schulz (1996, 2001), for example, included only seven questions on the role of CF in her survey administered to both L2 and FL teachers and learners of English. Loewen et al. (2009), in turn, allocated four prompts on the topic. Finally, Jean and Simard's (2011) survey on the teaching and learning of grammar, administered to a large number of L2 English and French learners in Quebec high schools, dealt with the issue using only three questions. In contrast, the questionnaire designed for and employed in Study 3 (described below) consisted of 40 items, all of which focused exclusively on CF. Specifically, the statements were based on theoretical and empirical findings described in the literature on CF—the rationale for the questionnaire statements is provided in Section 4.2.1.3.

4.2 EVIDENCE: KARTCHAVA'S EXPERIMENTAL STUDY 3

The aim of Study 3 was to answer the call for more research that examines the impact of learner beliefs on their ability to notice and learn from the feedback supplied in the L2 classroom. If beliefs influence L2 learning, then there could be a link between beliefs and noticing and between beliefs and learning. Hence, the research question posed by this study is: Do learner beliefs about CF mediate their noticing and learning of L2 norms?

4.2.1 Method
4.2.1.1 Participants

Three highly experienced ESL teachers and their 197 high-beginner college students (mean age: 20.75 years old) participated in the study. All the students came from intact classes and spoke French as their first language (see Section 2.2.1.1 in Chapter 2 for a detailed description of the context). All 197 participants completed a beliefs questionnaire (see 4.2.1.3 for details) at the beginning of the term, and 99 of these, from six intact classes, took part in the intervention to ensure experimental comparability. The number of learners across groups and teachers is the same as that described in Table 2.1 (Chapter 2). The participants' prior exposure to ESL instruction amounted to 120 hours in primary school and 670 hours in high school. The college English classes they were enrolled in met once a week for three hours, two of which were spent in the classroom and one in the language laboratory. The courses were taught by the same teachers for the entire term.

The teachers, bilingual in English and French, were observed and interviewed prior to the investigation in order to identify if and how each provided CF. The three teachers addressed most of the learners' errors but did so using different methods. While one teacher (Albert) responded to errors primarily with recasts, another (Brian) showed a clear preference for prompts. The third teacher (Charles) consistently alternated between recasts and prompts. Because it was not possible to find another teacher from the same college who provided no feedback, Kartchava taught the control group.

4.2.1.2 CF Conditions

The CF conditions were operationalized in accordance with the CF types documented by Lyster and Ranta (1997) and Sheen (2004). Recasts were operationalized as the teacher's reformulation of a learner's incorrect utterance. The Recast teacher was allowed to react with a full, partial, interrogative, or integrated reformulation. For example, in response to a student's utterance *He go to the movies yesterday*, any of the following approaches could be adopted:

Full reformulation: Okay. He went to the movies yesterday.
Partial reformulation: (He) Went.

Interrogative reformulation: Where did you say he went yesterday?
Integrated reformulation: He went to the movies yesterday. Did he go alone or with someone?

Prompts were defined as techniques that elicited the correct form from the learner. These techniques included: (1) repetition, where the teacher repeated the student's incorrect utterance, either as a whole with rising intonation or partly by zooming in on the error while withholding the correct form; (2) elicitation, where the teacher repeated part of the learner's utterance and paused at the error to provide a clue as to the problem, as well as to invite the student to self-repair; and (3) metalinguistic information, where the teacher provided metalinguistic clues but did not provide the correct form, thus pushing the learner to self-correct. Hence, the Prompt teacher could adopt any of the following in response to *He go to the movies yesterday*:

Full repetition: He go to the movies yesterday?
Partial repetition: Go yesterday? Go?
Elicitation: He *what* [stressed] yesterday?
Metalinguistic information: It happened yesterday. So what should we say?
    (How do we form the past in English?)

The Mixed group's teacher was asked to alternate between recasts and prompts as equally as possible during the activities. The need for a combination of techniques stems from Lyster and Ranta's (1997) early observation that language teachers regularly use combinations of feedback types to address learners' errors. As such, the use of a mixed group is warranted not only to provide pragmatically justified evidence for the noticeability and effectiveness of CF types, but to also answer the call of "moving away from dichotomous comparisons of CF strategies that isolate CF from other relevant instructional variables and towards an examination of combinations of CF types that more closely resemble teachers' practices in classroom setting" (Lyster et al., 2013, p. 30).

Please note that the same linguistics targets and instructional intervention as in Study 1 (described in Chapter 2) were used in this study—for full details, please refer to sections 2.2.1.4 and 2.2.1.5 respectively.

4.2.1.3 Learner Beliefs

To uncover learner beliefs about CF, a two-part questionnaire (Appendix 4.1,[34] available on the Features tab at www.rowman.com/ISBN/9781498536776) was created; this was done in line with recommendations for questionnaire design in Dörnyei and Csizér (2012). In Part 1, demographic information on the participants was gathered, including their linguistic background. For each of the languages spoken, the participants then indicated: (1) where they learned it (i.e., classroom, home, other); (2) the number of years they have been speaking it; and (3) how well they spoke, wrote, listened, and read in each using a 3-point scale of "poor" (1) to "excellent" (3). Part 2 of the questionnaire consisted of 40 statements about CF, which were based on theoretical and empirical findings in the CF literature (e.g., Horwitz, 1988, 1999; Mohamed, 2011; Schulz, 1996, 2001). Specifically, the statements, the rationale for which is described below, centered on the (1) importance and (2) expectations for feedback, the (3) mode, (4) timing, and (5) amount of CF, as well as (6) recasts, (7) prompts, and (8) the manner and (9) by whom the CF should be delivered. On a scale of 1 to 5 ("1" = strong disagreement and "5" = strong agreement) the participants indicated the degree to which they agreed with each statement. The questionnaire was written in French (the participants' L1) and the items were randomized prior to the administration during Week 1 of the term.

The rationale for the questionnaire statements follows. Researchers (e.g., Long, 1996; Schmidt, 1990, 1995, 2001) and L2 learners (Chenoweth, Day, Chun, & Luppescu, 1983; Schulz, 1996, 2001) agree that CF is important in language learning. In fact, learners across different contexts expect to have their oral and written errors corrected (Schulz, 1996, 2001; Sheen, 2011) and in large amounts (Chenoweth et al., 1983; Jean & Simard, 2011). If they are not, learners' motivation to learn an L2 may decrease and they may question their teacher's credibility (Horwitz, 1990; Schulz, 1996, 2001). In terms of timing, while some methodologists believe that CF interrupts the communicative flow (e.g., Bartram & Walt, 1991; Harmer, 2007) and recommend that teachers address errors at the end of a task (e.g., Willis, 1996; Hedge, 2000), learners value teachers who provide immediate feedback to oral errors (Brown, 2009). While it is not clear how much feedback is necessary to affect learning, methodologists promote and some learners prefer (Lasagabaster & Sierra, 2005) selective correction (e.g., Harmer, 2007), suggesting that only errors that are prevalent and impede the message transmission should be treated. Regarding learner preferences for specific CF techniques, the research is scarce, with studies showing that lower-proficiency learners favor prompts over recasts (Mohamed, 2011; Yoshida, 2008), but that more advanced learners prefer recasts to prompts (Brown, 2009). Similarly, little is known about learners' preferences for who should correct—the teacher or the students. While Hendrickson (1980) argued for learner involvement in correcting their own errors, Hedge (2000) claimed that this might not always be possible due to the learners' inability or unwillingness to effect correction.

4.2.1.4 Noticing and Learning Measures

Immediate recall (administered during class activities) and lesson reflection sheets (completed at the end of each session) were used to measure the noticeability of the supplied feedback. The two instruments are described in detail in Chapter 2 (Section 2.5.1.6). While the immediate recall protocols were analyzed for the types of noticing reported and to calculate learner average noticing scores, the lesson reflection sheets, adapted from Mackey (2006), were analyzed qualitatively to provide additional evidence of noticing. To ensure that the coding was representative, an independent rater analyzed and categorized 10% of the data, randomly selected; inter-rater reliability was 93% based on simple agreement.

Please note that the same learning measures as those described in Chapter 2 (Section 2.2.1.7) were also used in this study.

4.2.1.5 Data Analysis

To examine common themes in the participants' beliefs as a group, the responses on Part 2 of the questionnaire were subjected to an exploratory factor analysis. The suitability of the data was confirmed by the Kaiser-Meyer-Oklin value of .82 and the statistically significant Bartlett's Test of Sphericity ($\chi 2 = 2968.542, p < .001$). Cronbach's alpha for the 40-item scale was .84, indicating internal item consistency. To determine to what extent the confirmed factors distinguished among the learners in all conditions, average scores for each learner were generated to represent values for the identified beliefs and to use in subsequent analyses investigating possible relationships between beliefs and learning and between beliefs and noticing.

Pearson analyses of the correlation between each learner's beliefs score and noticing score were conducted; the same was done for the beliefs and learning relationship. The noticing scores were calculated by dividing the total number of times a learner reported noticing by the total number of recall instances provided, which were then converted into percentages. This analysis was carried out for each target and feedback condition. The scores were used to determine the differential noticing of recasts, prompts, and the mixture of the two. Similarly, percentage accuracy scores were computed for each target across test times. For the past tense, the total number of verbs accurately supplied in the obligatory contexts was divided by the maximum score of 10 and then multiplied by 100. If the same verb was used more than once, only its initial use was counted to offset overuse. To account for the different number of questions produced by each learner, the number of correctly formed questions was divided by the total number of questions supplied and then multiplied by 100.

4.2.2 Results

4.2.2.1 Learner Beliefs

The factor analysis revealed five components, explaining a total of 44.3% of the variance. Interpretation of the components proved difficult because the output indicated that while the participants saw CF as important and expected it in the L2 classroom, they appeared unsure as to how, when, and by whom they prefer to be corrected. Hence, it was decided to run another analysis on only those items ($n = 26$) that dealt with the expectation for and importance of CF as well as the two CF techniques of interest (recasts and prompts). The resulting factor analysis (.85 Kaiser-Meyer-Oklin value and statistically significant Bartlett's Test of Sphericity value, $\chi2 = 1821.755$, $p < .001$, Cronbach's coefficient alpha: .855) produced a three-component solution, explaining a total of 43% of the variance, with Component 1 contributing 26.72%, Component 2 contributing 9.13%, and Component 3 contributing 7.15%. Oblimin rotation helped in interpreting the resulting factors, which were named using the highest loading items on each component (Pallant, 2007). Because the 16 items that loaded on Factor 1 were concerned with the expectation of CF (Questions 7, 16, 17, 20, 21, 22, 23, 25, 26, and 32) and with recasts as the technique of choice (Questions 6, 11, 12, 14, 18, and 40), this factor was labeled as "Expectation of CF and Recasts as CF Method." Among the six items that loaded on Factor 2, five items (Questions 3, 15, 33, 34, and 39) represented the belief that the best way to provide CF is through prompts; one item (Question 36), with the lowest loading score, attributed the importance to recasts. Because the majority of the items with high loadings spoke of prompts as the corrective technique of choice, this factor was named "Prompts as CF Method." Finally, because the two items (Questions 2 and 35) that loaded on Factor 3 pertained to the negative consequences that CF may yield, this factor was tagged as "Negative Consequences of CF." Table 4.1 shows the resulting factor loadings for the 26-item analysis. It is important to note that two items (Question 8 and Question 19) did not load onto any of the three factors.

Calculation of average scores per factor for each learner proved difficult because both Factor 1 and Factor 2 were composed of diverging items. Factor 1 contained items that spoke to the importance/expectation of CF and to recasts as the method of treating errors. Similarly, while the majority of the items in Factor 2 centered on prompts as the desired CF technique, one item spoke of recasts. It was decided to separate the loaded items according to the concept they represented. Factor 1 was split into two sets of beliefs: (1) importance and expectation of CF (Questions 7, 16, 17, 20, 21, 22, 23, 25, 26, and 32) and (2) recasts as a CF technique (Questions 6, 11, 12, 14, 18, and 40). Factor 2 spoke to prompts as a CF technique (Questions 3, 15, 33, 34, and 39). The internal consistency of the

Table 4.1. Rotated Factor Loadings for Learner Beliefs about CF (26 Items, *n* = 197)

Item	Factor 1	Factor 2	Factor 3
I. Expectation of CF and Recasts as CF method (26.72% of variance)			
6. Provision of the correct form is helpful for the beginner students. *(Fournir la forme correcte est bénéfique pour les étudiants de niveau débutant.)*	.512		
7. The correction of speaking errors is necessary in an English class. *(La correction des erreurs orales est indispensable en classe d'anglais.)*	.528		
11. Provision of the correct form is the best technique to correct vocabulary errors in English. *(Fournir la forme correcte est la meilleure technique pour corriger les erreurs de vocabulaire en anglais.)*	.575		.402
12. Provision of the correct form is the best technique to correct grammatical errors in English. *(Fournir la forme correcte est la meilleure technique pour corriger les erreurs grammaticales en anglais.)*	.567		
14. In light of my oral errors in English, I prefer that my teacher explicitly lets me know that my utterance is incorrect and that he/she supplies the correct form. *(Face à mes erreurs orales en anglais, je préfère que mon professeur m'indique de façon explicite que mon énoncé n'est pas acceptable et qu'il me fournisse la forme correcte.)*	.536		
16. If my English teacher does not correct my speaking errors, my determination to learn English will diminish. *(Si le professeur d'anglais ne corrige pas mes erreurs orales, ma détermination d'apprendre l'anglais diminuera.)*	.636		
17. The English teacher must inform the student of the aspects that he must improve so that the student acquires them. *(Le professeur d'anglais doit informer l'étudiant des aspects qu'il doit améliorer pour que ce dernier arrive à les maîtriser.)*	.654		
18. Provision of the correct form is the best technique to correct pronunciation errors in English. *Fournir la forme correcte est la meilleure technique pour corriger les erreurs de prononciation en anglais.*	.683		
20. I expect my teacher to correct my vocabulary errors in English. *(Je m'attends à ce que mon professeur corrige mes erreurs de vocabulaire en anglais.)*	.710		

Item	Factor 1	Factor 2	Factor 3
21. If the teacher lets students make errors from the start, it will be difficult to remedy them later on. *(Si le professeur laisse les étudiants faire des erreurs au départ, il sera difficile de les en débarrasser plus tard.)*	.521		
22. I like it when the teacher corrects me in an English class. *(J'aime que le professeur me corrige en classe d'anglais.)*	.577		−.454
23. I expect my teacher to correct my grammatical errors in English. *(Je m'attends à ce que mon professeur corrige mes erreurs de grammaire en anglais.)*	.734		
25. I expect my teacher to correct my pronunciation errors in English. *(Je m'attends à ce que mon professeur corrige mes erreurs de prononciation en anglais.)*	.723		
26. Correction of speaking errors in English reinforces the student's oral production. *(La correction des erreurs orales en anglais est un moyen privilégié pour renforcer la production des étudiants.)*	.546		
32. Correction of oral errors in English attracts my attention to the correct form given by my teacher. *(La correction des erreurs orales en anglais attire mon attention sur la forme correcte donnée par mon enseignant.)*	.402		
40. Provision of the correct form is the best technique to correct speaking errors in English. *(Fournir la forme correcte est la meilleure technique de correction des erreurs à l'oral en anglais.)*	.484		
II. Prompts as CF method (9.13% of variance)			
3. Encouraging learners to self-correct is helpful for students at the beginner level. *(Inciter les élèves à se corriger par eux-mêmes est bénéfique pour les étudiants de niveau débutant.)*		.690	
15. Pushing learners to correct their own errors helps them to acquire English. *(Pousser les étudiants à corriger leurs propres erreurs les aide à acquérir l'anglais.)*		.699	
33. Encouraging learners to self-correct is helpful for students at the advanced level. *(Inciter les élèves à se corriger par eux-mêmes est bénéfique pour les étudiants de niveau avancé.)*		.640	

(continued)

Table 4.1. *(Continued)*

34. I prefer it when my English teacher encourages me to correct myself on my own. *(Je préfère que mon professeur d'anglais m'incite à me corriger moi-même.)*	.800
36. Provision of the correct form is helpful for advanced students. *(Fournir la forme correcte est bénéfique pour les étudiants de niveau avancé.)*	.446
39. My teacher always provides a comment or linguistic information to help me correct myself on my own. *(Mon professeur fournit toujours un commentaire ou un renseignement linguistique pour m'aider à me corriger moi-même.)*	.485
III. Negative Consequences of CF (7.15% of variance)	
2. The correction of speaking errors in English makes me anxious. *(La correction des erreurs orales en anglais me rend anxieux.)*	.682
35. The correction of speaking errors in an English class leads to a negative attitude towards the study of English. *(La pratique de la correction des erreurs orales en classe d'anglais mène à une attitude négative envers l'apprentissage d'anglais.)*	.539

new beliefs was assured with a Cronbach alpha coefficient, which is considered acceptable above .7 (DeVellis, 2003), though the preferred value is above .8 (Pallant, 2007). The Cronbach alpha for Belief 1 was .83 and .79 for Belief 2, suggesting very good internal consistency and reliability for the scale with this sample. The reliability coefficient for Belief 3 was deemed satisfactory at .73. In light of this, each learner's average score for each belief item was calculated and compiled in terms of group means, which are presented in Table 4.2.

Table 4.2. Group Mean Belief Scores (Maximum Score: 5.0)

Group	Importance of CF (Belief 1)		Recasts (Belief 2)		Prompts (Belief 3)		Affective Consequences (Belief 4)	
	M	SD	M	SD	M	SD	M	SD
Recast	3.90	.46	4.05	.56	3.50	.63	4.25	1.36
Prompt	3.83	.77	4.06	.83	3.47	.92	3.70	1.37
Mixed	4.04	.84	4.13	.84	3.43	.96	3.88	1.51
Control	3.99	.53	4.23	.49	3.62	.74	4.05	1.35
Total	3.93	.65	4.11	.68	3.50	.79	4.00	1.40

4.2.2.2 Learner Beliefs and Noticing

Correlation analyses were performed to determine (1) whether there is a relationship between the learners' beliefs about Belief 1 (Importance of CF), Belief 2 (Recasts), Belief 3 (Prompts) and Belief 4 (Negative consequences of CF) and their overall noticing scores, and (2) whether such a relationship exists across the two grammatical targets.

Table 4.3. Pearson Correlations Between Noticing and Beliefs ($n = 79$)

Beliefs	1	2	3	4
Noticing	.221*	.255*	.063	−.157

* $p < .05$ (2-tailed)

The relationship between the overall noticing scores and the four beliefs was investigated using the Pearson correlation coefficient (Table 4.3). Preliminary analyses ensured no violation of the assumptions of normality, linearity, and homoscedasticity (Pallant, 2007). There was a weak, positive correlation between overall noticing and Belief 1 (Importance of CF), $r = .221$, $n = 79$, $p < .05$. Belief 1 helps to explain nearly 5% of the variance in the respondents' noticing scores, suggesting that the more students believe in the importance of CF, the more likely they are to notice its corrective intent. There was a weak, positive relationship between the overall noticing scores and Belief 2 (Recasts as CF), $r = .255$, $n = 79$, $p < .05$. Belief 2 helps to explain 6.5% of the variance in the respondents' noticing scores, suggesting that the more students believe in the effectiveness of recasts as a feedback technique, the more likely they are to notice the corrective intent of feedback. No significant correlation was found for Belief 3 (Prompts as CF), $r = .063$, or Belief 4 (Negative consequences of CF), $r = −.157$, suggesting that noticing appears to be independent from beliefs about prompts and negative consequences of feedback.

No significant correlations between group beliefs and noticing across the two target types were found (Table 4.4), implying that, for these learners, noticeability of feedback delivered in response to errors in questions and/or the past tense does not seem to be informed by beliefs about CF.

Table 4.4. Pearson Correlations Between Group Beliefs and Noticing Across the Two Targets ($n = 79$)

Group	Past Tense				Questions			
	Belief 1	2	3	4	Belief 1	2	3	4
Recast	.197	.268	−.201	−.134	−.047	.080	−.022	−.150
Prompt	.087	.080	.149	−.330	.185	.157	.029	−.161
Mixed	−.051	−.053	−.064	.100	.111	.203	.199	.056

4.2.2.3 Learner Beliefs and Learning

Correlation analyses were performed to determine (1) whether there is an overall relationship between the learners' beliefs about Belief 1 (Importance of CF), Belief 2 (Recasts), Belief 3 (Prompts), and Belief 4 (Negative consequences of CF) and their post-test scores; and (2) whether such a relationship exists on a group level.

The relationship between the four beliefs and the test scores was investigated using the Pearson correlation coefficient, the results of which are presented in Table 4.5. No significant correlations were found, suggesting that improvement from pre-test to post-test for these learners was independent from the four beliefs investigated. Similarly, no significant correlations were found between the beliefs and the test outcomes across the groups (Table 4.6), implying that, for this sample, improvement on the two morphosyntactic features appears to be independent from beliefs.

To summarize, learner beliefs were composed of several underlying factors: (1) the importance of CF and recasts as the CF technique, (2) prompts as a CF technique, and (3) negative consequences of CF. Specifically, the participants believed in the importance of oral CF overall and expected the teacher to use recasts in response to errors. They also saw a positive role for self-correction (facilitated by prompts) and were aware of the negative effects that CF can invoke. The correlation analyses between the learners' reports of noticing and their beliefs about CF revealed a positive relationship between overall noticing and the belief in the importance of CF as well as noticing and the belief in recasts as an effective feedback technique. There were, however,

Table 4.5. Pearson Correlations Between Test Scores and Beliefs ($n = 99$)

Beliefs	1	2	3	4
Simple Past	.060	.052	.083	−.135
Questions	−.003	.002	−.083	−.080

Table 4.6. Pearson Correlations Between Group Beliefs and Test Scores Across the Two Targets ($n = 79$)

	Past Tense				Questions			
Group	Belief 1	2	3	4	Belief 1	2	3	4
Recast	.041	.249	−.127	−.014	−.271	.233	−.143	−.034
Prompt	.087	.080	.149	−.330	.185	.157	.029	−.161
Mixed	−.051	−.053	−.064	.100	.111	.203	.199	.056

no significant correlations between beliefs and the noticing of either grammatical target across the three groups. Finally, no significant relationship was found between beliefs and the test scores across the groups.

4.2.3 Discussion

The goal of this study was to determine whether learner beliefs about CF mediate the noticeability and effectiveness of feedback delivered in the classroom. Beliefs appear to have an association with the noticeability of feedback in general and recasts in particular, but did not mediate the relationship between beliefs and learning. The beliefs-noticing relationship found here echoes the general agreement among SLA researchers that learner beliefs may affect how learners view and perform language tasks (Horwitz, 1988; Kern, 1995) and that learners generally favor feedback on errors in the classroom (Cathcart & Olsen, 1976; Chenoweth et al., 1983; Jean & Simard, 2011; Mohamed, 2011; Schulz, 1996, 2001). The learners' beliefs about the importance and effectiveness of feedback in this study seemed to have positively affected their ability to notice the supplied corrections, paving the way for a more productive learner experience and longer-lasting learning (Mantle-Brompley, 1995).

However, the lack of a statistically significant relationship between beliefs and noticing across the two grammatical targets may be seen as contrary to previous research (Kern, 1995; Peacock, 1999; Schulz, 1996, 2001) that associated higher concerns for grammatical accuracy and CF with learners rather than teachers. In those studies, the learners enjoyed grammar instruction and CF more than their teachers (Peacock, 1999), who appeared less concerned about the value of grammar teaching than did their students (Schulz, 1996). In Kern's (1995) study, the learners, more than their teachers, were concerned about the effect of fossilization in the case of no CF and agreed with the need for grammar rules. So, if grammar is important and feedback is a gateway to accuracy, then why was there no association between beliefs about CF and the noticing scores for either grammatical feature? One of the reasons may be that there were no direct questions regarding the role of grammar instruction in the beliefs' questionnaire, thus preventing an evaluation of learner preference in this regard. Another reason may be that "students may not be universally motivated to be accurate, generally, or grammatically accurate, specifically" (Chavez, 2007, p. 555). Chavez's study revealed that first, second, and third year learners of German, as well as their teachers, perceived grammatical accuracy as having a stronger emphasis than they felt it needed to have. That is, although they recognized its importance, the learners appeared to show a strong concern for accuracy only because they wanted to receive a good grade or because they felt that this concern would be in line with their teacher's expectations. The teachers, in turn, might have overestimated the course requirements and the role of grammatical practice. In the current study, because the participants were surveyed during the first class of the term, it may be argued that they were not concerned with or did not have the time necessary to form opinions about the course requirements, the teacher's expectations for accuracy, or the evaluation criteria.

The lack of a relationship between beliefs and L2 development is in line with previous research (Ellis, 2008b; Mori, 1999; Tanaka, 2004) in that the amount of learning the students engage in depends, for the most part, on the actions they take to improve their language knowledge, not on their perceptions of what constitutes language learning. This speaks to the limitation of the instrument used to measure beliefs in this study. Specifically, the fact that the topic and phrasing of the Likert-style questionnaire items were identified by the researcher, and the participants were simply asked to respond to these "ready-made" constructs, raises questions about the extent to which "a construct as intellectually and affectively complex and rich as is one's personal belief system . . . [can] be fully captured by people's responses to a set of normative statements" (Bernat & Gvozdenko, 2005, p. 7). The use of such a questionnaire, however, allowed for a large number of respondents and ensured a statistically reliable instrument that helped to uncover an emergent picture of learner beliefs regarding feedback.

Another reason there was no association between beliefs and test scores might have to do with the length of the intervention and the fact that no delayed post-test was used. Because the process of language learning takes time and effort on the part of the student, it is unlikely that the learning measured after a four-hour intervention would show a relationship with beliefs; more time may be necessary for beliefs to affect learning outcomes (Ammar & Spada, 2006; Mackey & Goo, 2007). The comparison of the results on a delayed post-test with belief scores might have yielded a connection between beliefs and the test scores. More research is needed in this area to determine to what extent beliefs can influence learning.

Finally, this result may be rooted in the participants' dependence on their teachers, a finding corroborated in Kartchava (2016). Having been exposed for much of their academic life to the traditional model of teaching, where the instructor is in charge of the classroom, the learners may rely on the teacher not only for CF in response to their errors, but also for information on their learning progress. The activities used in this study gave the learners opportunities to create and express content, ask questions, and to interact with peers. This new instructional context, though brief, may have given the participants a reason to start seeing the teacher more as a facilitator than as an authority figure in the classroom (Cotterall, 1995)—an idea that could, in the long run, prompt them to view learning "as a learner-centered and self-regulated process in which proactive participation and initiatives are important" (Amuzie & Winke, 2009, p. 376). This, of course, remains a speculation until empirically observed.

4.3 CONCLUSION

This study suggests that learners' positive attitudes towards CF can positively affect the noticing of CF in the classroom. Specifically, the more learners believe in the importance of feedback, the more likely they are to notice its corrective intent, especially if the CF is in the form of a recast. A major concern with this finding, however, is that while it represents the opinions of all the participants in the study, it is not clear what the results would have been had the learners assigned to the Control group been given a chance to receive CF. Discussing findings of the research on the effects of beliefs about CF on learning outcomes (where Study 3 and the work of Sheen [2008, 2011] were assessed), Li (2017), in his recent synthesis of CF research, characterized this finding in the following way (p. 155):

> It would seem that learners that were enthusiastic about feedback did benefit more from feedback when the corrective intention was salient, and that these learners were also more sensitive to the corrective force of the feedback.

On the other hand, no relationship was found between beliefs and test scores, suggesting that the test results were not mediated by the learners' beliefs about CF. It can also be argued that beliefs "correlate with learning outcomes when feedback [is] effective" and do not correlate with them when "feedback [has] no effect" (Li, 2017, p. 155). Conversely, the lack of such a connection may be due to the absence of delayed post-tests for it may be that more than four hours of instruction is necessary for beliefs to affect outcomes. Still, these findings point to the influential role that beliefs about CF play in the learning of an L2. Study 4, described in the next chapter, echoes the importance of helping learners to identify the corrective intent of CF by delving into the role of non-verbal behavior in the provision of oral CF.

Chapter Five

Nonverbal Behavior and Corrective Feedback

This chapter examines the role of nonverbal behavior in the provision of CF. This focus is prompted by the limited body of research that, to date, has examined this very common, yet often overlooked, component of feedback. Because nonverbal behavior and speech tend to co-occur to express meaning (McNeill & Duncan, 2000), ignoring the former may be imprudent, especially in the language classroom. Furthermore, since nonverbal behavior has been shown to be an integral part of human communication (Bancroft, 1997; Pennycook, 1985), engaging only one modality of meaning-making may be limiting, unwise, and even, detrimental to the study of language. This is because asking language learners to rely primarily on the auditory channel to process instruction can not only "cause a huge part of the communication process to go unnoticed" (Gregersen & MacIntyre, 2017, p. 4), but may also yield negative learner-internal emotions about the adequacy of their L2 knowledge; these, in turn, may lead to a pause in or cessation to their L2 development.

As CF research has shown, learners often struggle to recognize and take advantage of the corrective intent behind teacher's feedback, especially if that feedback is in the form of recasts. The noticeability and effectiveness of CF in general has been shown to depend on a number of variables, including classroom context, learner cognitive and affective differences, error type, grammatical feature, and saliency of a particular CF technique. Consequently, it may be that the use of nonverbal cues, a primary and universal feature of human interaction, alongside oral CF may positively impact learner awareness of the feedback and its utility in the classroom. Study 4, reported here, considers this point and investigates the extent to which a teacher's use of nonverbal cues during in-class CF episodes can enhance the noticeability of CF. The chapter begins with a review of the literature on nonverbal behavior in general and in language learning in particular. Then, studies that have specifically considered nonverbal behavior in the provision of corrective feedback are detailed. Following this, the design and findings of Study 4 are presented and examined in light of the possible implications they may generate for the language classroom.

5.1 BACKGROUND

5.1.1 Nonverbal Behavior

In their recent publication on nonverbal behaviors in interpersonal relations, Richmond, McCroskey, and Hickson (2012) define nonverbal behavior as "any of a wide variety of human behaviors that also have the potential for forming communicative messages. Such nonverbal behavior becomes communication if another person interprets it as a message and attributes meaning" (p. 6). In this view, nonverbal behavior is limited to exchanges between people. Extending this notion to the context of language education, Gregersen and MacIntyre (2017) argue that nonverbal communication should also include the "intrapersonal function." which involves an individual's self-talk (p. 7). They claim that widening the definitional aspects of nonverbal behavior in such a way allows for a far-reaching examination of "the full array of communicative, affective, and cognitive functions of nonlinguistic and paralinguistic codes [. . .] that language teachers and learners can capitalize on to increase communicative, affective and cognitive competence" (p. 8).

Because nonverbal behavior and speech constantly co-exist, separating the two is impossible, and even unnecessary (Arndt & Janney, 1987), since each contributes a different, yet vital, piece of meaning to an interaction (McNeill, 1992). In fact, when the verbal and nonverbal channels are at odds with the information they transmit, the resulting message may come across as not only confusing, but also as something to distrust. This is because nonverbal information is trusted more than the verbal in that the former is seen as more spontaneous, genuine, and, unlike speech, less prone to intentional manipulation. Letting learners know that these two channels are interdependent and are in constant interaction to create meaning is essential, argue Gregersen and MacIntyre, for the development of learners' communicative and affective competences. From the cognitive standpoint, because nonverbal behavior can enhance learning by reducing the cognitive load, improving information comprehension, recall, and retention, can aid thinking for speaking, enact the abstract, and help achieve self-regulation, Gregersen and MacIntyre call on educators to train learners to recognize the power of nonverbal behavior and capitalize on it both in their interactions with others and the self.

While Gregersen and MacIntyre (2017) see gesture, posture, facial expression, and eye behavior as all being components of the overarching concept of nonverbal behavior, some researchers have used the term "gesture" to encompass nonverbal behaviour.[35] Gestures can occur by themselves or accompany speech. They can control the flow of interaction, regulate turn-taking, emphasize or clarify intended meanings, capture and maintain attention, facilitate comprehension (especially in noisy or ambiguous L1 contexts, Kelly, Barr, Breckinridge Church, & Lynch, 1999), and display emotions (Knapp & Hall, 2010; Richmond et al., 2012). Gestures have been classified into various frameworks, one of the more popular of which is that by McNeill (1992). This classification entails five gestural types: emblems, iconic, metaphoric, deictic, and beats (see Chapter 1 for definitions and examples). McNeill's framework is said to be based on a portion of the four-type gestural classification—illustrators, regulators, emblems, and affect displays—proposed by Ekman and Freisen (1969). McNeill further divided the "illustrators" classification into the five types mentioned earlier. Illustrators generally occur with speech for the purpose of complementing or accentuating verbal input. Regulators, in turn, monitor turn-taking in conversations. Finally, emblems are culturally-specified gestures whereas affect displays are generally universal, emotional nonverbal reactions to speech. Study 4 detailed in this chapter has operationalized nonverbal behavior in terms of a teacher's body movements and gestures.

5.1.2 Nonverbal Behavior and Language Learning

In general education, research on nonverbal behavior, and gesture in particular, has shown that gestures frequently occur in the classroom (e.g., Goldin-Meadow & Sandhofer, 1999), are used to capture learner attention (e.g., Flevares & Perry, 2001), and are effective in moving the learning forward when combined with verbal explanations (e.g., Goldin-Meadow, Cook, & Mitchell, 2009; O'Neill, Topolovec, Stern-Cavalcante, 2002). In SLA, however, few studies have investigated the distribution of nonverbal behaviors in L2 classrooms as well as considered the link between nonverbal cues in the L2 input and language learning.

Observational studies have described various nonverbal behaviors language teachers use for pedagogical purposes (e.g., Allen, 2000; Lazarton, 2004; Smotrova, 2017). Working with a high school teacher of Spanish, Allen (2000), for example, observed several types of nonverbal behavior present in the teacher's classroom practice. Specifically, using the Ekman and Freisen's (1969) classification, she found instances of illustrators, regulators, emblems, and affect displays. Similary, in the L2 context, Lazarton (2004) investigated the use of gestures in the teaching of vocabulary. One female Japanese L1 graduate student taught an intensive ESL university-level course, three 50-minute sessions of which were video-recorded and analyzed. The examination focused on the teacher's speech and gestures used in the explanations of unplanned vocabulary items. The analysis revealed that the teacher was an active user of a variety of nonverbal cues, including hand gestures, nodding, and acting out problem words. This finding, argued Lazarton, was a clear indication that nonverbal behavior was part of L2 input and "mattered" (p. 107). As such, SLA research needed to consider and investigate nonverbal input that language learners may encounter as part of the L2 classroom discourse.

Most recently, Smotrova (2017) investigated the use of gesture in the teaching and learning of L2 pronunciation. Having analyzed two 50-minute beginner-level ESL reading lessons, the researcher found the teacher used different kinds of gestures, some of which were employed spontaneously, whereas others were planned. While the teacher used unplanned gestures when explaining grammar and vocabulary, her gestural practice in the teaching of pronunciation was often pre-planned. This was because the teacher wanted the learners to use these gestures as they worked on pronunciation. Although she did not explicitly train the learners in these gestures, they would imitate her body movements that accompanied explanations of syllabification (i.e., identification production of syllables), word stress, and rhythm, appropriating them in their subsequent study of the English suprasegmentals. These results, argues Smotrova, suggest that teachers need to understand the gestures they themselves use and should, in turn, encourage learners to incorporate these pedagogical behaviors (i.e., "intentional instructional gestures") in their language learning.

To determine whether or not the presence of nonverbal behavior and/or their production results in L2 learning, several experimental studies have been undertaken. Working with young (mean age 5:5) French L1 learners of English (n = 20), Tellier (2008), for example, investigated the effect of gesture on the learning of L2 vocabulary. The learners were divided into two groups, one of which was taught eight English (animal-related) words with pictures, and the other group was taught the same words but was also shown accompanying gestures; this group was asked to imitate the gestures as they engaged in word repetition practice. The findings showed that the group that was shown gestures and was asked to reproduce them was more successful at memorizing and retaining the words than the group that was only shown pictures. Similarly, working with adults, Macedonia and Klimesch (2014) investigated the effect of gestures on the learning of 36 artificial vocabulary items (in Tessetisch, the artificial language). Twenty-nine German-speaking college students were divided into two groups. One of the groups saw the words written in Tessetisch along with their German translation. In addition, one of the researchers pronounced the words aloud, and the students were asked to repeat them. The second group was presented with the same words, but in addition to hearing their pronunciation, the researcher also used gestures to demonstrate the word meanings (e.g., a gesture to illustrate the meaning of "large"—/takra/); the students were also asked to repeat the pronunciation of the words and to imitate the accompanying gestures. The results showed superior retention for the "gesture" group.

Nakatsukasa and Loewen (2017) discuss other research that has attempted to determine the impact of gesture on the learning of L2 pronunciation and grammar. While they found no conclusive evidence for the positive link between the use of gesture and pronunciation learning, the recent study by Smotrova (2017), described above, may potentially indicate the possibility of such a connection. As for the gestural studies that considered L2 grammar, there is only one—by Nakatsukasa (2016). The study investigated the learning of the English locative prepositions as a function of gesture and CF, and it is described in the section that follows.

5.1.3 Nonverbal Behavior and Corrective Feedback

There is a limited body of studies that have examined the use of nonverbal cues during CF episodes (Davies, 2006; Schachter, 1981) and the impact of these cues on the L2 learning (Davies, 2006; Nakatsukasa, 2016; Wang, 2009; Wang & Loewen, 2016). Arguably, the first call for teachers to use nonverbal cues in their provision of CF came from Schachter (1981), who having devised a "hand signal system," proposed that teachers abandon oral feedback and, instead, use "nonverbal visual devices" to attend to the issues of form. She argued that oral feedback was ineffective because teachers used it to interchangeably address issues of form and to confirm the intended meaning, making the practice more confusing than helpful. To reduce "the student's analytical burden while at the same time enhancing the possibility that the student will be able to self-correct appropriately" (p. 128), Schachter advocated for a use of gestures that would indicate the type of error a learner was making, suggesting that this would be more effective in terms of communicating the intended input and obtaining a desired outcome. Her hand system contained six gestures, with each corresponding to a particular error type that included errors of tense, agreement, pluralization, prepositions, word order, and articles. Schachter argued that a limited number of gestures was sufficient to make the corrective intention clear to the learner and that using more hand signals than the suggested six "would put a great learning burden on the student" (p. 129). Training in the use of the hand signals was deemed essential, and, as such, Schachter saw it as an effective use of class time. Specifically, she identified five benefits for the practice: (1) a clear unambiguous indication to the learner that an error of form had occurred and (2) the source of the error, (3) opportunity for self-correction, (4) a chance at several attempts of correction, and (5) "the impetus to bridge the gap between [learners'] current production and their goal" (p. 135). Furthermore, to her, the use of gestures was natural in that the teachers "constantly communicate nonverbally anyway" (p. 135) and incorporating hand signals into one's practice was not only easy but also meaningful. As such, Schachter called for research that would examine the effectiveness of teacher gestures on language development.

One of the first to respond to the call was Davies (2006), who examined the distribution of "purely paralinguistic" features (i.e., feedback instances devoid of "any verbal feedback at all," p. 845) in four Japanese EFL classrooms (n = 12) and their impact on the number of uptake instances that occurred as a result. Using 24 hours of classroom data, Davies found that when purely paralinguistic feedback was used, it resulted in 100% uptake. Similarly, when implicit types of feedback (i.e., recasts and clarification requests) were combined with paralinguistic features, the feedback was more effective in producing uptake compared to when it was used alone. Stimulated recall interviews conducted with two of the four teachers showed that in order to highlight the corrective focus of an implicit CF strategy, the teachers chose to incorporate paralinguistic features; conversely, whenever their intention was to focus on meaning, the teachers would use implicit CF without paralinguistic support. Davies (2006) argued that implicit CF techniques should not be seen as unsuccessful in yielding uptake; rather, "they are very successful at resulting in exactly what teachers intend them to" (p. 854). Yet, while teacher intention appears to drive the choice of CF technique, it is unclear whether this conclusion is generalizable beyond the sampled context and the limited number of paralinguistic episodes identified. Furthermore, because the term "paralinguistic" was not explicitly identified, the specific nonverbal cues used and their impact on the reported uptake results are difficult to reproduce.

Heeding these limitations, Wang and Loewen (2016) observed nine ESL university-level classes in the United States to determine ways in which the teachers used nonverbal cues during the provision of CF. The analysis of 65 hours of classroom observations revealed that nonverbal behavior (i.e., "a variety of bodily movements [. . .] not restricted to a particular body part," p. 461) accompanied CF episodes 60.2% of the time. Unlike Davies (2006), the observed teachers used nonverbal cues with both implicit and explicit (prompts or metalinguistic explanations) CF types. Using the McNeill's (1992) gestural framework (described in Chapter 1), the researchers identified various gestures (e.g., deictics, iconics, and beats) and nonverbal cues (e.g., head shaking, nodding) used to accompany CF in these classrooms. Of these, nodding and shaking of the head (32%) as well as pointing to an object or person (27%) were the most frequent types. To compare the effects of verbal versus nonverbal CF on L2 learning, Wang (2009, cited in Nakatsukasa & Loewen, 2017) designed and administered tailor-made tests to those learners from the nine classes who had received CF. The results showed that the inclusion of nonverbal cues in verbal feedback episodes improved learners' accuracy on the immediate (73%) and delayed (61%) post-tests; conversely, the use of verbal feedback alone resulted in lower totals (56% post-test, 47% delayed post-test). What's more, because the overall accuracy rate was 59% on the post-test and 47% on the delayed post-test, oral CF alone (i.e., without accompanying nonverbal cues) did not seem to make a difference.

Similarly, Nakatsukasa (2016) investigated the impact of nonverbal feedback used alongside oral CF (i.e., recasts) on the acquisition of the English locative prepositions among 48 low-intermediate ESL learners. Three groups were created to participate in 30 minutes of information-gap tasks, during which two of the groups received feedback and one did not (control group). While verbal recasts were provided to one of the treatment groups, the other group received both recasts and gestures. To assess the learning of prepositions, all groups completed a pre-test, post-test, and a delayed post-test, which consisted of an oral production test and a grammar test. The results showed that recasts were effective in leading to higher post-test values for both treatment groups whereas the control group's scores did not improve. Yet, on the delayed post-test, the group that received both verbal recasts and accompanying nonverbal cues (i.e., gestures illustrating the locations of *under*, *above*, *on*, and *next to*) not only maintained its post-test gains, but also outperformed the recasts-only and control groups. Hence, it appears that nonverbal cues used alongside recasts helped learners to understand the linguistic target of the feedback, which, in turn, helped them to retain the corrective information contained in the CF episodes, leading to long-term improvements. While encouraging, these results cannot be generalized and need to be investigated with other student populations, instructional contexts, linguistic targets, developmental measures, and nonverbal cues. The need for such research is further precipitated by the very limited body of investigations that have considered the link between nonverbal behavior, CF, and L2 learning. This is precisely why Nakatsukasa and Loewen (2017) have called for continued research in the area "to understand what kind of linguistic structures or what types of non-verbal behavior benefit L2 development" (p. 167).

5.2 EVIDENCE: KARTCHAVA'S EXPERIMENTAL STUDY 4

The study reported here aimed to contribute to the existing research on nonverbal behavior in the provision of oral CF. To this end, it examined one ESL teacher's spontaneous use of body movements and gestures during the act of verbal feedback provision. To understand the impact of this practice on noticing, learner reactions to such feedback were also studied. The following research questions guided this study: (1) What nonverbal behavior accompanies the teacher's verbal CF episodes? and (2) Do learners notice the verbal CF that involves nonverbal cues?

5.2.1 Method

5.2.1.1 Setting

The study was carried out in an intensive English program at a university in Eastern Canada. The non-credit program is offered throughout the year and is attended by more than 1,000 students from various countries around the globe. It aims to help learners develop their listening, reading, speaking and writing skills while immersing them in regular socio-cultural activities that promote Canadian culture and enhance their language learning experience. Course levels range from beginner to advanced, and learners receive a certificate of completion upon graduation. For placement purposes, at the beginning of their studies, learners are required to take an in-house test to determine their proficiency level. Once placed, learners spend 15 weeks in a course that meets 25 hours a week. Although each level is guided by a set curriculum, instructors are free to decide how to achieve them. Two instructors are assigned per course, with each teaching 2.5 days a week. A teaching assistant responsible for designing and carrying out laboratory work is also allocated to each course. Upon completion of a course, the students are required to pass an exit test to advance to the next level or to graduate. Unlike the government-regulated program of Quebec (described in Studies 1 through 3), the students here are free to enter and leave the program at any point. Many, however, choose to complete all the courses and enter various degree programs offered at the University. This is why all but the beginner level courses also offer a focus on academic language.

5.2.1.2 Participants

One teacher and her intact class participated in the study. The teacher was a female native speaker of English, with over 20 years of teaching experience in Canada and other countries. At the time of the study, she held a Ph.D. in Education and a certificate in Teaching English as a Second Language. The teacher described herself as someone who ensures that both authentic interaction and a focus on form are consistently present in her classroom. While she sees herself primarily as a facilitator of the learning process, she is also aware of the learners' needs, which she attempts to identify early in the term and meet by adapting her materials and approaches as needed. Her students appreciate her efforts as is evidenced by the consistently high scores she receives on end-of-term teaching evaluations.

A total of twelve students of 18–25 years of age participated in the study. Ten of the learners came from mainland China (Chinese L1), with the remaining two being from Morocco (Arabic L1). For many this was their first course in the program, and the amount of time they had spent in Canada ranged between one and five months. They all had extensive exposure to English instruction in their countries of origin but little practice with non-scripted L2 use. They were attending a low-intermediate course that aimed to help them develop a variety of language-related skills that would be equally effective in formal and informal L2 contexts. In terms of the academic skills, learners were instructed in the use of such strategies as note-taking, skimming, and scanning as well as employing contextual clues to comprehend academic texts, presentations, lectures, and media podcasts.

5.2.1.3 Teacher's Verbal Feedback Preferences

Whenever providing feedback, the teacher used both recasts and prompts. Based on a previous observation, mixing feedback types is the teacher's regular practice. The teacher was not asked to change anything in her CF provision prior to the investigation. Recasts were operationalized as the teacher's reformulation of the learner's incorrect utterance. Whenever using recasts, the teacher did not comment on the grammaticality of the students' incorrect utterances nor did she push learners to correct their ungrammatical utterances. Instead, the teacher reacted with a full, partial, interrogative, or integrated reformulation. She used prompts whenever the target was to elicit self-correction from the learner. She could either repeat the student's incorrect utterance either as a whole with rising intonation or partly by zooming in on the error while withholding the correct form (repetition), repeat part of the learner's utterance and pause at the error to provide a clue as to the problem, as well as to invite the student to self-repair (elicitation), or provide metalinguistic clues without supplying the correct form, pushing the learner to self-correct (metalinguistic feedback). To her, recasting felt "more like correction" whereas prompting was "a bit more organic—it is like almost I

150   Chapter Five

did not understand you." Furthermore, the teacher characterized her feedback provision as naturally involving body movements. This, to her, was especially apparent when she used prompts, "For me, part of the prompting is my body moves. Like I lean forward, spread my arms in a gesturing format, I pause with my hand."

5.2.1.4 Linguistic Targets

The past tense and questions in the past were again the linguistic targets of choice. As mentioned previously, they: (1) are problematic for ESL learners, regardless of L1; (2) represent different levels of complexity (DeKeyser, 1998, 2005); (3) are subject to L1 interference (Ammar, Sato & Kartchava, 2010; Collins, 2002); (4) occur frequently in the input (Doughty & Varela, 1998), which facilitates their elicitation during communicative tasks (McDonough, 2007); and (5) have been shown to be good candidates for learner improvement when they are targeted with CF (Mackey & Philp, 1998; McDonough, 2005; McDonough & Mackey, 2006; Mackey, 2006 for questions; Doughty & Varela, 1998; Ellis et al., 2006; McDonough, 2007; Yang & Lyster, 2010 for past tense). Research has also shown that the noticing of CF leads to language development, though it largely depends on the technique employed and on the nature of the error (Mackey et al., 2000; Ammar, 2008; Ammar & Sato 2010a).

5.2.1.5 Communicative Task

As part of their class, in Week 3 of the course, the learners engaged in a communicative 60-minute task designed to promote the use of both past tense and questions in the past. The task was adapted from Gatbonton (1994) and was deemed appropriate by the teacher in terms of level and focus. The students worked in groups to create accounts of their whereabouts, which were then questioned by the whole class. CF was provided during the student-fronted portion of the activity, which lasted approximately 36 minutes. No instruction on the two targets was provided prior to the intervention.

5.2.1.6 Noticing Measure

As in Study 2, noticing was measured with uptake, operationalized as the learner's immediate *verbal* reaction[36] following feedback. While the use of uptake as a measure of noticing may be problematic (Leeman, 2007), it provides evidence that the CF has been perceived in one way or another (Ohta, 2000; Sheen, 2006). The 36-minute student-fronted portion of the activity carried out during the communicative task was analyzed for instances of uptake (see Chapter 1 for information about the uptake measure). Examples of uptake were then classified into "repair" and "needs repair" whereas instances of repair were further classified into the "repetition" and "incorporation" types. While the repetition type of repair entails a learner repeating the teacher's feedback, the incorporation type of repair has the learner repeat the correction, incorporating it into a longer utterance.

5.2.1.7 Nonverbal Measures

The same 36 minutes of the student-fronted portion that were analyzed for instances of uptake were also coded for any accompanying nonverbal cues. The teacher's nonverbal behavior was operationalized in terms of body movements and gestures. In line with previous research on nonverbal behavior and CF (Wang, 2009; Wang & Loewen, 2016), the gestures were classified using McNeill's (1992) gestural framework described in Chapter 1. Specifically, the gestures were classified in terms of type: emblems, iconic, metaphoric, deictic, and beats. Classification of the body movements, in turn, did not follow a specific framework or coding scheme, but was, instead, data-driven. It is important to note that only nonverbal behaviors that were particular to feedback episodes of the error-feedback-uptake sequence and that targeted the two linguistic features investigated (past tense and questions in the past) were considered; all other nonverbal episodes were ignored. The accuracy of the results for both the uptake and nonverbal instances was ascertained by an independent second rater, who assessed 100% of the data. The inter-rater reliability percentage was 90%, with any disagreements being settled through discussion.

5.2.2 Results

The data were analyzed in two phases. First, all CF episodes that targeted the use of the past tense statements and questions were identified. As Table 5.1 shows, a total of 35 episodes occurred during the student-fronted portion of the communicative task. This means that, on average, the teacher corrected learners every minute. Of the 35 episodes, 26 targeted the use of the past tense in statements (74%) and the remaining 9 focused on the errors with questions (26%). In terms of the CF techniques, 25/35 errors were corrected using recasts (71%) and 10/35 errors were addressed with prompts (29%). Of these, 17/26 statements (65%) and 8/9 questions (89%) were corrected with recasts whereas 9/26 statements (35%) and 1/9 question (11%) were addressed with prompts.

In terms of uptake, 17/26 statements (65%) and 7/9 questions (77%) were repaired, and 4/26 statements (15%) resulted in a needs-repair; feedback to 5/26 statements (19%) and 2/9 questions (22%) produced no uptake. Of the

Table 5.1. Uptake Following Teacher's CF

Error	Total	CF		Uptake					
				Recast			Prompt		
		Recast	Prompt	Repair	Needs-Repair	No Uptake	Repair	Needs-Repair	No Uptake
Statements	26	17	9	11	1	5	6	3	0
Questions	9	8	1	6	0	2	1	0	0
	35	25	10	17	1	7	7	3	0

repaired statements, 11/26 were corrected with recasts (42%) and 6/26 with prompts (23%); 1/26 statement was addressed with a recast (4%) and 3/26 were targeted with prompts (11.5%) needed further repair. Six of nine recasts (67%) and 1/9 prompt (11%) were used to facilitate learner repair of the nine questions; there was no uptake to the remaining 2/9 questions (22%) targeted with recasts.

To examine the teacher's nonverbal behavior (NB), in Phase 2, the identified CF episodes were examined to identify whether they were accompanied by nonverbal cues. As illustrated in Table 5.2, of the 35 episodes, 27 included a nonverbal cue (77%) and 8 did not (i.e., they were purely verbal). Of the 27 CF episodes accompanied by NB, 23 targeted statements (85%) and 4 question (15%) errors. In terms of the CF type, 17/27 recast (63%) and 10/27 prompt (37%) episodes included the use of a nonverbal cue. Of the 17 recast + NB episodes, 14 contained statement errors (82%) and 3—question errors (18%). Similarly, of the 10 prompt + NB episodes, 9 targeted errors in statements (90%) and 1—a question error (10%). Of the 14 statement errors addressed by a recast, 9 resulted in a repair (64%), 1 in a needs-repair (7%), and 4 produced no uptake (29%); all 3 recasted question errors were repaired (100%). Of the 9 statement errors targeted by a prompt, 6 resulted in a repair (67%) and 3 in a needs-repair (33%); the sole question error addressed with a prompt was repaired (100%). Hence, overall, 13/17 (76%) recasts accompanied by NB and 10/10 (100%) prompts supplemented with nonverbal cues resulted in noticing or CF. Of note, 63% of recasts without NB (2/3 statements and 3/5 questions) also showed repair.

As for the different types of nonverbal behavior, the teacher predominantly used her head, face (n = 14), and hands (n = 13) to accompany her verbal feedback.[37] She would, for example, raise her head and arch eyebrows to get the learner to self-correct (Example 1) or she would raise her head, speak slower, and enunciate the correct form, all the while maintaining her gaze on the learner (Example 2). Although the teacher chose to use recasts in Example 2, she appeared to prompt the learner to recognize the form-related issue. First, to alert the learner to the problem, she raised her head and slowed down her output. When this appeared insufficient, she then enunciated the correction and waited for the learner to react. The corrective information provided allowed the learner to not only understand the problem but to also self-correct. At times, the teacher would alert learners to an error by raising her head and once a successful repair was achieved, she would nod once as if to encourage the learner and to confirm the successful uptake (Example 3). The teacher would also nod while speaking to alert the learner to the target form (Example 4). Albeit this often did not generate uptake, the teacher maintained her gaze on the learner, nodded, and recasted the error.

Table 5.2. Uptake and Nonverbal Behavior (NB) Following Teacher's CF

| Error | Total | NB | CF | | | Uptake | | | | | |
| | | | | | | Recast | | | Prompt | | |
			Recast	Prompt	Repair	Needs-Repair	No Uptake	Repair	Needs-Repair	No Uptake
Statements	26	23	14	9	9	1	4	6	3	0
Questions	9	4	3	1	3	0	0	1	0	0
	35	27	17	10	12	1	4	7	3	0

Example 1 (@1:30)
Student: Eight thirty, eight thirty, so before eight thirty, uh anybody can anybody prove you are . . .
Teacher: You . . . [Prompt—elicitation]
[raises head and arches eyebrows, observing the student]
Student: You were sleeping [Repair—incorporation]

Example 2 (@5:18)
Student: Lunch, uh, we drunk some
Teacher: Drank. [Recast—partial]
[raises head while speaking slower]
Student: Drink.
Teacher: Drank.
[raises head and enunciates "drank"]
Student: Drank. Drank some coffee and ate some snacks in the cafeteria inside of the Center. [Repair—incorporation]

Example 3 (@18:08)
Student: Yeah, uh which shops do you . . .
Teacher: Did you go to. [Recast—partial]
[raises head, arches eyebrows, glancing at student asking question]
Student: Yeah, did you go. [Repair—repetition]
Teacher: [Nods once, turns attention to answering students]

Example 4 (@6:56)
Student 1: We make appointment at nine thirty.
Student 2: Nine thirty. Hmm.
Teacher: You made an appointment for nine thirty? [Recast—interrogative]
[nods while speaking, gaze on Student 1]
Student 1: Yeah. [no uptake]

The other type of nonverbal cue that dominated the teacher's feedback behavior was pointing, which she did primarily with her hand (Example 5), finger (Example 6), or entire body (Example 7). Because the communication activity required that the past tense be used, it is not surprising that deictic gestures were the ones used throughout the student-questioning portion of the task. Specifically, the teacher would point to an imaginary point in the past, which was located either behind her, to her (right/left) side, or away from the area where the conversation was taking place. In Example 7, the teacher signaled the problem with her body by leaning it away from the center and providing a verbal prompt. When this proved insufficient, she used a verbal recast to highlight the correct form; after another unsuccessful attempt to repair, the teacher repeated the correct form and coupled it with a nod to show appreciation of the learner's efforts and to confirm the correct form. The teacher would also use her outstretched index finger to point in a direction away from her body or her thumb pointing behind her (Example 8) as if to indicate the required temporal distance. This pointing (illustrated in Examples 5, 6, and 8) appeared particularly effective in that it resulted in almost immediate successful repair.

Example 5 (@16:37)
Student: So, I come to
Teacher: I came to [Recast—full]
  [full hand pointing palm down to side of body, away from center]
Student: I came to his house. [Repair—incorporation]

Example 6 (@22:10)
Student: Shayari found he at the mag, and then we go to the shopping centre.
Teacher: We . . . [Prompt—elicitation]
  [outstretched right index finger moving towards the left of body]
Student: Went to the shopping center. Uh, went shopping. [Repair-incorporation]

Example 7 (@8:19)
Student: I wake up at about five thirty.
Teacher: You . . . [Prompt—elicitation]
  [leans away from the center to an invisible point to indicate the need for the past tense]
Student: Wolk. [Uptake—Needs repair]
Teacher: Woke. [Recast—partial]
Student: Wawlk. [Uptake—Needs repair]
Teacher: Woke up. [Recast—partial]
  [nods in appreciation of learner's effort and to confirm the target form]

Example 8 (@13:19)
Student: Yeah, Matthew and I wake up at six a.m.
Teacher: You wake up? [Prompt—repetition]
  [thumb pointing behind and silently enunciating the correct form]
Student: Woke up. [Repair]

To summarize, the teacher provided verbal CF on average every minute during the 35-minute student-centered portion of the communicative task.

Of the 35 CF episodes, 77% contained a nonverbal cue, which most often involved either the use of the head and/or face (52%) or pointing (48%). Nonverbal cues accompanied verbal recasts 63% of the time (17/27 instances) whereas prompts were used alongside nonverbal feedback 37% of the time (10/27 instances). In terms of learner CF noticing, the corrective nature of recasts accompanied by nonverbal cues was recognized 76% of the time (13/17 episodes); for prompts, the value was 100% (10/10 episodes).

5.2.3 Discussion

The goal of this study was two-fold: (1) to identify the types of nonverbal behavior that an experienced English language teacher used to accompany her verbal feedback and (2) to investigate whether the use of the identified nonverbal cues made a difference in helping learners to recognize the corrective focus of the verbal CF techniques used.

5.2.3.1 Nonverbal Cues

The raw frequency results show that the teacher used nonverbal cues 77% of the time during CF, which is more than the rates reported in Davies (2006) and Wang and Loewen (2016), 47.4% and 60.2% respectively. The differences may lie in the research contexts investigated and data analyses performed. While Davies examined the nonverbal behavior of four EFL teachers, Wang and Loewen studied eight ESL teachers; this study, in turn, looked at only one ESL teacher, who by her own admission, was naturally a physically-expressive teacher. Furthermore, the focus of the present study was on two grammatical features that were task-essential and the sole focus of the teacher's feedback during the 35-minute whole-class activity. Both Davies and Wang and Loewen, however, studied the teachers' nonverbal behavior using several hours of classroom data (24 hours for Davies and 65 hours for Wang & Loewen) that were spread over four to ten weeks and included recordings of various language errors (grammatical, lexical, phonological, register, discourse) and learning tasks, not only those that involved whole-class communication.[38] Hence, it may be argued that the data they yielded are more representative than the findings here. As for the data analyses, Davies concentrated on describing nonverbal cues that accompanied recasts and clarifications requests (implicit CF) only; Wang and Loewen, in turn, analyzed nonverbal cues co-occurring with both implicit and more explicit (prompts) CF types. Similarly, this study looked at both recasts and prompts, finding that both were often supplemented with nonverbal cues.

As for the types of nonverbal behavior used to accompany the teacher's verbal feedback, head movements and pointing dominated. These results find support in Wang and Loewen's (2016) work, where similar conclusions were described. They argued that head movements provide students with learning opportunities in that they supply both positive and negative evidence about the learner's error. That is, if a teacher nods, the learner may interpret the gesture as a confirmation of his/her effort and/or the accuracy of the produced output. This, in fact, was how the teacher investigated here used nodding. As illustrated in Example 3, she would nod to confirm successful uptake following a verbal CF move; this nonverbal move could have then amplified the corrective intent of the verbal recast that the teacher used to address the error. Negative evidence, in turn, can be provided by shaking of the head to indicate disagreement or to disconfirm learners' output. Although the teacher here did not shake her head to indicate error, she often raised her head, arched her eyebrows, and established eye contact with a learner (Examples 1 and 3) to, arguably, provide the same negative evidence.[39] This practice appeared effective since it produced uptake, regardless of the type of verbal CF (recasts or prompts) it accompanied.

Pointing (deictic gestures) was also employed frequently by the teacher. Given that the target feature was metalinguistic in scope and required a focus on the past tense, this is not surprising. In fact, Wang and Loewen (2016) found a grammar teacher in their sample use deictic gestures to indicate various verb tenses. They argued that it is "the nature of the classes that teachers taught and the teaching materials they used in class" (p. 474) that determined the kind of nonverbal behavior they were likely to adopt. It, then, stands to reason that the teacher's pointing in this study was precipitated by the grammatical focus and the nature of the task. Furthermore, pointing may have allowed the teacher to draw specific learners' attention to their errors (Wang & Loewen, 2016); this gesture may have been perceived as particularly effective with lower-level learners that have been shown to "[benefit] from seeing a speaker's facial expression and gestures in L2 comprehension" (Nakatsukasa & Loewen, 2017, p. 169).

5.2.3.2 Nonverbal Cues and Uptake

The second goal of the study was to determine whether the teacher's use of nonverbal cues amplified the corrective focus of the verbal CF techniques used. The findings reveal that the presence of nonverbal cues helped learners to notice more recasts (76%) than they would have otherwise (63%); such comparison, however, was not possible for the prompts since their use was accompanied with nonverbal cues 100% of the time. The high rate of uptake following recasts with a nonverbal cue is noteworthy. One of the explanations could, of course, lie in the presence of a nonverbal cue that highlighted the corrective nature of recasts by alerting the learner to an issue of form. The cue (e.g., pointing) may have located the error and subsequently, the teacher giving the learner time to attempt correction (the practice usually limited to prompts) may also have encouraged uptake. Additional body movements such as nodding supplied after the uptake may have rewarded the learner's corrective attempts and encouraged the practice in the instances that followed. In this way, the nonverbal cues were instrumental in helping learners to notice the corrective intent behind recasts, satisfying the two basic prerequisites for CF effectiveness: locating the locus of the problem and eliciting correction (Gass & Varonis, 1994; Schmidt, 1983, 1990).

Furthermore, studies that have examined the impact of gestures on L2 development (Davies, 2006; Nakatsukasa, 2016; Wang, 2009) unequivocally show that nonverbal cues provided alongside verbal feedback contribute to L2 development and yield higher levels of uptake than verbal CF alone, especially in the long-term. The lasting effect of verbal and gestural recasts (compared to recasts-only and control groups) was exactly what Nakatsukasa (2016) found in her investigation. Similarly, Davies (2006) showed higher uptake rates for CF that incorporated paralinguistic features than feedback that did not. In fact, in the same study, when paralinguistic features were used alone, they yielded 100% uptake. Although the teacher in the present study did not use purely nonverbal cues (without the oral component), future research that investigates the effectiveness of such practice may be worthwhile. Still, even today, Nakatsukasa and Loewen (2017) already recommend that teachers use gestures to signal the source of learner error, to save instructional time and corrective effort, and to promote long-term retention of knowledge. They see the use of gestures especially effective "when providing implicit forms of feedback such as recasts" (p. 170).

Yet, the use of uptake as a measure of noticing may have not been sufficiently adequate to capture the differences in the noticing rates for each CF type employed in the study. That is, a simple repetition of the provided correction (as was often the case with recasts) cannot constitute evidence of noticing (Gass, 1997, 2003). Similarly, the reverse is true in that absence of uptake does not necessarily denote lack of noticing. Nakatsukasa (2016), for example, was unable to have her participants articulate any noticing of the feedback provided during her study. Surprisingly, the learners' comments focused on the quality of the tasks used and not on the supplied recasts or the target structures (prepositions of place). Despite this, learners in both the recasts only and recasts with gestures groups displayed learning gains on the immediate post-test; these gains were maintained by the recasts + gesture group a week later. Furthermore, uptake examined in the present study was *verbal* uptake in that the learners had to orally react to the corrective information supplied by the teacher. As such, nonverbal uptake was not examined. However, it may be possible that nonverbal responses did occur. For this reason, Nakatsukasa and Loewen (2017) call for more research that not only considers nonverbal uptake but also investigates its impact on the noticing results, especially in studies of CF. Still, one caveat is in order. As with verbal uptake, absence or limited occurrence of nonverbal uptake should not be taken as evidence of not noticing. After all, learners are different, with some being more inclined to use nonverbal cues to accompany speech and others less so. In addition, what someone says and in what amounts may affect how much nonverbal uptake takes place; what's more, social circumstances and affective factors (e.g., nervousness, anxiety) may limit nonverbal uptake even further (Gullberg, 2010).

Another explanation for the high uptake rates following recasts (with and without nonverbal cues) may be attributed to the fact that the teacher used both prompts and recasts to address the issues of form. In fact, she is a self-identified "mixer" of the two CF types, believing that each has a role to play in the learning process. This line of thinking finds support in the Counterbalance Hypothesis (Lyster & Mori, 2006) that argues that a balanced provision of recasts and prompts in a classroom setting may contribute to their effectiveness and their noticeability. Hence, similar to Kartchava and Ammar's (2014a) position, it is possible that the teacher's use of prompts may have alerted the learners to expect attention to form and that when recasts were provided, the students were more likely to recognize their corrective nature. This interpretation is strengthened by the fact that in this study the recasts without nonverbal cues were also noticed, 63% of the time. Furthermore, because the provided recasts were of short length and as such, made the locus of the problem more evident, this may have accentuated their saliency even more. Also, the fact that the teacher focused exclusively on the errors with the past (in statements and questions) may have highlighted the corrective focus of all CF types. Finally, the task itself could have contributed to the noticing results. According to Ortega (2007b), tasks that promote the use of a target structure and provide target-specific CF encourage learners to focus on the accuracy of their output.

Lastly, as with any study, the results of this investigation need to be interpreted with care. This is due to a number of limitations incurred. First, the results depict nonverbal behavior of one language teacher, without comparing the findings with other teachers or groups of learners. Furthermore, because no experimental conditions were included, it is difficult to know whether manipulation of teacher input and/or task would have yielded different results. Second, noticing was measured by verbal uptake only, without consideration of the possible nonverbal uptake generated by learners in response to the teacher's CF. This is exacerbated further by the fact that, due to various logistical restrictions, neither the teacher nor the learners were interviewed post study to determine their views and preferences. Third, because no developmental measures were used, it is difficult to ascertain an impact of the observed noticing on the learners' L2 development. Moreover, only past tense statements and questions in the past were considered and other linguistics targets (lexis and pronunciation) present in the input were not analyzed. Still, this study provides support for the existing research on teacher nonverbal behavior and its role in contributing to the noticeability of verbal feedback. Additional research on the topic is urgently needed. It should consider other noticing tools, tasks (e.g., Gregersen & MacIntyre, 2017), learners (in terms of proficiency and background), teachers, and linguistic targets.

5.3 CONCLUSION

The results of this study provide additional evidence to support previous research that has found language teachers using nonverbal cues alongside verbal CF; it also suggests that the presence of these cues amplifies the saliency of recasts. These findings are encouraging in that, like recasts, nonverbal behavior is a natural and frequent classroom occurrence. As such, understanding the power of nonverbal cues, especially in the delivery of verbal CF, may improve teachers' pedagogical practices and encourage learners to make use of the information contained in the teacher's input. As research on CF training (e.g., Bouffard & Sarkar, 2008; Fujii, Mackey, & Ziegler, [2016]; Sato & Lyster 2012; Study 2 this volume) has shown, letting learners know why a teacher or peer is using certain practices in class or during interaction may not only highlight the intended corrective purpose, but may also involve students in the learning process, encouraging equal teacher-learner and learner-learner partnerships, learner autonomy, and continued improvement. Moreover, once teachers become aware of their nonverbal practices, they may become open to ameliorating the practice in line with their teaching/cultural context, learner preferences, and expected outcomes. After all, since nonverbal behavior is "an integral part of our communication efforts" (Gullberg, 2008, p. 75) and "a fundamental aspect of [the teacher's] pedagogical repertoire" (Lazarton, 2004, p. 107), ignoring it may carry significant repercussions to our understanding of the classroom, classroom discourse, and "the teaching act" (Allen, 2000) itself.

Chapter Six

Conclusion

The goal of this chapter is to summarize the findings of the four research studies described in the book and to highlight the resulting implications for the language classroom. The chapter also discusses the overall significance and contribution of the volume as well as identifies its limitations. Directions that future investigations of CF may pursue are suggested at the end.

6.1 CONTRIBUTIONS OF THE VOLUME

Allen (2000) once posited that "in order to improve teaching, we must first have an adequate description of the teaching act" (p. 169). This volume has attempted to describe a portion of the teaching act, namely the provision of corrective feedback to L2 learners and ways to ameliorate its noticeability and effectiveness. To this end, it synthesized the available CF research conducted in and out of the language classroom and linked it to four classroom-based investigations that examined: (1) learners' ability to notice and learn from the CF supplied in the classroom, (2) the impact of training learners to notice CF, (3) the relationship between learner beliefs about CF and the noticing of feedback, and (4) the role of nonverbal behavior in improving the saliency of verbal feedback. While the findings reiterate the facilitative nature of corrective feedback in the learning of an L2, they also highlight the need to make CF and its pedagogical purpose more explicit to learners. In addition, the four studies provide new practical insights into what language teachers could do to take advantage of the power of CF and help them to understand why some practices may prove more effective than others in certain contexts, with particular learners, and at specific developmental periods. Arguably, it is through self-reflection as well as consistent analysis of one's teaching and the resulting classroom discourse that teachers can not only become informed users of CF, but can also empower their students to become confident decoders of verbal and nonverbal input they are exposed to in the classroom.

Before summarizing the main findings of the studies reported here, it is important to note that as with any academic pursuit, this publication is not without limitations. The first limitation concerns the particular theoretical perspective taken. That is, the research described has largely been influenced by the cognitive-interactionist theories of SLA. It is further limited by the adopted narrow view of attention (i.e., whether attention is necessary for L2 success) and the examination of the impact of attention on the early (versus other) stages in L2 learning. Yet, such narrowing of the viewpoint is intentional. This is primarily due to how theories are constructed and confirmed. According to McLaughlin (1987), theories have three functions to perform. First, they need to group large amounts of information into meaningful generalizations. Second, theories ought to explain these generalizations and/or their interactions. In this sense, theories *transform* the current understanding of a phenomenon. Third, theories need to stimulate research by generating hypotheses that predict and test where the theory is heading. In short, theories interpret, criticize, and synthesize knowledge (arrived at via empirical observation) about natural phenomena. Hence, empirical investigations require that some boundaries be placed on the construct under investigation. At the same time, the choice of boundaries may affect the resulting interpretations of the observed phenomena. The differences may lie in the scope, content, type, and form that a theory takes (Long, 2006). While SLA as a field tends to welcome a multitude of perspectives on how L2 learning happens and the processes that underlie it, there is opposition to unwarranted "proliferation" of theories (Larsen-Freeman & Long, 1991; Long, 2006; VanPatten & Williams, 2015a). Specifically, although theorizing is viewed as a healthy way to stimulate research, scholars have objected to the "let all the flowers bloom" (Long, 2006, p. 151) attitude of Lantolf (1996), who does not see the need to subject the proposed theories to either critical or comparative evaluation. Recently, however, an effort has been made to blur the boundaries and bridge the cognitive and sociocultural views on L2 learning (Hulstijn, Young, Ortaga, Bigelow, DeKeyser, Ellis, Lantolf, Mackey & Talmy, 2014) since, it is argued, working exclusively within one theoretical perspective without acknowledging potential insights from the other may prove limiting and unconstructive. While such efforts are worthy, they merely point to the fact that both an overlap in perspectives (i.e., "different marital viewpoints," Leow, 2015, p. 271) and a gap in viewpoints "can be an opportunity to open up new paths to knowledge creation" (Hulstijn et al., 2014, p. 54).

The second limitation lies in the fact that all the studies described in the book examined only English past tense and questions in the past. While the range is admittedly small, the choice of the target features was prompted by their pervasiveness in L2 input and the challenge that ESL learners experience when using them, regardless of L1. Yet, because the communicative tasks that naturally required the use of the past tense were employed, the elicitation and consequently, treatment of the learners' ill-formed utterances and questions have arguably proved ecologically valid and genuine. Furthermore, the tasks themselves have been argued to help make the corrective intent of the CF more salient, allowing for "in-time learning" and possibly promoting Transfer Appropriate Processing (Lightbown, 2008) that posits L2 learning to be context-dependent in that "knowledge is easier to retrieve if we are returned to or can recreate those circumstances and thinking processes" (Lightbown & Spada, 2013, p. 224). The latter is possible because if learners are focused on the form of their oral production while engaged in a classroom communicative task, they are more likely to attend to accuracy in real-life communications later on.

The third limitation has to do with the focus of the investigations being exclusively on oral CF, foregoing any consideration of the possible contributions that written and/or computer-mediated CF could have brought to the forefront, especially if these were considered individually, in addition to the oral CF, or compared between the delivery modes (e.g., face-to-face written/oral CF versus computer-mediated interactions). Comparisons of interaction enacted in the face-to-face (F2F) versus computer-mediated contexts (CMC) are of special value to the study of CF since a recent review of the literature (Ziegler & Mackey, 2017) has shown CMC to bring about more noticing of form and consequently, more L2 learning opportunities than F2F interaction. It was argued that this was due to "the possibility of increased saliency, more opportunities to review input and output, and longer times for processing and planning production" (p. 83); these advantages were especially pronounced in the noticing of lexical versus morphological errors (Gurzynski-Weiss & Baralt, 2014; Smith, 2012). Similarly, CF delivered in such Computer-Assisted Language Learning (CALL) environments as Tutorial CALL (where "the computer takes on the role of a *tutor* [. . .] by evaluating [sentence-based] learner responses and presenting new material in one-to-one interactions," Heift & Hegelheimer, 2017, p. 52) and Automatic Writing Evaluation (AWE) systems (where whole essays are evaluated) can yield development in L2 writing, albeit the findings of the empirical investigations to date have been mixed (Heift & Hegelheimer, 2017).

Not considering peer feedback in any of the studies may also be considered a limitation. This is in light of a growing body of research that has found peers to be effective providers and users of oral, written, and computer-mediated CF. Still, teacher feedback is the primary type of corrective input that learners have come to expect in the classroom context. In fact, research has shown L2 students to shy away from peer feedback without appropriate training and classroom environment that supports the process. Sato (2017) has shown peer oral CF to be effective when both partners value each other's L2 knowledge, remain open to receiving and supplying correction, as well as have confidence in the value of CF and their mutual ability to supply it appropriately. However, when it comes to teacher CF, while students may need help and possibly training (Study 2, Chapter 3) to recognize the teacher's CF intentions and methods, learners have been shown to value CF and expect attention to form in the L2 classroom (Study 3, Chapter 4). Furthermore, while peer CF may be a useful tool to incorporate in L2 classrooms, it should be provided *in addition to* teacher CF and *with* the teacher's "ongoing assistance" (Nassaji & Kartchava, 2017b, p. 177). After all, as mentioned elsewhere, peer CF is "fundamentally different from teacher CF because it does not (or cannot) necessarily contain the pedagogical intent to assist language development of another learner" (Sato & Ballinger, 2012, p. 159).

This volume considered the mediating role of only learner beliefs about CF on the noticeability and effectiveness of CF. This is despite evidence that individual differences may affect how CF is perceived and used in L2 learning. Sheen (2011), having examined the effect of anxiety, language aptitude, and beliefs on the learners' ability to learn from the provided oral and written CF, suggested that age and motivation could be other variables to consider when evaluating CF effectiveness. Yet, because learner beliefs, an affective individual difference, have recently been shown to permeate and regulate much more of the learning process than previously understood, learner beliefs may prove to "become the most versatile of all learner characteristics, potentially entering into combined characteristic adaptations with most other [learner characteristics—] motivational beliefs, beliefs about aptitude, [and] affective beliefs" (Dörnyei & Ryan, 2015, p. 191). As such, investigations into learner beliefs about CF and/or its various types (e.g., Study 3, Chapter 4) may need to continue to: (1) evaluate the impact of the instructional context, teaching approaches, learner characteristics (proficiency, background, cognitive variables, etc.), as well as teacher attitudes/preferences towards feedback on the effectiveness of the CF practices in place, and to (2) tease out the contributions these (and possibly other) factors may bring to affect feedback efficacy.

Finally, the studies described here were intended to be exploratory and pushed to ask the "what if?" question about the various factors that could be considered in making CF more noticeable to learners in the classroom context. As such, the investigations are limited by methodological and data-related issues that future research may choose to address. Among these is insufficient triangulation to explain the noticing and learning results in Study 1 and the reported beliefs in Study 3; using multiple methods, such as interviews, stimulated recall, and/or open-ended statements in addition to the closed statements on the beliefs questionnaire, could have helped to better explain the obtained results and support the conclusions. Limited training and practice time made available to learners in Study 2 preclude any generalizations as does not giving participants a chance to verbalize analyses they may have engaged in when processing CF. Limited data in Study 4 prevent comparisons of prompts provided alongside nonverbal cues and those without.

The research reported in this publication has, however, produced important contributions to the study of CF. First, all the investigations described were conducted in the L2 classroom. Results of CF research have found the classroom to be more representative of the kinds of learning that is likely to take place than the results yielded in the language laboratory (Lyster et al., 2013; Nassaji, 2016), even though the language classroom often presents a complex and unpredictable environment in which to learn. This is because studies conducted in the laboratory setting tend to involve primarily dyadic interactions, with the researcher being one of the interlocutors, and focus on feedback provided intensively, on a limited number of linguistic targets (Nicholas et al., 2001). Classroom studies, on the other hand, tend to focus on CF provision directed to the class as a whole, with teachers focusing on a variety of target forms (Nassaji, 2016). The findings yielded by the research in this book, then, represent a more realistic reflection of what can happen in an L2 classroom when certain CF-related actions are pursued.

Second, with the exception of Study 2, all the studies involved an examination of more than one CF type. Lyster et al. (2013) have called for more CF research that moves "away from dichotomous comparisons of CF strategies that isolate CF from other relevant instructional variables and towards an examination of combinations of CF types that more resemble teachers' practices in classroom settings" (p. 30). After all, one CF technique might not work for everyone and in the words of Ellis (2012), "the single 'best' strategy may be a chimera" (p. 263). This, of course, is not surprising given that the success of L2 learning very much depends on a number of learner-internal and learner-external factors, some of which may include learner factors (e.g., age, proficiency, affective and cognitive variables), teacher differences (e.g., attitudes, training, teaching experience, preferred teaching approaches), the instructional context (e.g., L2 vs. FL, intensive vs. regular, grammar vs. communicatively-based, technology-oriented vs. traditional, but see Nassaji, 2013), and program-specific objectives (e.g., ESL, English for Academic Purposes (EAP), English for Specific Purposes (ESP), Content and Language Integrated Learning (CLIL), immersion).

Third, this volume reported on two important initiatives in the study of CF. Study 2 investigated the impact of classroom-based CF training on learners' ability to benefit from implicit recasts. The results pointed to positive effects of such training in that the trained learners produced fewer errors overall, higher CF-uptake ratio, and more repair than their counterparts who were exposed to recasts without the training. Adding to a limited body of research on the use of nonverbal behavior in the provision of CF, Study 4, in turn, investigated one ESL teacher's spontaneous use of body movements and gestures during the act of verbal feedback provision. The findings revealed the teacher using nonverbal cues with both prompts and recasts; yet, the use of nonverbal cues alongside recasts appeared to have highlighted their saliency. Together, these studies point to the need for teachers to communicate the pedagogical purpose of their in-class practices because, as the interviews with the participants in Study 2 showed, letting learners know why a certain practice is used and/or why they are asked to engage in a particular activity may not only demystify the practice, but also show learners what they can do to more effectively develop their L2.

Finally, the importance of noticing is the theme running through the four studies. Specifically, Study 1 indicated that while learners were able to notice oral CF, the rates of noticing depended on the type of CF strategy used. That is, the CF techniques that push learners to self-correct (i.e., prompts) as well as a combination of prompts and recasts were found more effective in alerting learners to the corrective intent of the CF move. Recasts alone, however, resulted in the least amount of reported noticing. With this result in mind, Study 2 questioned whether training learners to notice the corrective focus of recasts before supplying them in the context of a communicative task would help them recognize the accuracy-driven focus of recasts. Although no clear quantitative differences between the trained and non-trained groups were found, it was argued that the learners who were alerted to the premise of recasts and their intended function in the classroom discourse reacted to recasts in a qualitatively different way than their uninstructed counterparts. Study 3 investigated the impact of learner beliefs on their ability to notice and learn from the supplied CF. The findings indicated that learner beliefs about CF can mediate the noticeability of classroom-based CF. This was especially the case for recasts in that learners who believed in the importance of CF were more likely to notice feedback in general and the corrective intent of recasts in particular. Finally, Study 4 showed that learners can take advantage of a teacher's nonverbal cues to decipher their CF intentions. The learners were able to accurately interpret the teacher's body movements as cues to attend to the form of their ill-structured utterances. These interpretations, in turn, resulted in uptake and repair for both recasts and prompts and amplified the corrective intent of recasts. Although no direct link between uptake and learning was established in the four studies described, taken together, the findings support the general consensus that noticing CF may help learners to attend to the form of their output. This attention to form may then turn input into intake, enabling L2 development (Schmidt, 1993, 1995). The importance of noticing in CF effectiveness was shown to be a key theme in Nassaji and Kartchava's (2017) volume on CF, with several studies providing support for the role of feedback explicitness and noticing.

6.2 PEDAGOGICAL IMPLICATIONS

If CF noticeability is important, then what can teachers do to enable this noticing? The studies in this volume, along with previous research, support the notion that teachers can be instrumental in helping their students notice oral feedback supplied in the classroom. Specifically, they can:

1. Alert learners to the presence of CF in their classroom practice;
2. Provide CF to various target language forms (intensively and extensively), ensuring as much as possible that learners understand the focus of the correction and/or able to self-repair;
3. Employ a range of CF techniques alone or in combination;
4. Explain the CF techniques teachers regularly use and the reasons for their use;
5. Engage learners in a practice with these CF techniques as a class and in dyadic interactions;
6. Probe learner preferences about feedback in general and particular CF techniques;
7. Facilitate discussions on the perceived effects and/or shortcomings of certain CF strategies, amending their use as needed;
8. Demystify the teacher's nonverbal behavior and identify the meaning of the different cues used, possibly providing training and/or establishing a "code" system;
9. Consider the role of a given teaching context, tasks, lesson formats, topics, and the learner participation structure (whole class, small group, individual one-on-one) on the success of the intended CF (Nassaji, 2016); and
10. Make CF a regular feature of the classroom discourse.

While these suggestions may prove helpful, it is important to note that any "utterance can count as feedback or correction only if a learner is willing to construe some bit of language as expressing a corrective intention on the part of some speaker" (Carroll, 2001, p. 348). Hence, it is *both* a teacher's intention and a learner's comprehension of the said intention that together are needed to make CF noticeable. Furthermore, the complex nature of the instructional context, the teaching approach in place, and any changes in the lesson organization can determine the noticeability and effectiveness of CF. This is what Nassaji (2013) found in his investigation of the extent to which changes in the organization of classroom talk (i.e., interactions in groups, pairs, or as a whole class) affected the amount, type, and effectiveness of CF. An examination of 54 hours of classroom interaction across three proficiency levels (beginner, intermediate, advanced) revealed that while whole-class interactions received the most CF, learners were more likely to benefit from CF when interacting with peers in small groups or one on one. Hence, "the same classroom context and [. . .] differences in participation structure may impact both the provision and usefulness of [CF]" (Nassaji, 2013, p. 862).

6.3 FUTURE RESEARCH DIRECTIONS

It is apparent that more work remains to be done to understand the many unknowns about CF. A promising direction in such endeavor is the use of technology and the opportunity to explore real-time processing that learners engage in when attending to feedback. After all, such tools as uptake and verbal protocols not only provide indirect measures of attention and noticing, but can also affect the quality and outcomes of a language task. Recent advances in psycholinguistics have identified techniques and resources that may be used for L2 acquisition research (Roberts, 2012). Specifically, such measures as eye-tracking have gained acceptance and produced important findings about what learners focus on and for how long (gaze fixation) when engaged in a language learning task (e.g., Smith, 2012). Long (2017) argues that tracking eye movements and gaze fixations can provide an alternative to the uptake measure. While uptake results can be affected by a number of affective variables (learner differences, opportunities for uptake, task, etc.) and require researchers to infer the occurrence of noticing, the eye-tracking tool records eye movements and gaze in real time, without relying on learners to report noticing. Furthermore, such measures can enable triangulation and allow "test[ing] of rival claims to the effect that noticing at the level of awareness is necessary for acquisition [Schmidt's Noticing Hypothesis] or that noticing at the level of attention to input, i.e., detection, is sufficient as claimed by Tomlin and Villa (1994)" (Long, 2017, p. 14). Moreover, Long (2017) describes the use of an aptitude measure (Hi-Lab, developed at the University of Maryland) that has already been used to investigate the impact of aptitude on learners' ability to learn from recasts and explicit correction (Granena & Yulmaz, to appear, cited in Long, 2017).

CF research in general may benefit from replication of existing studies to confirm and expand on what is already known about feedback. At the same time, more investigations are needed to address currently known methodological, participant, and contextual challenges in the study of CF. Furthermore, additional research on oral, written, computer-mediated teacher and peer feedback as well as the need for feedback training is needed. Studies that explore nonverbal behavior in the study of verbal CF are also important to determine learners' ability to interpret and respond to teachers' nonverbal feedback; this research should also focus on teachers' use of nonverbal feedback, their reasons for using it, and whether or not it is susceptible to modification (Wang & Loewen, 2016).

Finally, because "pedagogy should be research informed and [...] research will benefit from being pedagogy informed" (Ellis, 2017, p. 13), teachers can help identify important CF-related issues they face on a daily basis to inform future research agendas.

6.4 FINAL REMARKS

Corrective feedback is an important yet complex phenomenon. While a number of factors have been shown to mediate its effectiveness, attention to form remains a constant in the study and teaching of second languages. Currently, when it comes to CF, there are no unequivocal answers to the question as to what exactly teachers should do in the L2 classroom with particular linguistic targets, learners, programs, etc. What is known, however, is that both teachers and learners have a role to play to bring about language learning. In other words, "the L2 classroom [is] a context in which the responsibility of learning is on the student [... and] it is the teacher's role to maximize such learning by providing well-designed tasks and activities and the opportunity to practice the L2" (Leow, 2015, p. 276). When both learners and teachers understand the intention of CF and decide to play an active role in using the information it entails, it is possible that these efforts may demystify classroom discourse for learners and result in measurable yet realistic expectations in terms of feedback effectiveness for teachers. After all, corrective feedback is the reason many learners enter the L2 classroom; it should, then, be one of the reasons they succeed in the learning of a second language.

Endnotes

1. For a description of other theoretical perspectives on attention, please see Leow (2015).
2. For a full account of the Noticing Hypothesis and the debate about it, please see Chapter 2.
3. It is important to note that corrective feedback is generally not provided outside the classroom or other instructional settings. Yet, its provision during instruction (in these contexts) is not guaranteed (Foster, 1998).
4. Errors usually refer to any deviation from the target language in terms of pronunciation, vocabulary and morphosyntax (Lyster, 1999).
5. To date, there has been little research done on the impact of CF on L2 pragmatics. For a brief overview, see Lyster et al. (2013).
6. The "prompt" category in Lyster (2004), for example, includes both implicit and explicit moves (Ellis, Loewen, & Erlam, 2006).
7. It is important to note that some researchers (e.g., Mackey & Philp, 1998; Nassaji, 2011a) qualify uptake as more than a learner's immediate response to feedback; instead, they see it as learner's attempts to modify or repair the problematic utterance. To them, "uptake usually denotes that learners have somewhat benefitted from the feedback, whereas responses of acknowledgement [i.e., Lyster & Ranta's (1997) definition of uptake] do not necessarily do so" (Nassaji, 2016, p. 539).
8. Contrastive Analysis refers to detailed comparisons of the phonology, morphology, syntax and even the cultural systems of two languages to determine the similarities and differences between the two. Similarities between the structures were seen as the candidates for *positive transfer* because learners would not need to change their old habits but would simply apply them "as is" to a new context. *Negative transfer*, however, signalled differences between the languages, resulting in learner difficulty (errors).
9. The five hypotheses of Krashen's monitor model are: (1) the acquisition-learning hypothesis, (2) the monitor hypothesis, (3) the natural order hypothesis, (4) the input hypothesis, and (5) the affective filter hypothesis.

10. Long-term memory can be differentiated further to include semantic memory (knowledge of facts known to everyone) and episodic memory (privately experienced events; see Tulving, 2002).

11. Kartchava, E. & Ammar, A. (2014a). The noticeability and effectiveness of corrective feedback in relation to target type. *Language Teaching Research, 18*(4), 428–452. Portions of that article reprinted with permission.

12. But see Smith (2012), who used eye-tracking to measure noticing of explicit recasts in computer-mediated communication.

13. Dörnyei (2003) provides a list of published questionnaires used to investigate a range of research topics, including those used in L2 research (e.g., language attitudes, teacher/learner beliefs, preference for instructional activities, etc.).

14. The fundamental assumption for verbal reporting is that information that is noticed as a task is being performed is represented in short-term memory and may be reported during or after the completion of the task (Ericsson & Simon, 1993). To enable this "noticing," "the subjects should verbalize the corresponding thought or thoughts [so that] the new incoming information is maintained in attention until the corresponding verbalization of it is completed" (ibid, p. 32).

15. The remaining nineteen participants carried out a delayed post-test instead.

16. The following tests were done to measure individual differences described herein: (1) a test of phonological memory measuring phonemic coding skills, (2) a test of working memory measuring the executive function of working memory, (3) a test of attention control measuring executive attention management, and (4) a test of analytical ability measuring grammatical sensitivity (Trofimovich et al., 2007).

17. For Ellis (2001), FFI is "any planned or incidental instructional activity that is intended to induce language learners to pay attention to linguistic form" (pp. 1–2).

18. While reactive FFEs refer to feedback *in reaction* to the student's erroneous utterance made by any interlocutor, pre-emptive FFEs involve drawing attention to a potentially difficult linguistic item before it results in error.

19. The information presented in this section is partially reproduced from Kartchava & Ammar (2013). Although Study 1 does not specifically focus on the link between noticeability of CF and L2 development, I believe it is important to include this information to show that this type of research has been done.

20. Studies 1, 2 (Chapter 3), and 3 (Chapter 4) were conducted in this setting.

21. In French-medium CEGEPs, English is taught as a second language and in English-medium colleges, French is taught as a second language.

22. English schools "were allowed to accept only children with a *certificate of eligibility* based on having at least one parent schooled in English at the primary level in Quebec [. . .] and elsewhere in Canada" (Winer, 2007, p. 492).

23. Adapted from Watcyn-Jones, P. (1995). *Grammar games and activities for teachers*. London, UK: Penguin Books.

24. With the exception of clarification requests that signal to the learner that the utterance has been misunderstood since these can be more implicit than explicit.

25. The questionnaires were designed to determine: (1) instances when the learners and their classmates were corrected, (2) the target of correction, and (3) instances of language learning.

26. Although the two conditions were recalled the least, it is important to note that the recast + repetition condition yielded slightly more recalls than the recasts condition. Nevertheless, in terms of the post-test performance, no significant differences between these two conditions were identified.

27. The feedback was provided verbally during the oral presentations and in writing on the written reports. The errors in writing were circled and the correct version was provided next to the error.

28. "The NSs were instructed to recast fully any non-targetlike utterance given by the NNSs and to target and recast question forms as much as possible" (Mackey & Philp, 1998, p. 346).

29. In fact, a number of review articles (Nicholas et al., 2001; Ellis & Sheen, 2006) and the meta-analysis of interaction studies (Mackey & Goo, 2007) jointly point out that the learning outcomes yielded in the laboratory and classroom settings vary significantly.

30. Kartchava, E. & Ammar, A. (2014b). Learners' beliefs as mediators of what is noticed and learned in the language classroom. *TESOL Quarterly, 48*(1), 86–109. DOI: 10.1002/tesq.101

31. "La perception constitue le processus par lequel toute personne ou un groupe de personnes prennent conscience des objets qui leur sont présentés ou des événements qui surviennent" (Gagné, 1979, p. 25).

32. Although Horwitz is usually credited with initiating the study of beliefs about language learning, by some accounts this recognition should go to Papalia (1978), who studied the beliefs of 316 grade 9 students (Bernat, 2004).

33. The Big Five paradigm comprises five broad dimensions that identify the traits that underlie the concept of personality. These include: (1) openness to experience, (2) conscientiousness, (3) extraversion—introversion, (4) agreeableness, and (5) neuroticism—emotional stability (Dörnyei, 2005, pp. 14–18).

34. Please note that the original questionnaire was in French. The version provided here has been translated into English and was published in Kartchava (2016).

35. It is, however, important to note that there are researchers who have restricted the definition of gesture specifically to the hands, arms, and even to the head (e.g., Sime, 2006).

36. Nakatsukasa and Loewen (2017) note that despite the possibility that uptake can be nonverbal, in CF research, it has been operationalized primarily as verbal. To date, only one study has attempted to document both verbal and nonverbal instances of uptake (Wang, 2009) albeit inconclusively.

37. Of the 27 feedback episodes that contained nonverbal cues, 14 included head movements and 13—pointing.

38. While Davies (2006) did not specify the tasks the students engaged in, his context choice was precipitated by the opportunity to observe fluency-based activities. Wang and Loewen (2016), however, described the different task types that dominated the observed classes. These included: discussing reading and listening materials, comparing answers, and performing information gap activities (p. 463).

39. It is difficult to know the teacher's exact intention since no follow-up interview or stimulated recall was conducted.

References

Abraham, R. & Vann, R. (1987). Strategies of two language learners: A case study. In A. Wenden & J. Rubin (Eds.), *Learner strategies in language learning* (pp. 85–102). Englewood Cliffs, N.J.: Prentice Hall.

Abselson, R. (1979). Differences between systems and knowledge systems. *Cognitive Science, 3*, 355–366.

Alanen, R. (1995). Input enhancement and rule presentation in second language acquisition. In R. Scmidt (Ed.), *Attention and awareness in foreign language learning and teaching* (pp. 395–411). Honolulu, HI: University of Hawai'i Press.

Algarawi, B. S. (2010). The effects of repair techniques on L2 learning as a product and as a process: A CA-for-SLA investigation of classroom interaction. Unpublished doctoral dissertation, University of Newcastle Upon Tyne, UK.

Alexander, P. A. & Dochy, F. J. (1995). Adults' views about knowing and believing. In R. Garner & P. A. Alexander (Eds.), *Beliefs about text and about instruction with text* (pp. 223–244). Hillsdale, NJ: Erlbaum.

Allen, L. Q. (2000). Nonverbal accommodation in foreign language teacher talk. *Applied Language Learning, 11*, 155–176.

Almarza, G. G. (1996). Student foreign language teacher's knowledge growth. In D. Freeman & J. C. Richards (Eds.), *Teacher Learning in Language Teaching* (pp. 50–78). New York: Cambridge University Press.

Ammar, A. (2008). Prompts and recasts: Differential effects on second language morphosyntax. *Language Teaching Research, 12*, 183–210.

Ammar, A. & Sato, M. (2010a). *Corrective feedback, noticing, and individual differences: Exploration into their relationship with second language acquisition.* Paper presented at the annual conference of Canadian Association of Applied Linguistics, Montreal, Quebec, Canada.

———. (2010b). *The importance of noticing in meaning-oriented second language classrooms.* Paper presented at the 10th International Conference of the Association for Language Awareness, University of Kassel, Germany.

Ammar, A., Sato, M. & Kartchava, E. (2010). *How should noticing be measured? Evidence from classroom research on corrective feedback.* Paper presented at the annual conference of American Association of Applied Linguistics, Atlanta, Georgia, U.S.A.

Ammar, A. & Spada, N. (2006). One size fits all? Recasts, prompts and L2 learning. *Studies in Second Language Acquisition, 28*, 543–574.

Amuzie, G. L. & Winke, P. (2009). Changes in language learning beliefs as a result of study abroad. *System, 37*, 366–379.

Anderson, J. R. (1983). *The architecture of cognition.* Cambridge, MA: Harvard University Press.

———. (1985). *Cognitive Psychology and Its Implications.* San Francisco, CA: Freeman

Anderson, J. R., Fincham, J. M., & Douglass, S. (1997). The role of examples and rules in the acquisition of a cognitive skill. *Journal of Experimental Psychology: Learning, Memory, and Cognition, 23* (4), 932–945.

Arndt. H. & Janney, R. (1987). *InterGrammar: Toward an integrative model of verbal, prosodic and kinesic choices in speech.* Berlin: Mouton de Gruyter.

Baddeley, A. D. (2007). *Working memory, thought and action.* Oxford: Oxford University Press.

Bancroft, W. J. (1997). Nonverbal communication: How important is it for the language teacher? *Mosaic*, 4, 3–12.

Bardovi-Harlig, K. (1998). Narrative structure and lexical aspect: Conspiring Factors in Second Language Acquisition of Tense-Aspect Morphology. *Studies in Second Language Acquisition, 20, 471–508.*

Barcelos, A. M. F. (2003). Researching beliefs about SLA: A critical review. In P. Kalaja & A. M. F. Barcelos (Eds.), *Beliefs about SLA: New research approaches* (pp. 7–33). Dordrecht: Kluwer Academic Publishers.

———. (2015). Unveiling the relationship between language learning beliefs, emotions, and identities. *Studies in Second Language Learning and Teaching, 5*(2), 301–325.

Barcelos, A. M. F. & Kalaja, P. (2011). Introduction to beliefs about SLA revisited. *System, 39*(3), 281–289.

Bartels, N. (2003). How teachers and researchers read academic articles. *Teaching and Teacher Education, 19*(7), 737–753.

Bartram, M. & Walt, R. (1991). *Correction. Mistake management: A positive approach for language teachers.* Hove: Language Teaching Publications.

Benson, P. & Lor, W. (1999). Conceptions of language and language learning. *System, 27*, 459–472.

Bernat, E. (2004). Investigating Vietnamese ESL learners' beliefs about language learning. *EA Journal, 21*, 40–54.

Bernat, E. & Gvozdenko, I. (2005). Beliefs about language learning: Current knowledge, pedagogical implications, and new research directions. *TESL-EJ, 9*, 1–21.

Biron, D. (1991). Étude *du rôle de l'activité de représentation extreme dans la résolution de problèmes mathématiques complexes par des enfants du primaire.* Unpublished doctoral dissertation, Université de Montréal, Canada.

Bloom, B. (1954). The thought processes of students in discussion. In S. J. French (Ed.), *Accent on teaching: Experiments in general education* (pp. 23–46). New York: Harper.

Borg, S. (2007). Research engagement in English language teaching. *Teaching and Teacher Education, 23*(5), 731–747.

Bouffard, L. A. & Sarkar, M. (2008). Training 8-year-old French immersion students in metalinguistic analysis: An innovation in Form-focused pedagogy. *Language Awareness, 17*(1), 3–24.

Bowles, M. A. (2010). *The think-aloud controversy in language acquisition research.* Routledge.

Braidi, S. M. (2002). Reexamining the role of recasts in native-speaker/nonnative-speaker interactions. *Language Learning, 52*, 1–42.

Breen, M. P. (2001). *Learner contributions to language learning: New directions in research.* Harlow, Essex: Pearson Education Limited.

Brown, A. V. (2009). Students' and teachers' perceptions of effective foreign language teaching: A comparison of ideals. *The Modern Language Journal, 93*(1), 46–60.

Brown, D. (2016). The type and linguistic foci of oral corrective feedback in the L2 classroom: A meta-analysis. *Language Teaching Research, 20*, 436–458.

Brown, R. (1973). *A first language: The early stages.* Cambridge: Harvard University Press

Brown, R., & Hanlon, C. (1970). Derivational complexity and order of acquisition in child speech. In J. R. Hayes (Ed.), *Cognition and the development of language* (pp. 11–53), New York, NY: Wiley.

Carroll, S. (1995). The irrelevance of verbal feedback to language learning. In L. Eubank, L. Selinker & M. Sharwood Smith (Eds.), *The current state of interlanguage* (pp. 73–88). Amsterdam: John Benjamins.

———. (2001). *Input and evidence: The raw material of second language acquisition: Volume 25.* Philadelphia, PA: John Benjamins.

Carroll, S. & Swain, M. (1993). Explicit and implicit negative feedback: An empirical study of the learning of linguistic generalizations. *Studies in Second Language Acquisition, 15*, 357–386.

Cathcart, R. L., & Olsen, J. E. W. B. (1976). Teachers' and students' preferences for correction of classroom conversation errors. In J. F. Fanselow & R. H. Crymes (Eds.), *On TESOL '76* (pp. 41–53). Washington, DC: TESOL.

Chaudron, C. (1977). A descriptive modal of discourse in the corrective treatment of learners' errors. *Language Learning, 27*, 29–46.

———. (1988). *Second language classrooms.* New York: Cambridge University Press.

Chavez, M. (2007). Students' and teachers' assessments of the need for accuracy in the oral production of German as a foreign language. *The Modern Language Journal, 91*, 537–563.

Chenoweth, N. A., Day, R. R., Chun, A. E., & Luppescu, S. (1983). Attitudes and preferences of ESL students to error correction. *Studies in Second Language Acquisition, 6*, 79–87.

Chomsky, N. (1957). *Syntactic Structures*. The Hague: Mouton.
———. (1966). Linguistic theory. In J. P. B. Allen & P. Van Buren (eds.), *Chomsky: Selected Readings* (pp. 152–159). London: Oxford University Press.
———. (1981). Principles and parameters in syntactic theory. In N. Hornstein & D. Lightfoot (eds.), *Explanation in linguistics: The logical problem of language acquisition*. London: Longman.
Collins, L. (2002). The roles of L1 influence and lexical aspect in the acquisition of temporal morphology. *Language Learning, 52*, 43–94.
———. (2007). L1 differences and L2 similarities: teaching verb tenses in English. *ELT Journal Volume 61*(4), 295–303.
Collins, L., Trofimovich, P., White, J., Cardozo, W., & Horst, M. (2009). Some input on the easy/difficult grammar question: An empirical study. *The Modern Language Journal, 93*(3), 336–353.
Corder, S. P. (1967). The significance of learners' errors. *International Review of Applied Linguistics*, 5, 161–170.
Cotterall, L. S. (1995). Readiness for autonomy: Investigating learner beliefs. *System, 23*, 195–205.
———. (1999). Key variables in language learning: What do learners believe about them? *System, 27*, 473–492.
Courchêne, R. (1980). The error analysis hypothesis, the contrastive analysis hypothesis and the correction of error in the second language classroom. *TESL Talk, 11*(3), 1–29.
Davies, M. (2006). Paralinguistic focus on form. *TESOL Quarterly, 40*(4), 841–855.
DeBot, K. (1996). The psycholinguistics of the output hypothesis. *Language Learning, 46*, 529–555.
DeKeyser, R. (1993). The effect of error correction on L2 grammar knowledge and oral proficiency. *Modern Language Journal, 77*, 501–514.
———. (1998). Beyond focus on form: cognitive perspectives on learning and practicing second language grammar. In C. Doughty & J. Williams (Eds.), *Focus on Form in Classroom Second Language Acquisition* (pp. 42–63). New York: Cambridge University Press.
———. (2005). What makes learning second-language grammar difficult? A review of issues. In R. M. DeKeyser (Ed.), *Grammatical Development in Language Learning* (pp. 1–25). Malden, MA: Blackwell Publishing.
———. (2007a). Introduction: Situating the concept of practice. In R. M. DeKeyser (Ed.), *Practice in second language: Perspectives from applied linguistics and cognitive psychology* (pp. 1–18). New York, NY: Cambridge University Press.
———. (2007b). Skill acquisition theory. In B., VanPatten & J. Williams (Eds.), *Theories in second language acquisition: An introduction* (pp. 97–113). Mahwah, NJ: Lawrence Erlbaum Associates, Publishers.
DeVellis, R. F. (2003). *Scale development: Theory and applications* (2nd ed.). Thousand Oaks, CA: Sage.
Dörnyei, Z. (2003). *Questionnaires in second language research: Constructing, administering and processing*. Mahwah, NJ: Lawrence Erlbaum Associates.

———. (2005). *The psychology of the language learner: Individual differences in second language acquisition.* Mahwah, NJ: Lawrence Erlbaum Associates, Inc.

Dörnyei, Z. & Csizér, K. (2012). How to design and analyze surveys in second language acquisition research. In A. Mackey & S. Gass (Eds.), *Research methods in second language acquisition: A practical guide* (pp. 74–94). Maiden, MA: Blackwell Publishing.

Dörnyei, Z. & Ryan, S. (2015). *The psychology of the language learner revisited.* New York, NY: Routledge.

Doughty, C. (1994). Fine-tuning of feedback by competent speakers to language learners. In J. E. Alatis (Ed.), *Georgetown University Round Table on Languages and Linguistics 1993* (pp. 96–108). Washington, DC: Georgetown University Press.

———. (2001). Cognitive underpinnings of focus on form. In P. Robinson (Ed.), *Cognition and second language instruction* (pp. 206–257). Cambridge: Cambridge University Press.

Doughty, C. & Pica, T. (1986). "Information gap" tasks: Do they facilitate second language acquisition? *TESOL Quarterly, 20*, 305–325.

Doughty, C., & Varela, E. (1998). Communicative focus on form. In C. Doughty & J. Williams (Eds.), *Focus on Form in Classroom Second Language Acquisition* (pp. 114–138). New York: Cambridge University Press.

Doughty, C., & Williams, J. (1998). Pedagogical choice in focus on form. In C. Doughty & J. Williams (Eds.), *Focus on Form in Classroom Second Language Acquisition* (pp. 197–262). New York: Cambridge University Press.

Egi, T. (2007a). Interpreting recasts as linguistic evidence. *Studies in Second Language Acquisition, 29*, 511–537.

———. (2007b). Recasts, learners' interpretations, and L2 development. In A. Mackey (Ed.), *Conversational interaction in second language acquisition: A collection of empirical studies* (pp. 249–267). Oxford: Oxford University Press.

Egi, T. (2010). Uptake, modified output, and learner perceptions of recasts: learner responses as language awareness. *The Modern Language Journal, 94*, 1–21.

Ekman, P. & Friesen, W. V. (1969). The repertoire of nonverbal behaviour: Categories, origins, usage, and coding. *Semiotica, 1*(1), 49–98.

Ellis, N. C. (2002). Frequency effects in language processing. *Studies in Second Language Acquisition*, 24, 143–188.

———. (2005). At the interface: dynamic interactions of explicit and implicit language knowledge. *Studies in Second Language Acquisition*, 27, 305–352.

Ellis, R. (2001). Non-reciprocal tasks, comprehension, and second language acquisition. In M. Bygate, P. Skehan, & M. Swain (Eds.), *Researching pedagogic tasks: Second language learning, teaching, and testing.* Harlow: Pearson.

———. (2006). Researching the effects of form-focussed instruction on L2 acquisition. *AILA Review, 19*, 18–41.

———. (2008). *The study of second language acquisition* (2 ed.). Oxford: Oxford University Press.

———. (2008b). Learner beliefs and language learning. *Asian EFL Journal, 10*(4), 7–25.

———. (2012). *Language teaching research and language pedagogy*. Oxford: Wiley Blackwell.

———. (2015). *Understanding Second Language Acquisition* (2nd ed.). Oxford, UK: Oxford University Press.

———. (2017). Oral corrective feedback in L2 classrooms: What we know so far. In H. Nassaji & E. Kartchava (Eds.), *Corrective Feedback in Second Language Teaching and Learning: Research, Theory, Applications, Implications* (pp. 3–18). Oxon, UK: Routledge.

Ellis, R., Basturkmen, H., & Loewen, S. (2001). Learner uptake in communicative ESL lessons. *Language Learning, 51*, 218–318.

Ellis, R., Loewen, S. & Erlam, R. (2006). Implicit and explicit corrective feedback and the acquisition of L2 grammar. *Studies in Second Language Acquisition, 28*, 339–368.

Ellis, R. & Sheen, Y. (2006). Re-examining the role of recasts in L2 acquisition. *Studies in Second Language Acquisition, 28*, 575–600.

Ericsson, K. A. & Simon, H. A. (1993). *Protocol analysis: verbal reports as data* (revised edition). Cambridge, MA: Bradford Books/MIT Press.

Fanselow, J. (1977). The treatment of error in oral work. *Foreign Language Annals, 10*, 583–593.

Farrar, M. J. (1990). Discourse and the acquisition of grammatical morphemes. *Journal of Child Language, 17*, 607–624.

———. (1992). Negative evidence and grammatical morpheme acquisition. *Developmental Psychology, 28*, 90–98.

Flevares, L. M. & Perry, M. (2001). How many do you see? The use of nonspoken representations in first-grade mathematics lessons. *Journal of Educational Psychology, 93*, 330–345.

Foster, P. (1998). A classroom perspective on the negotiation of meaning. *Applied Linguistics, 19*, 1–23.

Fox, C. A. (1993). Communicative competence and beliefs about language among graduate teaching assistants in French. *Modern Language Journal, 77*, 313–324.

Fujii, A., Ziegler, N., & Mackey, A. (2016). Peer interaction and metacognitive instruction in the EFL classroom. In M. Sato & S. Ballinger (Eds.), *Peer interaction and second language learning: Pedagogical potential and research agenda* (pp. 63–89). Amsterdam: John Benjamins.

Gagné, F. (1979). Étude de la perception par des enseignants et des étudiants des divers éléments de compétence des enseignants du niveau collégial. Unpublished doctoral dissertation, University of Montreal, Canada.

Gardner, R. C., & MacIntyre, P. D. (1992). A student's contributions to second language learning. Part I: Cognitive variables. *Language Teaching, 25*, 211–220.

Gass, S. M. (1997). *Input, interaction and the second language learner*. Mahwah, NJ: Lawrence Erlbaum.

———. (2003). Input and interaction. In C. Doughty & M. Long (Eds.), *The handbook of second language acquisition* (pp. 224–255). MA; Blackwell Publishing.

Gass, S. M., & Mackey, A. (2000). *Stimulated Recall Methodology in Second Language Research*. Mahwah, NJ: Lawrence Erlbaum Associates.

———. (2015). Input, interaction and output in second language acquisition. In B. VanPatten & J. Williams (Eds.), *Theories in second language acquisition: An introduction, 2nd edition* (pp. 180–206). New York, NY: Routledge.
Gass, S. M. & Selinker, L. (2001). *Second Language Acquisition: An Introductory Course* (2nd ed.). Mahwah, New Jersey: Lawrence Erlbaum Associates, Inc.
Gass, S. M. & Varonis, E. (1994). Input, interaction and second language production. *Studies in Second Language Acquisition, 16*, 283–302.
Gatbonton, E. (1994). *Bridge to fluency: Speaking (Book 1)*. Scarborough, Ontario: Prentice-Hall Canada Inc.
Goldin-Meadow, S., Cook, S. W., & Mitchell, Z. A. (2009). Gesturing gives children new ideas about math. *Psychological Science, 20*, 267–272.
Goldin-Meadow, S. & Sandhofer, C. M. (1999). Gesture conveys substantive information to ordinary listeners. *Developmental Science, 2*, 67–74.
Goo, J. (2012). Corrective feedback and working memory capacity in interaction-driven L2 learning. *Studies in Second Language Acquisition, 34*, 445–474.
Goo, J. & Mackey, A. (2013). The case against the case against recasts. *Studies in Second Language Acquisition, 35*, 127–165.
Good, T. & Brophy, J. (2000). *Looking in classrooms* (5th ed.). New York, NY: Harper Collins.
Green, A. (1998). *Verbal protocol analysis in language testing research: A handbook*. Cambridge, UK: Cambridge University Press.
Gregersen, T. and MacIntyre, P. D. (2014). *Capitalizing on language learners' individuality: From premise to practice*. Bristol: Multilingual Matters.
———. (2017). *Optimizing language learners' nonverbal behaviour: From tenet to technique*. Bristol, UK: Multilingual Matters.
Gullberg, M, (2008). Gestures and second language acquisition. In P. Robinson & N. C. Ellis (Eds.), *Handbook of cognitive linguistics and second language acquisition* (pp. 276–305). London: Routledge.
———. (2010). Methodological reflections on gesture analysis in second language acquisition and bilingualism research. *Second Language Research, 26*(1), 75–102.
Gurzynski-Weiss, L. & Baralt, M. (2014). Exploring learner perception and use of task-based interactional feedback in FTF and CMC modes. *Studies in Second Language Acquisition, 36*(1), 1–37.
Hall, G. (2011). *Exploring English language teaching: Language in action*. New York: Routledge.
Han, Z. (2002). A study of the impact of recasts on tense consistency in L2 output. *TESOL Quarterly, 36* (4), 543–572.
———. (2008). On the role of meaning in focus on form. In Z. Han (Ed.), *Understanding second language process* (pp. 45–79). Clevedon, UK: Multilingual Matters.
Harley, B., & Swain, M. (1984). The interlanguage of immersion students and its implications for second language teaching. In A. Davies, C. Criper, & A. Howatt (Eds.), *Interlanguage* (pp. 291–311). Edinburgh: Edinburgh University Press.
Harmer, J. (2007). *The practice of English language teaching* (4 ed.). London: Longman.
Hattie, J. & Timperley, H. (2007). The power of feedback. *Review of Educational Research, 77*(1), 81–112.

Havranek, G. (1999). The effectiveness of corrective feedback: Preliminary results of an empirical study. *Acquisition et Interaction en Language Étrangère, 2,* 189–206.

Hawkes, L. & Nassaji, H. (2016). The role of extensive recasts in error detection and correction by adult ESL students. *Studies in Second Language Learning and Teaching, 6,* 19–41.

Hedge, T. (2000). *Teaching and learning in the language classroom.* Oxford: Oxford University Press.

Heift, R. & Hegelheimer, V. (2017). Computer-assisted corrective feedback and language learning. In H. Nassaji & E. Kartchava (Eds.), *Corrective Feedback in Second Language Teaching and Learning: Research, Theory, Applications, Implications* (pp. 51–65). Oxon, UK: Routledge.

Hendrickson, J. M. (1978). Error correction in foreign language teaching: Recent theory, research, and practice. *The Modern Language Journal, 62*(8), 387–398.

———. (1980). The treatment of error in written work. *The Modern Language Journal, 64,* 216–221.

Hertel, T. J. (2003). Lexical and discourse factors in second language acquisition of Spanish word order. *Second Language Research, 19,* 273–304.

Horwitz, E. K. (1985). Using student beliefs about language learning and teaching in the foreign language methods course. *Foreign Language Annals, 18*(4), 333–340.

———. (1987). Surveying student beliefs about language teaming. In: Wenden, A. L., Robin, J. (Eds.), *Learner strategies in language learning* (pp. 119–132). Prentice Hall, London.

———. (1988). The beliefs about language learning of beginning university foreign language students. *The Modern Language Journal, 72*(3), 283–294.

———. (1990). Attending to the affective domain in the foreign language classroom. In S. Magnan (Ed.), *Shifting the instructional focus to the learner* (pp. 15–33). Middlebury, VT: Northeast Conference on the Teaching of Foreign Languages.

———. (1999). Cultural and situational influences on foreign language learners' beliefs about language learning: a review of BALLI studies. *System, 27*(4), 557–576.

———. (2015). Beliefs about language learning and the experience of second language learning: Asking useful questions about language learning. In H. M. McGarrell & D. Wood (eds.), *CONTACT—Refereed Proceedings of TESL Ontario Research Symposium, 41*(2), 20–30.

Hulstijn, J. H., Young, R. F., Ortega, L., Bigelow, M., DeKeyser, R., Ellis, N. C., Lantolf, J. P., Mackey, A., & Talmy, S. (2014). Bridging the gap: Cognitive and social approaches to research in second language learning and teaching. *Studies in Second Language Acquisition, 36*(1), 1–61.

Isaacs, T. & Trofimovich, P. (2012). Deconstructing comprehensibility: Identifying the linguistic influences on listeners' L2 comprehensibility ratings. *Studies in Second Language Acquisition, 34*(3), 475–505.

Ishida, M. (2004). Effects of recasts on the acquisition of the aspectual form of *–te i (ru)* by learners of Japanese as a foreign language. *Language Learning, 54,* 311–394.

Iwashita, N. (2001). The effect of learner proficiency on interactional moves and modified output in nonnative–nonnative interaction in Japanese as a foreign language. *System, 29*(2), 267–287.

Iwashita, N. (2003). Negative feedback and positive evidence in task-based interaction: Differential effects of L2 development. *Studies in Second Language Acquisition, 25*(1), 1–36.

Izumi, S. (2002). Output, input enhancement and the noticing hypothesis: An experimental study on ESL relativization. *Studies in Second Language Acquisition, 24*, 541–577.

Jean, G. & Simard. D. (2011). Grammar learning in English and French L2: Students' and teachers' beliefs and perceptions. *Foreign Language Annals, 44*(3), 467–494.

Kamiya, N. & Loewen, S. (2014). The influence of academic articles on an ESL teacher's stated beliefs. *Innovation in Language Learning and Teaching, 8*(3), 205–218.

Kartchava, E. (in press). The role of training in feedback provision and effectiveness. In H. Nassaji & E. Kartchava (Eds.), The Cambridge Handbook of Corrective Feedback in Language Learning and Teaching. Cambridge University Press.

———. (2012). Noticeability of corrective feedback, L2 development, and learners' beliefs. Unpublished doctoral dissertation, Université de Montréal, Canada.

———. (2013). The place of corrective feedback within the major SLA theories. *US-China Foreign Language, 11*(2), 136–151.

———. (2016). Learner beliefs about corrective feedback in the language classroom: Perspectives from two international contexts. *TESL Canada Journal, 33*(2), 19–45.

Kartchava, E. & Ammar, A. (2013). Noticing and learning: Relationship patterns. *Study in English Language Teaching, 1*(1), 8–25.

———. (2014a). The noticeability and effectiveness of corrective feedback in relation to target type. *Language Teaching Research, 18*(4), 428–452.

———. (2014b). Learners' beliefs as mediators of what is noticed and learned in the language classroom. *TESOL Quarterly, 48*(1), 86–109.

Kelly, S. D., Barr, D. J., Breckinridge Church, R., & Lynch, K. (1999). Offering a hand to pragmatic understanding: The role of speech and gesture in comprehension and memory. *Journal of Memory and Language, 40*, 577–592.

Kern, R. G. (1995). Students' and teachers' beliefs about language learning. *Foreign Language Annals, 28*, 71–92.

Kim, Y. (2013). Effects of pretask modeling on attention to form and question development. *TESOL Quarterly, 47*(1), 8–35.

Kim, J. H. & Han, Z. (2007). Recasts in communicative EFL classes: do teacher intent and learner interpretation overlap? In A. Mackey (Ed.), *Conversational interaction in second language acquisition: A collection of empirical studies* (pp. 269–297). Oxford: Oxford University Press.

Knapp, M. L. & Hall, J. A. (2010). *Nonverbal communication in human interaction* (7th ed.). Belmont, CA: Wadsworth, Cengage Learning.

Kramsch, C. (2003). Metaphor and the subjective construction of beliefs. In P. Kalaja & A. M. F. Barcelos (Eds.), *Beliefs about SLA: New research approaches* (pp. 109–128). Kluwer Academic Press, Dordrecht.

Krashen, S. (1981). *Second language acquisition and second language learning*. Oxford: Pergamon.

———. (1982). *Principles and practice in second language acquisition*. Englewood Cliffs, NJ: Prentice-Hall.

Krashen, S. (1985). *The Input Hypothesis: Issues and implications*. New York: Longman.
Kulhavy, R. W. (1977). Feedback in written instruction. *Review of Educational Research, 47*(1), 211–232.
Lantolf, J. P. (1996). SLA theory building: "Letting all the flowers bloom!" *Language Learning, 46*(4), 713–749.
Larsen-Freeman, D., & Long, M. H. (1991). *An introduction to second language acquisition research*. New York, NY: Longman.
Lasagabaster, D. & Sierra, J. M. (2005). Error correction: Students' versus teachers' perceptions. *Language Awareness, 14*, 112–127.
Lazarton, A. (2004). Gesture and speech in the vocabulary explanations of one ESL teacher: A microanalytic inquiry. *Language Learning, 54*, 79–117.
Leeman, J. (2003). Recasts and second language development: Beyond negative evidence. *Studies in Second Language Acquisition, 25*, 35–63.
———. (2007). Feedback in L2 learning: Responding to errors during practice. In R. M. DeKeyser (Ed.), *Practice in second language: Perspectives from applied linguistics and cognitive psychology* (pp. 111–137). New York, NY: Cambridge University Press.
Leif, J. (1987). Croyance et connaissance. *Savoir et pouvoir*. Les editions E S F, Paris.
Leow, R. P. (1997). Attention, awareness, and foreign language learning. *Language Learning, 47*, 467–506.
———. (1998). The effects of amount and type of exposure on adult learners' L2 development in SLA. *Modern Language Journal, 82*, 49–68.
———. (2001). Attention, awareness, and foreign language behavior. *Language Learning, 51*, 113–155.
———. (2015). *Explicit learning in the L2 classroom: A student-centered approach*. Oxon, UK: Routledge.
Levelt, W. (1983). Monitoring and self-repair in speech. *Cognition, 14*, 41–104.
Li, S. (2010). The effectiveness of corrective feedback in SLA: A meta-analysis. *Language Learning, 60*, 309–365.
———. (2013). The interactions between the effects of implicit and explicit feedback and individual differences in language analytic ability and working memory. *The Modern Language Journal, 97*, 634–654.
———. (2017). Student and teacher beliefs and attitudes about oral corrective feedback. In H. Nassaji & E. Kartchava (Eds.), *Corrective Feedback in Second Language Teaching and Learning: Research, Theory, Applications, Implications* (pp. 143–157). Oxon, UK: Routledge.
Lightbown, P. M. (1998). The importance of timing in focus on form. In C. Doughty & J. Williams (Eds.), *Focus on form in classroom second language acquisition* (pp. 177–196). New York: Cambridge University Press.
———. (2008). Transfer appropriate processing as a model for classroom second language acquisition. In Z. Han (Ed.), *Understanding second language process* (pp. 27–44). Bristol, UK: Multilingual Matters.
Lightbown, P. M., & Spada, N. (1990). Focus-on-form and corrective feedback in communicative language teaching: Effects on second language learning. *Studies in Second Language Acquisition, 12*, 429–448.

———. (1994). An innovative program for primary ESL in Quebec. *TESOL Quarterly, 28,* 563–573.

———. (2006). *How Languages are Learned* (3rd ed.). Oxford: Oxford University Press.

———. (2013). *How Languages are Learned* (4th ed.). Oxford: Oxford University Press.

Little, D., & Singleton, D. (1990). Cognitive style and learning approach. In R. Duda & P. Riley (Eds.), *Learning styles* (pp. 11–19). Nancy, France: University of Nancy.

Lochtman, K. (2002). Oral corrective feedback in the foreign language classroom: how it affects interaction in analytic foreign language teaching. *International Journal of Educational Research, 37* (3/4), 271–283.

Loewen, S. (2004). Uptake in incidental focus on form in meaning-focused ESL lessons. *Language Learning, 54,* 153–188.

———. (2005). Incidental focus on form and second language learning. *Studies in Second Language Acquisition, 27,* 361–386.

———. (2015). *Introduction to instructed second language acquisition.* New York, NY: Routledge.

Loewen, S., Li, S., Fei, F., Thompson, A., Nakatsukasa, K., Ahn, S., & Chen, X. (2009). Second language learners' beliefs about grammar instruction and error correction. *The Modern Language Journal, 93,* 91–104.

Loewen, S., & Philp, J. (2006). Recasts in the adult L2 classroom: characteristics, explicitness and effectiveness. *Modern Language Journal, 90,* 536–556.

Long, M. (1983). Native speaker/non-native speaker conversation and negotiation of comprehensible input. *Applied Linguistics, 4*(2), 126–141.

———. (1991). Focus on form: A design feature in language teaching methodology. In K. de Bot, R. Ginsberg, & C. Kramsch (Eds.), *Foreign language research in cross-cultural perspective* (pp. 39–52). Amsterdam: John Benjamins.

———. (1996). The role of the linguistic environment in second language acquisition. In W. C. Ritchie & T. K. Bhatia (Eds.), *Handbook Of Language Acquisition: Vol. 2. Second Language Acquisition* (pp. 413–468). New York: Academic Press.

———. (2006). *Problems in SLA.* New York, NY: Lawrence Erlbaum Associates.

———. (2017). Instructed second language acquisition (ISLA): Geopolitics, methodological issues, and some major research questions. *Instructed Second Language Acquisition, 1*(1), 7–44.

Long, M., Inagaki, S., & Ortega, L. (1998). The role of implicit negative feedback in SLA: Models and recasts in Japanese and Spanish. *The Modern Language Journal, 82*(3), 357–371.

Long, M. H., & Robinson, P. (1998). Focus on form: Theory, research, and practice. In C. Doughty & J. Williams (Eds.), *Focus on Form in Classroom Second Language Acquisition* (pp. 15–41). New York: Cambridge University Press.

Lyster, R. (1998a). Recasts, repetition, and ambiguity in L2 classroom discourse. *Studies in Second Language Acquisition, 20,* 51–81.

———. (1998b). Negotiation of form, recasts and explicit correction in relation to error types and learner repair in immersion classrooms. *Language Learning, 48,* 183–218.

———. (1999). La négociation de la forme: la suite . . . mais pas la fin. *The Canadian Modern Language Review/La Revue canadienne des langues vivantes, 55*(3), 355–381.

———. (2002). Negotiation in immersion teacher-student interaction. *International Journal of Educational Research, 37*, 237–253.

———. (2004). Differential effects of prompts and recasts on form-focused instruction. *Studies in Second Language Acquisition, 26*, 399–432.

Lyster, R., & Izquierdo, J. (2009). Prompts versus recasts in dyadic interaction. *Language Learning, 59*(2), 453–498.

Lyster, R., Lightbown, P. M., & Spada, N. (1999). A response to Truscott's "What's wrong with oral grammar correction." *Canadian Modern Language Review, 55*, 457–467.

Lyster, R., & Mori, H. (2006). Interactional feedback and instructional counterbalance. *Studies in Second Language Acquisition, 28*, 269–300.

Lyster, R. & Ranta, L. (1997). Corrective feedback and learner uptake: Negotiation of form in communicative classrooms. *Studies in Second Language Acquisition, 19*, 37–66.

———. (2013). Counterpoint piece: The case for variety in corrective feedback research. *Studies in Second Language Acquisition, 35*, 167–184.

Lyster, R. & Saito, K. (2010). Oral feedback in classroom SLA. *Studies in Second Language Acquisition, 32*, 265–302.

Lyster, R., Saito, K., & Sato, M. (2013). Oral corrective feedback in second language classrooms. *Language Teaching, 46*, 1–40.

Macedonia, M. & Klimesch, W. (2014). Long-term effects of gestures on memory for foreign language words trained in the classroom. *Mind, Brain, and Education, 8*(2), 74–88.

Mackey, A. (1999). Input, interaction, and second language development: an empirical study of question formation in ESL. *Studies in Second Language Acquisition, 21*(4), 557–587.

———. (2006). Feedback, noticing and instructed second language learning. *Applied Linguistics, 27*(3), 405–430.

Mackey, A., & Gass, S. (2006). Pushing the methodological boundaries in interaction research: An introduction to the special issue. *Studies in Second Language Acquisition, 28*, 169–178.

———. (2016). *Second Language Research: Methodology and Design* (2nd ed.). New York, NY: Routledge.

Mackey, A., Gass, S. M. & McDonough, K. (2000). How do learners perceive implicit negative feedback? *Studies in Second Language Acquisition, 22*, 471–497.

Mackey, A. & Goo, J. (2007). Interaction research in SLA: A meta-analysis and research synthesis. In A. Mackey (Ed.), *Conversational interaction in second language acquisition: A collection of empirical studies* (pp. 407–452). Oxford: Oxford University Press.

Mackey, A., & Oliver, R. (2002). Interactional feedback and children's L2 development. *System, 30*, 459–477.

Mackey, A., Oliver, R., & Leeman, J. (2003), Interactional Input and the Incorporation of Feedback: An Exploration of NS–NNS and NNS–NNS Adult and Child Dyads. *Language Learning, 53*, 35–66.

Mackey, A. & Philp, J. (1998). Conversational interaction and second language development: Recasts, responses, and red herrings? *The Modern Language Journal, 82*, 338–356.

Mackey, A., Philp, J., Egi, T., Fujii, A. & Tasumi, T. (2002). Individual differences in working memory, noticing of interactional feedback in L2 development. In P. Robinson (Ed.), *Individual differences and instructed language learning* (pp. 181–209). Amsterdam: John Benjamins Publishing Company.

Mantle-Bromley, C. (1995). Positive attitudes and realistic beliefs: Links to proficiency. *The Modern Language Journal, 79*, 372–386.

McDonough, K. (2005). Identifying the impact of negative feedback and learners' responses on ESL development. *Studies in Second Language Acquisition, 27*(1), 79–103.

———. (2007). Interactional feedback and the emergence of simple past activity verbs in L2 English. In A. Mackey (Ed.), *Conversational interaction in second language acquisition: A series of empirical studies*. Oxford: Oxford University Press.

McDonough, K. & Mackey, A. (2006). Responses to recasts: repetitions, primed production and linguistic development. *Language Learning, 56*(4), 693–720.

McLaughlin, B. (1987). *Theories of second language learning*. London, UK: Edward Arnold.

McNeill, D. (1992). *Hand and mind: What gestures reveal about thought?* Chicago, IL: The University of Chicago Press.

McNeill, D. & Duncan, S. D. (2000). Growth points in thinking-for-speaking. In D. McNeill (Ed.), *Language and gesture* (pp. 141–161). Cambridge: Cambridge University Press.

Mito, K. (1993). The effects of modeling and recasting on the acquisition of L2 grammar rules. Unpublished manuscript, University of Hawai'i at Manoa.

Mohamed Hassan Mohamed, R. (2011). *Les croyances des enseignants et des apprenants* adultes quant à la rétroaction corrective à l'oral et la pratique réelle en classe de français langue étrangère en Égypte. *Unpublished doctoral dissertation, Université de Montréal, Canada.*

Mori, Y. (1999). Epistemological beliefs and language learning beliefs: What do language learners believe about their learning? *Language Learning, 49*, 377–415.

Morgan, J. L., Bonamo, K. M., & Travis, L. L. (1995). Negative evidence on negative evidence. *Developmental Psychology, 31*, 180–197.

Muranoi, H. (2000). Focus on form through interaction enhancement: Integrating formal instruction into a communicative task in EFL classrooms. *Language Learning, 50*, 617–673.

Nabei, T., & Swain, M. (2002). Learner awareness of recasts in classroom interaction: A case study of an adult EFL student's second language learning. *Language Awareness, 11*(1), 43–63.

Nakatsukasa, K. (2016). Efficacy of recasts and gestures on the acquisition of locative prepositions. *Studies in Second Language Acquisition, 38*, 771–799.

Nakatsukasa, K. & Loewen, S. (2017). Non-verbal feedback. In H. Nassaji & E. Kartchava (Eds.), *Corrective Feedback in Second Language Teaching and Learning: Research, Theory, Applications, Implications* (pp. 158–173). Oxon, UK: Routledge.

Nassaji, H. (2009). Effects of recasts and elicitations in dyadic interaction and the role of feedback explicitness. *Language Learning, 59*, 411–452.

———. (2011a). Correcting students' written grammatical errors: The effects of negotiated versus nonnegotiated feedback. *Studies in Second Language Learning and Teaching, 1*, 315–334.

———. (2011b). Immediate learner repair and its relationship with learning targeted forms in dyadic interaction. *System, 39*, 17–29.

———. (2013). Participation structure and incidental focus on form in adult ESL classrooms. *Language Learning, 63*, 835–869.

———. (2015). *The interactional feedback dimension in instructed second language learning: Linking theory, research, and practice.* London: Bloomsbury.

———. (2016). Anniversary article. Interactional feedback in second language teaching and learning: A synthesis and analysis of current research. *Language Teaching Research, 20*(4), 535–562.

———. (2017). The effectiveness of extensive versus intensive recasts for learning L2 grammar. *The Modern Language Journal, 101*(2), 353–368.

Nassaji, H. & Kartchava, E. (Eds.) (in press). *The Cambridge Handbook of Corrective Feedback in Language Learning and Teaching.* Cambridge University Press.

Nassaji, H. & Kartchava, E. (Eds.) (2017). *Corrective Feedback in Second Language Teaching and Learning: Research, Theory, Applications, Implications.* Oxon, UK: Routledge.

Nassaji, H., & Kartchava, E. (2017b). Conclusion, reflections, and final remarks. In H. Nassaji & E. Kartchava (Eds.), *Corrective Feedback in Second Language Teaching and Learning: Research, Theory, Applications, Implications* (pp. 174–182). Oxon, UK: Routledge.

Netten, J. (1991). Towards a more language oriented second language classroom. In L. Malav & G. Duquette (Eds.), *Language, culture and cognition* (pp. 284–304). Clevedon, UK: Multilingual Matters.

Nicholas, H., Lightbown, P. M., & Spada, N. (2001). Recasts as feedback to language learners. *Language Learning, 51*, 719–758.

Nisbett, R., & Ross, L. (1980). *Human inferences: Strategies and shortcomings of social judgment.* Englewood Cliffs, NJ: Prentice-Hall.

Nobuyoshi, J., & Ellis, R. (1993). Focused communication tasks and second language acquisition. *ELT Journal, 47*, 719–758.

Norris, J., & Ortega, L. (2000). Effectiveness of L2 instruction: A research synthesis and quantitative meta-analysis. *Language Learning, 50*, 417–528.

Ohta, A. (2000). Rethinking recasts: A learner-centered examination of corrective feedback in Japanese classroom. In J. K. Hall & L. Verplaeste (Eds.), *The construction of second and foreign language learning through classroom interaction* (pp. 47–71). Mahwah, NJ: Erlbaum.

———. (2001). *Second language acquisition processes in the classroom: Learning Japanese*. Mahwah, NJ: Lawrence Erlbaum Associates.

Oliver, R. (1995). Negative feedback in child NS-NNS conversation. *Studies in Second Language Acquisition, 17*, 459–481.

———. (2000). Age differences in negotiation and feedback in classroom and pair work. *Language Learning, 50*, 119–151.

O'Neill, D. K., Topolovec, J. & Stern-Cavalcante, W. (2002). Feeling sponginess: The importance of descriptive gestures in 2- and 3-year-old children's acquisition of adjectives. *Journal of Cognition and Development, 33*, 243–277.

Ortega, L. (2007b). Meaningful L2 practice in foreign language classrooms: A cognitive-interactionist SLA perspective. In R. DeKeyser (Ed.), *Practice in a second language: Perspectives from applied linguistics and cognitive psychology* (pp. 180–207). New York, NY: Cambridge University Press.

———. (2009). *Understanding second language acquisition*. London, UK: Hodder Education.

Pallant, J. (2007). *SPSS Survival Manual* (3rd ed.). London, UK: Open University Press.

Panova, I. & Lyster, R. (2002). Patterns of corrective feedback and uptake in an adult ESL classroom. *TESOL Quarterly, 36*, 573–595.

Peacock, M. (1999). Beliefs about language learning and their relationship to proficiency. *International Journal of Applied Linguistics, 9*(2), 247–265.

———. (2001). Pre-service ESL teachers' beliefs about second language learning: A longitudinal study. *System, 29*, 177–195.

Pennycook, A. (1985). Actions speak louder than words: Paralanguage, communication, and education. *TESOL Quarterly, 19*, 259–282.

Philp, J. (2003). Constraints on "noticing the gap": Nonnative speakers; noticing of recasts in NS-NNS interaction. *Studies in Second Language Acquisition, 25*, 99–126.

Pica, T. (1992). The textual outcomes of native speaker/non-native speaker negotiation: what do they really reveal about second language learning? In C. Kramsch & S. McConnell-Ginet (Eds.), *Text in context: crossdisciplinary perspectives on language study* (pp. 198–237). Lexington, MA: D. C. Heath.

———. (1994). Research on negotiation: What does it reveal about second-language learning conditions, processes, and outcomes? *Language Learning, 44*(3), 493–527.

Pienemann, M., & Johnston, M. (1987). Factors influencing the development of language proficiency. In D. Nunan (Ed.), *Applying Second Language Acquisition Research*, Adelaide, Austria: National Curriculum Resource Centre, Adult Migrant Education Program.

Prudie, N., Hattie, J., & Douglas, G. (1996). Student conceptions of learning and their use of self-regulated learning strategies: A cross-cultural comparison. *Journal of Educational Psychology, 88*, 87–100.

Quinn, P. G. & Nakata, T. (2017). The timing of oral corrective feedback. In H. Nassaji & E. Kartchava (Eds.), *Corrective Feedback in Second Language Teaching and Learning: Research, Theory, Applications, Implications* (pp. 35–47). Oxon, UK: Routledge.

Ranta, L., & Lyster, R. (2007). A cognitive approach to improving immersion students' oral language abilities: The awareness-practice-feedback sequence. In R. DeKeyser (Ed.), *Practice in second language: Perspectives from applied linguistics and cognitive psychology* (pp. 141–160). New York: Cambridge University Press.

Rassaei, E. (2013). Corrective feedback, learners' perceptions, and second language development. *System, 41*, 472–483.

Richmond, V. P., McCroskey, J. C., & Hickson, M. L. (2012). *Nonverbal behavior in interpersonal relations.* Boston, MA: Allyn & Bacon.

Roberts, L. (2012). Psycholinguistic techniques and resources in second language acquisition research. *Second Language Research, 28*, 113–127.

Roberts, M. (1995). Awareness and the efficacy of error correction. In R. Schmidt (Ed.), *Attention and awareness in foreign language learning.* Honolulu: University of Hawai'i Press.

Robinson, P. (1995). Attention, memory and the "Noticing Hypothesis." *Language Learning, 45*, 283–331.

———. (2001). Individual differences, cognitive abilities, aptitude complexes, and learning conditions in second language acquisition. *Second Language Research, 17*, 368–392.

———. (2002). Learning conditions, aptitude complexes, and SLA: a framework for research and pedagogy. In P. Robinson (Ed.), *Individual differences and instructed language learning* (pp. 113–133). Amsterdam: John Benjamins.

———. (2003). Attention and memory during SLA. In C. Doughty & M. H. Long (Eds.), *Handbook of second language acquisition* (pp. 631–678). Oxford: Blackwell.

Robinson, P. & Gilabert, R. (2007). Task complexity, the Cognition Hypothesis and second language learning and performance. *IRAL—International Review of Applied Linguistics in Language Teaching, 45*(3), 161–176.

Rokeach, M. (1968). *Beliefs, attitudes, and values: A theory of organization and change.* San Francisco, CA: Jossey-Bass.

Rosa, E. M., & Leow, R. P. (2004). Awareness, different learning conditions, and second language development. *Applied Psycholinguistics, 25*, 269–292.

Russell, J., & Spada, N. (2006). The effectiveness of corrective feedback for second language acquisition: A meta-analysis of the research. In J. Norris & L. Ortega (Eds.), *Synthesizing research on language learning and teaching* (pp. 131–164). Amsterdam: Benjamins.

Sagarra, N. & Abbuhl, R. (2013). Optimizing the noticing of recasts via computer-delivered feedback: Evidence that oral input enhancement and working memory help second language learning. *The Modern Language Journal, 97*, 196–216.

Saito, K. & Lyster, R. (2012). Effects of form-focused instruction and corrective feedback on L2 pronunciation development of /ɹ/ by Japanese Learners of English. *Language Learning, 62*(2), 595–633.

Salaberry, R. (2000). *The development of past tense morphology in L2 Spanish.* Amsterdam: Benjamins.

Sarkar, M. (2004). Language education policy in Quebec: Access to which majority language and for whom? In S. May, M. Franken, & R. Barnard (Eds.), *LED2003:*

Refereed conference proceedings of the 1st International Conference on Language, Education and Diversity. Hamilton, New Zealand: University of Waikato, Wilf Malcolm Institute of Educational Research.

Sato, C. J. (1990). *The syntax of conversation in interlanguage development*. Tubingen: Gunter Narr.

Sato, M. (2013). Beliefs about peer interaction and peer corrective feedback: Efficacy of classroom interaction. *The Modern Language Journal, 97*(3), 611–633.

———. (2017). Oral peer corrective feedback: Multiple theoretical perspectives. In H. Nassaji & E. Kartchava (Eds.), *Corrective Feedback in Second Language Teaching and Learning: Research, Theory, Applications, Implications* (pp. 19–34). Oxon, UK: Routledge.

Sato, M. & Ballinger, S. (2012). Raising language awareness in peer interaction: A cross-context, cross-method examination. *Language Awareness, 21*(1–2), 157–179.

Sawyer, M., & Ranta, L. (2001). Aptitude, individual differences and instructional design. In P. Robinson (Ed.), *Cognition and second language instruction* (pp. 319–353). Cambridge: Cambridge University Press.

Saxton, M. (1997). The contrast theory of negative input. *Journal of Child Language, 24*, 139–161.

Schachter, J. (1981). The hand signal system. *TESOL Quarterly, 15*(2), 125–138.

Schmidt, R. (1983). Interaction, acculturation, and the acquisition of communicative competence. In N. Wolfson & E. Judd (Eds.), *Sociolinguistics and language acquisition* (pp. 137–174). Rowley, MA: Newbury House.

———. (1990). The role of consciousness in second language learning. *Applied Linguistics, 11*, 129–158.

———. (1993). Awareness and second language acquisition. *Annual Review of Applied Linguistics, 13*, 206–226.

———. (1994). Deconstructing consciousness in search of useful definitions for applied linguistics. *AILA Review, 11*, 11–26.

———. (1995). Consciousness and foreign language learning: A tutorial on the role of attention and awareness in learning. In R. Schmidt (Ed.), *Attention and awareness in foreign language learning* (pp. 1–63). Honolulu: Hawaii: University of Hawaii, Second Language Teaching and Curriculum Center.

———. (2001). Attention. In P. Robinson (Ed.), *Cognition and second language instruction* (pp. 3–32), Cambridge: Cambridge University Press.

Schmidt, R., & Frota, S. (1986). Developing basic conversational ability in second language: A case study of an adult learner of Portuguese. In R. Day (Ed.), *Talking to learn: Conversation in second language acquisition* (pp. 237–326). Rowley, MA: Newbury House.

Schulz, R. A. (1996). Focus on form in the foreign language classroom: students' and teachers' views on error correction and the role of grammar. *Foreign Language Annals, 29*(3), 343–364.

———. (2001). Cultural differences in student and teacher perceptions concerning the role of grammar instruction and corrective feedback: USA—Columbia. *The Modern Language Journal, 85*(2), 244–258.

Schumann, F., & Schumann, J. (1977). Diary of a language learner: An introspective study of second language learning. In H. D. Brown, C. Yorio, & R. Crymes (Eds.), *Teaching and learning English as a second language: Trends in research and practice* (pp. 241–249). Washington, DC: TESOL.

Schwartz, B. (1993). On explicit and negative data effecting and affecting competence and linguistic behavior. *Studies in Second Language Acquisition, 15*, 147–163.

Segalowitz, N. (2003). Automaticity and second languages. In C. Doughty & M. H. Long (Eds.), *Handbook of second language acquisition* (pp. 382–408). Maiden, MA: Blackwell.

Seliger, H. W. & Shohamy, E. (1989). *Second Language Research Methods*. Oxford: Oxford University Press.

Sheen, Y. (2004). Corrective feedback and learner uptake in communicative classrooms across instructional settings. *Language Teaching Research, 8*, 263–300.

———. (2006). Exploring the relationship between characteristics of recasts and learner uptake. *Language Teaching Research, 10*, 361–392.

———. (2007). The effects of corrective feedback, language aptitude, and learner attitudes on the acquisition of English articles. In A. Mackey (Ed.), *Conversational interaction in second language acquisition: A collection of empirical studies* (pp. 301–322). Oxford: Oxford University Press.

———. (2008). Recasts, language anxiety, modified output, and L2 learning. *Language Learning, 58*, 835–874.

———. (2011). *Corrective feedback, individual differences and second language learning*. Springer London Limited.

Sheen, Y. & Ellis, R. (2011). Corrective feedback in language teaching. In E. Hinkel (Ed.), *Handbook of research in second language teaching and learning* (pp. 593–610). New York, NY: Routledge.

Shkedi, A. (1998). Teachers' attitudes towards research: A challenge for qualitative researchers. *International Journal of Qualitative Studies in Education, 11*(4), 559–577.

Siebert, L. L. (2003). Student and teacher beliefs about language learning. *The ORTESOL Journal, 21*, 7–39.

Sime, D. (2006). What do learners make of teachers' gestures in the language classroom? *International Review of Applied Linguistics, 44*, 211–230.

Sinclair, B. & Ellis, G. (1992). Survey: Learner training in EFL course books. *ELT Journal, 46*(2), 209–225.

Skehan, P. (1998). *A cognitive approach to language learning*. Oxford: Oxford University Press.

Skinner, B. F. (1957). *Verbal Behavior*. New York: Appleton-Century-Crofts.

Slimani, A. (1989). The role of topicalization in classroom language learning. *System, 17*(2), 223–234.

———. (1991). Evaluation of classroom interaction. In C. Anderson & A. Berretta (Eds.), *Evaluating second language education* (pp. 197–220). Cambridge: Cambridge University Press.

Smith, B. (2012). Eye tracking as a measure of noticing: A study of explicit recasts in SCMC. *Language Learning and Technology, 16*(3), 53–81.

Smotrova, T. (2017). Making pronunciation visible: Gesture in teaching pronunciation. *TESOL Quarterly, 51*(1), 59–88.
Spada, N. (1997). Form-focussed instruction and second language acquisition: A review of classroom and laboratory research. *Language Teaching, 30*, 73–87.
Spada, N., & Lightbown, P. M. (1999). Instruction, first language influence, and developmental readiness in second language acquisition. *The Modern Language Journal, 83*(1), 1–22.
———. (2009). Interaction in second/foreign language classrooms. In A. Mackey & C. Polio (Eds.), *Multiple perspectives on interaction: Second language research in honor of Susan M. Gass* (pp. 157–174). London: Routledge.
Swain, M. (1985). Communicative competence: Some roles of comprehensible input and comprehensible output in its development. In S. Gass & C. Madden (Eds.), *Input in Second Language Acquisition* (pp. 235–253). Rowley, MA: Newbury House.
———. (1993). The output hypothesis: Just speaking and writing aren't enough. *The Canadian Modern Language Review, 50*, 158–164.
———. (1995). Three functions of output in second language learning. In G. Cook & B. Seidlhofer (Eds.), *Principle and practice in applied linguistics* (pp. 124–144). Oxford: Oxford University Press.
———. (2005). The output hypothesis: Theory and research. In E. Hinkel (Ed.), *Handbook on research in second language learning and teaching*. Mahwah, NJ: Lawrence Erlbaum Associates.
Swain, M., & Lapkin, S. (1995). Problems in output and the cognitive processes they generate: a step towards second language learning. *Applied Linguistics, 16*, 371–391.
Taddarth, A. (2010). Recasts, uptake and learning: Effects and relationships. Unpublished Master's thesis, Université de Montréal, Canada.
Tanaka, K. (2004). *Changes in Japanese students' beliefs about language learning and English language proficiency in a study-abroad context*. Unpublished doctoral dissertation, University of Auckland.
Tanaka, K., & Ellis, R. (2003). Study-abroad, language proficiency, and learner beliefs about language learning. *JALT Journal, 25*, 63–83.
Tellier, M. (2008). The effect of gestures on second language memorisation by young children. *Gesture, 8*, 219–235.
Thurstone, L. L., & Chave, B. (1980). The measurement of attitudes. In B. Sokoloff (Ed.), *L'attitude du Cegepien Face à la Méthode Audio-tutorale (appliquée en sciences) en Fonction du Nombre de Cours Suivis Selon Cette Méthode Dans Une Session*. Montréal: Université de Montréal.
Tomlin, R., & Villa, V. (1994). Attention in cognitive science and SLA. *Studies in Second Language Acquisition, 16*(2), 183–204.
Trofimovich, P., Ammar, A., & Gatbonton, E. (2007). How effective are recasts? The role of attention, memory, and analytical ability, In A. Mackey (Ed.), *Conversational interaction in second language acquisition: A collection of empirical studies* (pp. 171–195). Oxford, UK: Oxford University Press.
Truitt, S. (1995). Anxiety and beliefs about language learning: A study of Korean university students learning English. *Dissertation Abstracts International, 56* (06), 2155A. (UMI No. 9534977).

Truscott, J. (1996). The case against grammar correction in L2 writing classes. *Language Learning, 46*, 327–369.

———. (1999). What's wrong with oral grammar correction. *Canadian Modern Language Review, 55*, 437–456.

Tulving, E. (2002). Episodic memory: from mind to brain. *Annual Review of Psychology, 53*, 1–25.

Tumposky, N. R. (1991). Student beliefs about language learning: A cross-cultural study. *Carleton Papers in Applied Language Studies, 8*, 50–65.

Ur, P. (1996). *A course in language teaching: Practice and theory*. Cambridge: Cambridge University Press.

VanPatten, B. (1990). Attending to form and content in the input: An experiment in consciousness. *Studies in Second Language Acquisition, 12*(3), 287–301.

———. (2002). Processing instruction: an update. *Language Learning, 52*, 755–803.

———. (2004). Input and output in establishing form-meaning connections. In B. VanPatten. J. Williams, S. Rott, & M. Overstreet (Eds.), *Form-meaning connections in second language acquisition* (pp. 29–47). Mahwah, NJ: Lawrence Erlbaum.

———. (2007). Input processing in adult second language acquisition. In B. VanPatten & J. Williams (Eds.), *Theories in second language acquisition: An introduction* (pp. 115–136). Mahwah, NJ: Lawrence Erlbaum Associates, Publishers.

VanPatten, B., & Williams, J. (2015a). Introduction: The nature of theories. In B. VanPatten & J. Williams (Eds.), *Theories in second language acquisition: An introduction, 2nd edition* (pp. 1–16). New York, NY: Routledge.

———. (2015b). Early theories in second language acquisition. In B. VanPatten & J. Williams (Eds.), *Theories in second language acquisition: An introduction, 2nd edition* (pp. 17–33). New York, NY: Routledge.

Wang, W. (2009). *The noticing and effect of teacher feedback in ESL classrooms*. Unpublished doctoral dissertation, Michigan State University, US.

Wang, W. & Loewen, S. (2016). Nonverbal behaviour and corrective feedback in nine ESL university-level classrooms. *Language Teaching Research, 20*, 459–478.

Wenden, A. (1986). What do second language learners know about their language learning? A second look at retrospective accounts. *Applied Linguistics, 7*, 186–205.

———. (1987). How to be a successful language learner: Insights and prescriptions from L2 learners. In A. Wenden & J. Rubin (Eds.), *Learner strategies in language learning* (pp. 103–117). London: Prentice Hall.

———. (1991). *Learner Strategies for Learner Autonomy*. New York: Prentice Hall.

———. (1998). Metacognitive knowledge and language learning. *Applied Linguistics, 19*, 515–537.

———. (1999). An introduction to metacognitive knowledge and beliefs in language learning: Beyond the basics [Special issue]. *System, 27*, 435–441.

———. (2001). Metacognitive knowledge. In Breen, M. P. (Ed.), Learner contributions to language learning. *New Directions in research* (pp. 44–64). Harlow, Essex: Pearson Education Limited.

White, C. (1999). Expectations and emergent beliefs of self-instructed language learners, *System, 27*, 443–457.

White, L. (1987). Against comprehensible input: The input hypothesis and the development of L2 competence. *Applied Linguistics, 8*, 95–110.

Wickens, C. (2007). Attention to the second language. *IRAL—International Review of Applied Linguistics in Language Teaching, 45*(3), 177–191.

Willis, J. (1996). *A framework for task-based learning.* Harlow: Addison Wesley Longman.

Winer, L. (2007). No ESL in English Schools: Language Policy in Quebec and Implications for TESL Teacher Education. *TESOL Quarterly, 41*, pp. 489–508.

Yang, N. D. (1999). The relationship between EFL learners' belies and learning strategy use. *System, 27*, 515–535.

Yang, Y. & Lyster, R. (2010). Effects of form-focused practice and feedback on Chinese EFL learners' acquisition of regular and irregular past tense forms. *Studies in Second Language Acquisition, 32*, 235–263.

Yoshida, R. (2008). Teachers' choice and learners' preference for corrective-feedback types. *Language Awareness, 17*(1), 78–93.

———. (2010). How do teachers and learners perceive corrective feedback in the Japanese language classroom? *The Modern Language Journal, 94*, 293–314.

Zhong, M. (2008). *Report of a pilot study of the beliefs of one migrant learner of English.* Unpublished paper, Department of Applied Language Studies and Linguistics, University of Auckland, NZ.

Ziegler, N. & Mackey, A. (2017). Instructional feedback in synchronous computer-mediated communication: A review of the state of the art. In H. Nassaji & E. Kartchava (Eds.), *Corrective Feedback in Second Language Teaching and Learning: Research, Theory, Applications, Implications* (pp. 80–94). Oxon, UK: Routledge.

Index

accuracy, 1, 9, 10, 25, 34–35, 48, 49, 55, 56, 73, 89, 98–99, 110, 112, 123, 124, 126, 137, 138, 147, 158, 160, 165, 168
Adaptive Control of Thought Theory, 29
Associative-Cognitive CREED Framework, 20
affective filter, 24, 117
affective variables, 112–14, 166, 170. *See also* learner differences
attention, 1–5, 24, 25, 27, 28, 30–33, 48, 54, 56, 57, 74, 88, 98, 101, 112, 113, 163, 164; to meaning, 98
Audiolingual Method, 21
Autonomous Induction Theory, 20
automaticity, 27, 29

behaviorism, 20–22, 28

clarification requests, 12, 14, 15, 26, 27, 18–19, 49, 53, 55, 56, 83, 92, 93, 98, 99, 146, 157; output-promoting feedback, 93. *See also* conversational recasts
coarse-grained framework, 2
cognitive processing, 1, 9, 83, 96, 117
Cognitive Theories, 1, 20, 28, 119, 164

cognitive-interactionist theories, 164
communication strategies, 120–21
communicative tasks, 11, 12, 25, 28, 29, 43, 44, 58, 64, 78, 97, 101, 110, 150, 165, 171; collaborative, 96, 99; information gap, 50, 99, 147; meaning-focused, 97, 100; picture description, 45, 58, 67, 97, 99, 104, 114; problem-solving, 43, 99; spot-the-differences, 67, 85, 99; story sequencing, 91
comprehension check, 14, 26–27, 53
Concept-Oriented Approach, 20
confirmation check, 10, 26–27, 53, 90, 93, 99
content-based environments, 51, 88–90
corrective feedback definitions of, 6, 9–12; distribution of, 12–20, 52, 56; effectiveness of, 6, 7, 11, 12, 18, 36, 53–54, 56, 57, 76, 86, 94, 96–97,113, 115, 117, 125, 128, 137, 141, 159, 166, 169–71; future research directions, 170–71; input providing, 93–94; mode of, 5, 9–12; negative consequences of, 134; noticeability, 3, 4, 7, 11, 12, 20, 44, 46, 47, 57, 59, 61–62, 68–69, 73–77, 79, 81, 89, 94, 107–15,

126, 128, 137, 141, 163, 166, 168–70; relationship with age, 61; techniques, 12–20; timing of, 5, 9
Counterbalance Hypothesis, 56, 74

detection, 3, 4, 31, 32, 53, 66, 98, 170

elicitation, 11, 12, 14, 15, 19, 42, 46, 49, 59, 63, 64, 66, 67, 73, 83, 87, 92, 94, 101, 104, 128, 149, 150, 165
engagement, 24, 57, 100, 125, 169
environment. *See* behaviorism
error type, 45, 46, 48, 52, 58, 94, 141, 145; global, 35; lexicon. *See* lexical errors; local, 35; morphosyntax, 46, 48, 52; phonology. *See* phonological errors; semantics, 48, 52
explicitness, 5, 14–15, 36, 52, 55, 82, 94, 98, 123, 169
explicit feedback, 12, 19, 21, 93–94

form, 1, 3, 4, 9, 35, 55, 74, 77, *95*–96, 107; attention to, 9, 24, 25, 32, 33, 35, 39, 74, 101, 112, 149, 169; focus on, 40, 77, 82–83
Form-Focused Instruction 35, 49, 87. *See also* focus on form.
fluency, 9, 25, 34, 35, 98

gestures, 6, 7, 12, 16, 26, 73, 143–45, 151; and pronunciation, 144–45; and vocabulary, 144; classification of, 15; distribution of, 15–20; deictic, 16, 143, 146, 151, 155, 158
grammatical errors, 11, 101, 114; grammatical analysis of error, 102, 115
grammar features 11, 35, 68, 70, 79, 81, 104, 113, 119, 135, 137, 141, 157
grammatical knowledge 11, 21, 23–24, 57, 96, 125

habit formation. *See* behaviorism

imitation, 21, 22, 33; implicitness, 14–15, 82; implicit feedback, 56, 59, 90, 95

incorporation, 106, 151
input, 1, 2, 3, 4, 10, 11, 22–24, 27, 28, 31, 32, 36, 39, 46–48, 53, 54, 56, 57, 64, 78, 83, 89, 103, 112, 143, 144, 161, 169, 170; comprehensible, 24, 25, 25, 33
Input Processing hypothesis, 30
Input Processing Theory, 20
intake, 2, 3, 31, 32, 39, 169
interaction, 4, 5, 19, 25–28, 40, 41, 45, 47, 50, 51, 53, 55, 82, 84–85, 89, 98, 100, 120, 141–43, 161, 165; dyadic, 46, 59, 61, 92, 93, 114, 165, 169; with peers, 96–99
Interaction Framework. *See* Interactionism
Interaction Hypothesis. *See* Interactionism
Interactionism, 26–28, 53
interlanguage, 1–4, 24, 26, 27, 32, 51, 58, 78, 88, 89
intervention, 58, 64, 67, 71, 78, 88, 104, 107, 108, 113, 127, 128, 138, 150

Krashen's Monitor Theory, 22–25

learner attitudes, 5, 119, 123, 126. *See also* learner beliefs
learner beliefs, 6, 34, 96, 115, 117–28, 131–33, 166, 168; about corrective feedback, 125–26, 131–38; and noticing, 126–27, 135, 137–39; about L2 learning, 124–25, 136; dynamic and situated nature of, 118; reflections on, 121; relationship with learning experiences, 122–23; shaped by mental representations, 119; sources of, 121–24; types of, 120–21, 123
learner differences, 5, 94, 112–13, 115, 117, 123, 129, 166, 167
learner-internal factors. *See* learner differences
learning gains, 33, 59, 79, 86, 89, 96, 108–9, 111, 114–15, 159
lexis, 2, 11, 45, 161
lexical errors, 45, 85, 114

limited capacity model 28–29
linguistic targets, 9–12, 64, 67, 70, 73, 88, 93, 103–4, 106, 135, 137, 150, 161, 167, 171
listening, 23, 25, 60–61, 57, 122, 148, 175

meaning-focused, 4, 55, 83, 90, 95–96, 97, 100
metacognitive knowledge, 119–20
metalanguage, 102
metalinguistic cues, 15, 56, 82–83, 101, 128, 147, 158
metalinguistic feedback, 14, 19, 63, 73, 149
memory; capacity, 1–2, 30, 46, 48, 52; explicit-declarative, 30; implicit-procedural, 30; long-term, 3, 30, 83; short-term. *See* working; working, 1, 30, 39, 56, 83, 113
mimicking, 51, 111
models, 10, 21, 33, 90, 91
modification, 2, 26, 27, 48, 50, 56, 90, 171
morphosyntactic features, 11, 45, 60–70, 81, 114
motivation, 24, 33, 117, 121, 166

Nativism/Innatism, 22–25
needs repair, 16–18, 106, 151
negative evidence, 4, 10, 22, 28, 42, 82–86, 90, 93–94, 158
negative feedback, 9, 10, 82; implicit, 90
negotiation, 45, 48, 53, 99; of form, 14; for meaning, 26, 52, 58; sequences, 93
nonverbal behavior, 89, 141–48, 169, 171; and corrective feedback, 145–48; and language learning, 143–45; and oral feedback, 148; coexistence with speech, 141–42; definition, 142; noticeability of, 148; role of, 7; training, 142–44; types of 143, 156–58
nonverbal cues, 15, 141, 144, 146–47, 157, 161; and uptake, 158–61, 169; with prompts, 141, 149–50, 153, 168; with recasts, 147, 149, 153, 155, 159–60, 168; to enhance noticeability, 141. *See also* gestures
nonverbal feedback, 7, 36, 157, 171; role of, 5, 6
noticing, 3, 4, 5, 12, 20, 26, 45–50, 57, 59, 66, 73, 77–78, 85, 101, 111, 115; and error types, 58–60, 68, 94; and learner beliefs, 126–27, 135, 137–39; in the classroom, 61–62, 77, 79; measures of, 6, 39–52, 59, 150–51, 161; nonverbal behaviors, 148, 157; rate of, 77–79; relationship with second language development, 6, 56–58; training, 5, 95–97; theoretical importance of, 6

oral feedback, 6, 86, 94, 126, 145, 148, 169; and nonverbal behaviour, 148; types of, 6
orientation, 31, 32
output, 1, 2, 9, 21, 23, 25, 27, 33, 34, 41, 51, 53, 56, 83, 97, 99, 110, 131, 158, 160, 165, 169; comprehensible, 4, 26–28; modified, 85, 91, 93, 106, 153

paralinguistic cues. *See* nonverbal cues
paralinguistic features 146, 159
paralinguistic feedback, 15, 16
phonological errors 45, 48, 53, 101, 114
peer feedback, 5, 17, 73, 96–97, 101, 165–66, 171
pedagogical implications, 169–70
pedagogical perspectives, 33–36, 82
perceptions, 5, 6, 46, 49, 85, 112, 119, 121, 137; of training, 99
positive evidence, 10, 42, 82–83, 85, 85, 93, 94, 98, 113
positive feedback, 9, 21, 36, 82
practice, 1, 10, 21, 27, 29, 35, 75, 87, 98, 99, 105, 112, 115, 118, 119, 124, 138, 167, 169, 171
Processability Theory, 20
prompts, 12, 27, 33, 39, 44, 46, 49, 54–56, 60, 62–64, 68, 77, 87, 91,

101, 112, 127, 133, 158, 159, 168, 169; combined with recasts, 102; distribution of, 56, 74; effectiveness of, 87–88, 94, 114, 160, 163; explicit, 93, 102, 157, 163; implicit, 93, 147; noticeability of, 29, 54, 70, 73–75, 79, 81, 102, 160, 163; output-prompting, 82–84, 94; saliency of, 73, 84, 93; training, 97–98; with nonverbal cues, 141, 149–50, 153
pronunciation, 2, 41, 11, 144–45, 161. *See also* phonological errors
proficiency level, 46, 47, 54, 60, 77, 87, 94, 114, 117, 124, 148, 170; high-proficiency, 55, 77, 87; intermediate-proficiency, 77, 99; low-proficiency, 55, 77, 87, 105, 129; native-like, 25
psycho-cognitive theories, 28–33, 119
Psycholinguistic Theories, 20, 82

questionnaires, 40–42, 132–33

reading, 23, 24, 47, 60–61, 122, 144, 148
recall, 44–48, 51, 57, 66, 97; immediate, 43, 47, 64, 65, 66, 69, 76, 130; protocols, 20, 52, 54, 58, 60, 64, 130; stimulated, 43–46, 54, 57, 58, 85, 124, 146
recasts, 10, 26, 32, 39, 45–46, 54, 55, 58, 60, 62–64, 68, 81–96, 102–5, 112, 127, 131–32, 141, 146, 168, 169, 171; characteristics of, 19–20; communicative. *See* conversational; conversational, 14–15, 18, 93; conflated, 93. *See also* input-providing corrective feedback; definition, 81; didactic, 14–15; distribution of, 56, 74; effectiveness of, 88–89, 94–95, 160; explicit, 58–59, 82, 94–95, 101; frequency of, 19, 51; implicit, 58–59, 82, 159, 168; importance of, 57; in content-based classrooms, 88–89; intensive, 49, 91; length of, 14, 82, 94; noticeability

of, 39, 45–47, 49, 51–54, 70, 73–75, 77, 79, 81, 85, 94, 110–12, 126, 130, 131; pedagogical. *See* didactic; relationship with uptake, 50–52, 54, 113; role of, 89–90; saliency of, 47, 73, 75, 94, 110, 161; training in, 6, 79, 81–98, 103, 106–7, 109; with nonverbal cues, 147, 149, 153, 155, 159–60, 168
recognition, 4, 26, 53, 86, 99
reformulation, 12, 14, 18, 21, 26, 51, 56, 63, 82, 83, 88, 91, 96, 103, 127, 128, 149; immediate reformulation. *See* uptake. *See also* recasts
reinforcement. *See* positive feedback
repair, 10, 11, 16–17, 20, 51, 52, 56, 73, 95, 96, 101, 102, 106–7, 109, 112, 114, 151, 153, 156, 168, 169; partial, 18; peer-repair. *See* peer-feedback; self-repair, 17, 53, 63, 73, 79, 83, 86, 89, 96, 128, 133, 146, 149
repetition, 14, 15, 18, 19, 21, 27–28, 49, 51, 63, 65–66, 83, 84, 88, 101, 106, 149, 151
retrospective protocols, 42–43

saliency, 11, 20, 36, 47, 56, 76, 77, 83, 84, 88, 91, 93, 94, 110, 139, 141, 160, 163, 165
Schmidt's Noticing Hypothesis, 3, 31–32, 170, 173. *See also* noticing
self-assessment, 125
self-correction. *See* self-repair.
speaking, 25, 39, 60–61, 62, 88, 129, 132, 133, 134, 142, 145, 148, 153, 155
Skill Acquisition Theory, 20, 29
structuralist approach, 21
Swain's Comprehensible Output hypothesis, 26–28

teacher attitudes, 5, 123, 166. *See also* teacher beliefs
teacher beliefs, 96
teacher differences, 167

teacher provided feedback, 5, 62, 63, 74, 89, 128, 156, 166
theories of second language acquisition, 6, 20–33, 97
think-aloud protocols, 42–43, 101, 102
training 96–102, 104, 106, 115; increasing awareness of form, 100–102; in recasts, 6, 79, 81–98, 103, 106–7, 109; learners to notice feedback, 5, 81, 109–10, 163; metacognitive instruction session, 99; perceptions of, 99, 107; research in, 96–107; to provide peer-feedback, 97–99, 100; to recognize nonverbal behavior 142–44

uptake, 4, 6, 12–20, 40–41, 56, 65, 83, 85, 106–9, 113, 151; and nonverbal cues, 158–60, 169; definition of, 16, 48–49; relationship with recasts, 50–52, 54, 113

verbal protocols, 40, 42–48, 170; in corrective feedback, 45–48
vocabulary, 11, 41, 76, 119, 124, 132, 144, 145
Vygotskian Sociocultural Theory, 20, 164

writing, 23, 25, 58, 60–61, 88, 112, 114, 122, 148, 165

About the Author

Eva Kartchava is Associate Professor of Applied Linguistics and TESL in the School of Linguistics and Language Studies at Carleton University, Canada. Her main research interest is to explore the processes involved in the acquisition and teaching of second/additional languages in the classroom setting. Dr. Kartchava's research has focused on Form-Focused Instruction, corrective feedback, the role of noticing in L2 learning, individual differences, as well as teacher cognition and education.

www.ingramcontent.com/pod-product-compliance
Lightning Source LLC
Chambersburg PA
CBHW070830300426
44111CB00014B/2508